TOWARDS JUST AND SUSTAINABLE ECONOMIES

The social and solidarity economy North and South

Edited by Peter North and Molly Scott Cato

First published in Great Britain in 2018 by

Policy Press
University of Bristol
1-9 Old Park Hill
Bristol
BS2 8BB
UK
t: +44 (0)117 954 5940
pp-info@bristol.ac.uk
www.policypress.co.uk

North America office:
Policy Press
c/o The University of Chicago Press
1427 East 60th Street
Chicago, IL 60637, USA
t: +1 773 702 7700
f: +1 773-702-9756
sales@press.uchicago.edu
www.press.uchicago.edu

© Policy Press 2018

British Library Cataloguing in Publication Data
A catalogue record for this book is available from the British Library

Library of Congress Cataloging-in-Publication Data
A catalog record for this book has been requested

ISBN 978-1-4473-2723-3 paperback
ISBN 978-1-4473-2722-6 hardcover
ISBN 978-1-4473-2726-4 ePub
ISBN 978-1-4473-2727-1 Mobi
ISBN 978-1-4473-2725-7 ePdf

The right of Peter North and Molly Scott Cato to be identified as editors of this work has been asserted by them in accordance with the Copyright, Designs and Patents Act 1988.

Cover design by Andrew Corbett
Front cover image: Peter North
Printed and bound in Great Britain by by CPI Group (UK) Ltd, Croydon, CR0 4YY
Policy Press uses environmentally responsible print partners

MIX
Paper from
responsible sources
FSC® C013604

To the courageous people in Latin America and Europe who give their life and love to building a better world for us to share. Let us walk together, asking questions.

Contents

List of figures and tables

Figures

Tables

Notes on contributors

Luiz Roberto Alves is Professor in Culture and Management at the Methodist University of São Paulo, Brazil, focusing mainly on politics for education and culture in social movement. He is the author of *Cultura, Trabalho e Bem-Comum* (*Culture, Work and Common Good*) and *Políticas Públicas Integradas* (*Integrated Public Policies*) (São Paulo: Annablume FAPESP, 2008).

Dario Azzellini is Assistant Professor at the University of Linz, Austria. He has published several books and films, among them *Communes and Workers' Control in Venezuela: Building 21st Century Socialism from Below* (Brill, 2017), *An Alternative Labour History: Workers' Control and Workplace Democracy* (Zed Books, 2015) and (with M. Sitrin) *They Can't Represent Us: Reinventing Democracy From Greece to Occupy* (Verso, 2014).

Marco Aurelio Bernardes is an economist, university lecturer and researcher in the topics of economic solidarity and territorial dynamics. He is co-author of *Work, Solidarity Economy and Social Development: The Case of the Solidarity Economy in the Community Montanhão in SBC/SP*.

Lucas Becerra is an economist and Doctor in Social Science (Universidad de Buenos Aires, Argentina). He is currently a senior researcher in the Institute for the Study of Science and Technology at the National University of Quilmes (UNQ), Argentina. Lucas is an Ordinary Professor of Theories of International Trade and Social Innovation at UNQ and has a postdoctoral fellowship granted by the National Scientific and Technical Research Council (CONICET).

Molly Scott Cato is a Green Party member of the European Parliament, representing south-west England. She is a member of the Parliament's economics and agriculture committees and of its delegations to Brazil and the Mercosur countries. She was previously Professor of Green Economics at Roehampton University in London. Molly has helped to theorise the green economy, and is author of several books including *Green Economics* (Earthscan, 2009) and *The Bioregional Economy* (Earthscan, 2012). She has also worked on the economics of cooperatives and social enterprises, and in her home community of Stroud she is involved with organisations such as Transition Stroud,

Stroud Common Wealth and Stroud Community Agriculture. She was one of the founders of the town's local currency, the Stroud pound.

Paul Chatterton is a writer, researcher and social activist. He is currently Professor of Urban Futures in the School of Geography at the University of Leeds, UK, where he co-founded the Cities and Social Justice research cluster and MA in Activism and Social Change. He is currently Director of the university's Sustainable Cities Group. He has written extensively on urban change and renewal, civic experimentation and movements for social and ecological justice. Paul is also co-founder, first secretary and resident of the pioneering and award-winning Leeds-based low-impact housing cooperative, Lilac.

Penny Ciancanelli is an independent researcher, resident in Scotland, who retired from Strathclyde University in 2009. She is currently affiliated with the Department of Accounting and Finance at Glasgow University and with Roehampton University in London. Her research uses a political economy perspective to explore the relationship between globalisation and governance of the commons. Educated in the United States, she was awarded a BA in History by the University of Michigan, an MA in Educational Policy by Columbia University and a PhD in Economics from the New School for Social Research.

José Luis Coraggio is an economist. He is Emeritus Professor and Director of the Master's programme in Social Economics, Universidad Nacional de General Sarmiento, Argentina, and Professor at the Instituto de Altos Estudios Nacionales, Ecuador. He is a consultant in the field of social and solidarity economy to various Ecuadorian ministries, and the author of numerous publications on the subject, the most recent being *Economía Social y Solidaria: El Trabajo antes que el Capital* (*The Social and Solidarity Economy: Work before capital*) (2011, Abya Yala/FLACSO) and *Reinventar la Izquierda en el Siglo XXI: Hacia un Diálogo Norte-Sur* (*Reinventing the Left for the 21st Century: Towards a north-south dialogue*) (2011, UNGS/IAEN/CLACSO/DR&RD) (edited with Jean Louis Laville).

Andrew Cumbers is Professor of Regional Political Economy at the Adam Smith Business School, University of Glasgow, UK. His interests span the broad field of urban and regional development with a particular focus on alternative political economy and economic democracy. His recent book, *Reclaiming Public Ownership: Making Space for Economic*

Democracy (Zed Books, 2012), won the 2015 Gunnar Myrdal Prize for outstanding contributions to political economy.

Reinaldo Pacheco da Costa holds a degree in Mechanical Engineering from the Pontifical Catholic University of Rio Grande do Sul (1975), a Master's degree in Transport Engineering from the Federal University of Rio de Janeiro (1983) and a PhD in Engineering from the University of São Paulo (1998). He has been a Professor in the Department of Production Engineering, Polytechnic School of the University of São Paulo, Brazil, since 1992, and Coordinator of its Technological Incubator of Popular Cooperatives. His research focuses on production engineering and solidarity economics.

Ana Cecilia Dinerstein is Associate Professor of Sociology at the University of Bath, UK. She is an Open Marxist and critical sociologist, and writes about radical subjectivity; labour, social, rural and indigenous movements; Argentine and Latin American politics; autonomy; the uses of Ernst Bloch's concept of hope; and contemporary forms of Utopia. She is a research partner of the 'New Politics Project' (2016–2020) at the Transnational Institute, Amsterdam; and creator and convenor of two international research networks: 'Labour in Transition' and 'Women on the Verge'. Her publications include *The Labour Debate* (Ashgate, 2002; Otonom, 2006; Herramienta, 2009); *The Politics of Autonomy in Latin America: The Art of Organising Hope* (Palgrave Macmillan, 2015) and *Social Sciences for an other Politics: Women Theorising Without Parachutes* (editor and author) (Palgrave Macmillan, 2017).

David Fasenfest is Associate Professor of Sociology at Wayne State University as well as Editor of the journal *Critical Sociology*. His research focuses on community development, urban policy, social inequality and social change. His work has appeared in the *International Journal of Urban and Regional Research*, *Urban Affairs Quarterly*, *Journal of Correctional Education* and *International Journal of Economic Development*, as well as in many edited volumes. His most recent research is a monograph that deals with how to avoid market-based urban decline, *Detroit and New Urban Repertoires: Imagining the Cooperative City* (Policy Press, 2017).

Gilca Garcia de Oliveira works at the Universidade Federal da Bahia (UFBA), Brasil, as a teacher. She holds positions as agronomist at the Universidade Federal de Lavras, Brasil and gained her PhD in Rural Economy at the Universidade Federal de Viçosa, Brasil. She has been investigating conflicts and resistances, and especially work analogous to slave labour. She is also a member of the GeografAR research group at UFBA.

Guiomar Inez Germani is Professor of the Postgraduate Programme in Geography at the Universidade Federal da Bahia (UFBA), Brasil, and a member of the GeografAR research group at UFBA. She has a PhD in Geography from the University of Barcelona (UB) and is the author of the book *Land and Water: The conflict of Itaipu* (EDUFBA/ULIBRA, 2003). It is dedicated to the subject of the agrarian question, especially the actions and conflicts that involve social movements of the countryside, the struggle for agrarian reform and the traditional communities.

Erica Imbirussú is an economist at the Universidade Estadual de Feira de Santana, Brasil. She holds a Master's in Economics from the Universidade Federal da Bahia, Brasil. She is currently a PhD student in Economics, at the Universidade Federal do Rio Grande do Sul, Brasil. She is a member of the GeografAR research group at UFBA.

Waverli Maia Matarazzo-Neuberger is a biologist dedicated to conserving forested areas of the ABC region and the Director of the Sustainability Centre at the Methodist University of São Paulo, Brazil. Her research focuses on understanding and transforming cultural mindsets in order to achieve a sustainable and peaceful way of living.

Victor Gil Neto is a specialist in business administration and information technology, with 10 years' experience as a lecturer at the Methodist University of São Paulo, Brazil. As a Microsoft-certified professional, he has worked on infrastructure projects and solutions (servers, networks) and as a service-level manager.

Peter North is Reader in Alternative Economies in the Department of Geography and Planning at the University of Liverpool, UK. His research focuses on the transition to a convivial, just and sustainable world at a local level, in the context of the Anthropocene. He is the auther of four books, including *Money and Liberation* (University of Minnesota Press, 2007) and *Local Money* (Green Books, 2010). He helped set up Transition Liverpool.

Heloisa Helena Primavera is a biologist and neurophysiologist. She holds a Master's in Social Sciences from the Universidade de São Paulo, Brasil and is a PhD candidate at Facultad de Ciencias Económicas,

Universidad de Buenos Aires, Argentina. A lecturer in many universities in Latin America and Europe, she is a researcher and promoter of complementary currency systems worldwide. She is co-author with Bernard Lietaer of the Brazilian edition of *The Future of the Money* (RedLASES, 2014). Her current main interest lies in new information and communication technologies applied to education and electronic money models towards sustainable development.

Paola Raffaelli is finalising her PhD in Economics in the University of Roehampton, UK. Born in Argentina, she graduated in Sociology and has a Master's in Social Science of Labour from the Universidad de Buenos Aires, Argentina. Her interests include heterodox economics, social theory, power and inequalities in a globalised world. She is co-author of the book *Están Hablando de Drogas* (*They are talking about drugs*) (Buenos Aires: Gran Aldea, 2011), and the chapter 'Asociando cooperativas. De las unidades economics a las redes de organizaciones. El paso de la Red Gráfica Cooperativa' ('Associating co-operatives. From individual economic units to networks. The case of Co-operative Graphic Network Federation') in Ralon, G. (ed) *Condiciones y medio ambiente de trabajo, perspectivas de desarrollo en America* (*Working environment and conditions; development prospects in Latin America*) (Buenos Aires: ACILTRHA, 2012).

Paul Israel Singer was born in Austria and has been living in Brazil since early childhood. An economist with a PhD in Sociology, he is well known for his contribution to the field of social solidarity economy. Author of over 30 books and many articles, he has been an active member of Brazilian Socialist Party and lecturer at the University of São Paulo and the Catholic University of São Paulo. After an intense period of participation in the organisation of the Solidarity Economy movement in Brazil, he created the pioneering National Secretariat of Solidarity Economy, Ministry of Labour and Employment, which he led during the period 2003–16. His current area of interest is in community banks with social currencies as an instrument to eradicate poverty.

Marina Sitrin is an assistant professor of sociology and criminal justice at the State University of New York, Delhi, USA. She is the author of *Everyday Revolutions: Horizontalism and Autonomy in Argentina* (Zed Books, 2012), *Horizontalism: Voices of Popular Power in Argentina* (AK Press, 2006) and co-author of *They Can't Represent Us!: Reinventing Democracy from Greece to Occupy* (Verso Books, 2014). Her forthcoming book with the University of California Press addresses societies in movement.

Hernán Thomas has a doctorate in Science and Technology Policy from the Universidade Estadual de Campinas, Brasil and is Director of the Institute for the Study of Science and Technology at UNQ. Hernán is Professor of the Sociology of Technology at UNQ and Principal Researcher at CONICET.

Acknowledgements

There are too many people to thank for their contributions, some of which have made it into this collection, others who helped develop the ideas that have gone into it. We should start with thanks to the British Academy, without whose funding for our seminars in Liverpool and Buenos Aires none of this would have happened, and Marcelo Lopes de Souza from the Federal University of Rio de Janiero. Marcelo, you could not make it to Buenos Aires but your support, kindness, enthusiasm and guidance got us started. Thank you.

We would like to thank our partners who helped organise the seminars and study visits in Liverpool – especially Rosie Jolly, Debbie Felton and Patrick Hurley at Social Enterprise Liverpool. The staff at Blackburne House and Jerry Spencer, then at Liverpool Vision, also deserve a mention. In Buenos Aires José Luis Coraggio and Valeria Mutuberría Lazarini from the Universidad Nacional de General Sarmiento (UNGS) were central to organising the Buenos Aires seminar. We would like to send our thanks to everyone at the Cultural Centre of Cooperation 'Floreal Gorini' (CCC FG) who hosted the second seminar.

At the Liverpool seminar we would like to acknowledge contributions to our discussions from everyone who took part, but specifically Diana Raby, Adrian Smith, John Barry, Jenny Pearce, Robbie Davison and Colin Crooks.

In Buenos Aires we would like to thank Walter Pengue and the Urban Ecology Team from UNGS; Horacio López, the Sub-Director of CCC FG; the CCC and IDELCOOP team; Anabel Marin, Andres Ruggeri, Anabel Rieiro, Pablo Imen, Milton Maya, Alberto Gandulfo, and Edgardo Form. Kristofer Dittmer from the Autonomous University of Barcelona provided valuable translation assistance.

Finally we would like to thank Emily Watt, Laura Vickers and Jo Morton at Policy Press for their support in bringing this book to completion.

ONE

Introduction: new economies North and South – sharing the transition to a just and sustainable future

Peter North and Molly Scott Cato

The solidarity economy as an economy of hope

The globalised neoliberal economy encapsulated by the Washington Consensus and Fukuyama's famous (1992) declaration that the global acceptance of free markets and democracy has meant that we have reached the 'end of history' is increasingly beleaguered. Facing financial collapse on the one hand, and criticism for its failure to respond to social and environmental crises on the other, its central tenets are in need of radical reorientation. A new paradigm is developing – one that combines a commitment to social justice and a respect for the rights of other species, future generations and planetary limits. This will not be a new mono-cultural economy, but a diverse system of economies, within an overarching framework of social and environmental justice.

The emergence of movements as disparate as Occupy, Los Indignados, Transition initiatives, Momentum, Barcelona en Comú and Syriza is a recognition that the neoliberal economy that has been hegemonic, at the level of discourse at least, since the 1980s has not delivered the goods. It led to Latin America's 'lost decade' in the 1980s and to the global financial crisis of 2007–08, which has resulted in long-term austerity in many Eurozone countries. Worse, the urgency of the need to avoid dangerous climate change and the depletion of the core resources that fuel human development have not been recognised. This 'triple crisis' has called into question the extent to which growth-focused capitalist economies built on the huge throughput of resources can continue: is another economy both necessary and possible? Does the climate crisis 'change everything' or is this the latest version of capitalist crisis that is affecting, for example, what Paul Mason (2012) has identified as the 'student without a future' for whom capitalism is failing to provide a decent income and security? The shout 'Basta!'

('Enough!') emerging from Buenos Aires, Athens, Barcelona, Cairo, London and thousands of other places signals that the capitalist and climate crisis is a crisis of civilisation that means that for many it is, today, impossible to live a life with dignity.

While the central tenants of the global economy are increasingly being challenged by societies and citizens across the world and the protests from Wall Street to the Plaça Catalunya have given visibility to the feeling that something is seriously wrong, the concern is that, as Žižek put it in a speech to Occupy Wall Street in 2011:

> Carnivals come cheap – the true test of their worth is what remains the day after, how our normal daily life will be changed. The protesters should fall in love with hard and patient work – they are the beginning, not the end. Their basic message is: the taboo is broken; we do not live in the best possible world; we are allowed, obliged even, to think about alternatives.[1]

As Santos and Rodriguez-Garavito (2007, p xxi) argue:

> In contrast to a common perception within … the left in the past two centuries, today it is generally agreed that centralised socialist economies are neither feasible nor desirable as alternative systems to capitalism in the new millennium…. We know how to make an economic system based on self-interest, but not how to make one based on generosity.

We need better visions and examples of prosperous, resilient and sustainable livelihoods that allow everyone to live a life with dignity. The good news is that while neoliberalism might be ideologically hegemonic, it is not the only story in town. Since 2008, voices have both called for, and enacted, alternatives to continued crisis by recovering factories, voting for new participatory citizen-led movements, building ecohousing, challenging the right of elected parliamentarians to rule as they see fit, creating alternative currency networks, blocking coal trains and ships as a protest against the use of fossil fuels, growing their own food on wasteland, getting together to harvest fruit on common land, creating cooperatives to recover long lost skills such as boatbuilding, setting up social centres, sharing cars – millions of small scale acts that collectively show not only that 'another world is possible', but that we can bring into being the early days of a better world. We call this movement the 'social and solidarity economy' – an economy built on cooperation, not on competition. This book is about those acts, and what they mean.

The need for ideas to travel

As J.M. Keynes wrote in 1933:[2]

> Ideas, knowledge, science, hospitality, travel – these are things that of their nature should be international. But let goods be homespun whenever it is reasonably and conveniently possible, and above all, let finance be predominantly national.

This book is the result of a conference exchange funded under the British Academy's UK-Latin America/Caribbean Link Scheme. When we became aware of this funding, we immediately welcomed the opportunity to support the strengthening of relationships between scholars and activists working in the UK and Latin America. As Paul Chatterton and Marina Sitrin show in this volume, Latin American struggles have been incredibly inspirational for activists elsewhere, but in developing our response to the funding proposal, we were aware that there have been significant barriers to actors in the global North and South learning from each other. Latin American struggles can be largely invisible to those in the North who are not familiar with the blogosphere through which these experiences are exchanged, because of the language barrier, and by the fact that, like Molly Scott Cato, many of those involved in building more sustainable worlds do not want to needlessly contribute to global emissions and minimise the extent to which they fly. Sometimes, people don't think they have anything to learn from each other. Prejudices, such as the view often held by elite actors in the global North that we are unlikely to learn much from 'third world countries', are sometimes unwittingly reproduced by activists. The other side of the coin is that some Southern activists argue that that globally privileged actors from the 'imperialist' North, which continues to rape the resources of the global South and has caused climate change, cannot teach the South anything. We were aware of the need to be sensitive of our inherently powerful position as privileged academics from the global North. Finally, we wanted to avoid both a romantic celebration of the potential of movements attempting to bring a better world into being, and a structuralist denigration of their capacity to make change given global processes.

In our discussions, we were guided and inspired by Raúl Prebisch of the Economic Commission for Latin America:

> Nobody is in possession of the revealed truth today, neither in the North nor in the South.... It is essential that someday all of us, those of the North and South together, set ourselves to explore the nature of our problems, discarding dogmas and preconceived ideas, until we reach a measure of common ground. (Cited in Kay, 1989, p 1)

This is not a straightforward process. When there is a commitment to engage, there are significant problems associated with well-funded academics from the global North extracting the knowledge produced by Southern actors unless the exchange is genuinely two-way. To mitigate against this, we adopted a participatory and emancipatory approach to how we ran the seminars and associated visits that form the basis of this book, in line with Paolo Freire's conception that 'the world is emerging'. We shared our ideas with our partners, and listened to their ideas about what might and might not work, and what *they* wanted to get out of the exchange.

While the levels of mobilisation generated by the Latin American social and solidarity economy (SSE) sector have inspired Northern actors wanting to build an alternative reality, we recognise that, as Munck (2003, p xi) put it:

> For Latin Americans, [Latin America] is not an exotic land where they dance the samba and drink rum while talking revolution or carnival. For many outside observers, there is still this fascination with the exotic 'Other', however well-intentioned they may be.

We recognise that insecure, 'getting by' forms of informal economic activity, in which people struggle to survive on a day-to-day basis, has long been a feature of economies in the global South; it should not be inappropriately celebrated by those who do not have to survive in those conditions. On the other hand, given processes of structural adjustment and repeated economic crises, even relatively prosperous nations in both the South and the North have downscaled their social programmes with the result that people have increasingly to rely on their own resources or on non-governmental public action around work and livelihoods to get by. Insecurity is found in both the South and the North. Rather than hoping for the reintroduction of a lost world of welfare (Larner,

2003), however, we argue that in many contexts these activities are not just short-term, crisis-related coping mechanisms or solely responses to neoliberalisation; rather they problematise the relationship between the state, civil society and markets in interesting ways.

Given the failure of state-led strategies and of social democracy to provide credible alternatives to neoliberalism, we decided to look for alternatives in the social and solidarity economies. With the support of the British Academy, we worked with academic colleagues[3] in Latin America and with local social economy organisations to co-produce two international seminars that were held in Liverpool, UK in 2012, and Buenos Aires, Argentina in 2013. The following research questions, which we developed together, guided the exchanges:

- How do we understand the solidarity or social economy? Is it a sector of non-public sector social enterprises and cooperatives, trading to provide social benefits, or a counter-hegemonic project, an alternative to free market capitalism? Is it part of an alternative social and economic system, or, through concepts of social entrepreneurship, a bridge to, or even part of, the capitalist economy and as such a tool for neoliberalisation?
- How we can create enjoyable, socially inclusive, democratically managed jobs, enterprises, cooperatives and other forms of formal and informal economic organisation in a climate- and resource-constrained world?
- How do we define what it means to live the sort of life we want to live, while understanding that climate change and resource-constraint issues need to be recognised?
- How do we identify what we need and what we should produce?
- What is enjoyable, convivial, democratically controlled work, as opposed to exploitative, useless toil?
- How do we maintain and enable to flourish that which we hold in common and all depend on: wider ecosystems, social services, civic life, community?
- What does it mean to create wealth, to be entrepreneurial? How can we develop new, social and collective understandings of wealth creation?
- Are markets always 'capitalist', always illogical, prone to crisis and unequal rewards – or good allocation mechanisms? Can we reconfigure markets so they work to different rhythms?
- Can we 'change the world without taking power'? What are the possibilities and limits of grassroots action? Is this a naïve suggestion?

- What is the role of the state? Can the state facilitate, rather than co-opt, grassroots action? Do social democratic models in Scandinavian countries get the balance between civil society and a supportive state, underpinned by sufficient public spending, right?
- Are social democratic governments better or worse at working with civil society, without co-opting them? Paradoxically, are there more opportunities for grassroots change under neoliberal governments where citizens are expected to fend for themselves more? Or in the latter case, is this just a cover for privatisation, with social/solidarity economy organisations being set up to fail?
- What are the best conceptual and theoretical tools for thinking these issues through?

As well as taking part in the seminars, the participants visited a number of SSE projects in the two cities, and Molly Scott Cato then had an extended stay in Brazil before travelling back to Europe by sea. Peter North took part in a set of follow-up seminars in Paris, Rome and Thessaloniki organised by a network he was introduced to by one of the seminar participants, Dario Azzellini. We have collected together a series of chapters that engage with the issues encountered during these seminars and visits, or identified through resulting discussions. This volume differs from other books on SSE in that it reflects this North–South dialogue in poly-vocal ways, focusing on what actors in each continent can learn from each other: what is done better in the North and South? How have there been inspired by each other?

Defining the social and solidarity economy in a time of climate crisis and austerity

The SSE sector is not insignificant: the United Nations claims that it provides some 100 million jobs worldwide – 20% more than multinationals – through 761,221 cooperatives and mutual aid agencies with 813.5 million members. In the European Union, in 2009, 207,000 cooperatives provided employment for 4.7 million people. In Brazil, 3 million people work in the SSE sector, while Argentina has 250,000 to 300,000 cooperators (TFSSE, 2014, p 3). In India, 2.2 million self-help groups benefit 30 million people, and the SSE sector makes up a significant part of the economies of places such as Canada (Utting, 2015).

We conceptualise the social and solidarity economy as that sector between the public and private sectors that consists of grassroots-generated economic initiatives through which goods and services are produced by organisations that have social and environmental aims, and are guided by objectives and practices of cooperation, solidarity, ethics and democratic self-management. The SSE sector aims to replace fundamentally unjust or unequal social, economic and power relations with democratically run institutions providing sustainable livelihoods, in order to bring about democratically run, economically just, socially inclusive and environmentally sustainable futures. It includes cooperatives and worker-managed enterprises, community development trusts, social enterprises, community land trusts, local currency networks, and community-run food and renewable energy schemes. In making sense of this diversity, we advance the following conceptualisation of the sector:

- First, we identify **social enterprise** and **entrepreneurship**, the dominant approach in the United States and the United Kingdom in which business skills and entrepreneurship are deployed by a variety of voluntary and community sector organisations, often funded by the state, to address social issues in targeted, customised, user-focused ways. In the more neoliberal North Atlantic economies, reflecting hegemonic elite prejudices in favour of a supposedly 'efficient' private sector with 'get up and go' contrasted with what is appropriately denigrated as a 'lazy', 'bloated', 'trade union-dominated' public sector, social entrepreneurs and social enterprises are lauded as the new creative force that will provide better services at a cheaper cost in ways that meet citizens' needs and in ways that the centralised state never could (Norman, 2010). Recognising the way the state utilises, or incorporates, the SSE sector for its own end, North American authors talk about the 'shadow state' (Wolch, 1990).
- Second, we identify the **social economy** in Europe and Canada, especially Quebec (Mendell, 2009). Often influenced by Catholic social thinking, this approach looks to provide forms of economic activity that include those that profit-driven economies often ignore. Examples would be intermediate labour markets, customised training and guaranteed interview schemes that aim to ensure that socially excluded communities and individuals are included in sustainable growth. Through such support, members of households that are some way from the labour market can be helped to get 'good' jobs.
- Third, we identify the **solidarity economy** in Latin America and, more recently, those southern parts of Europe that have been suffering from the results of the Eurozone crisis (especially Spain and Greece). Elsewhere, this approach can be seen as the **community** (Dauncey,

1988; Pearce, 1993) or **diverse economy** (Gibson-Graham, 2008). Here, the question is less 'how can we include those that the profit-driven economy ignores?' (the social economy approach) than 'how can we live in inclusive ways, with dignity, safeguarding the needs of the environment and future generations, given that millions currently cannot do so?' (Barkin and Lemus, 2014). It might even mean 'how can we fight back against, or be antagonistic to, the pathologies of neoliberal capitalism?' – for example over work, poverty pay, poor working conditions, relocating manufacturing to areas with lower labour and environmental standards, closing a factory in a crisis, taking too much profit out and not reinvesting in future production.

• Finally, through what we call **antagonistic economies** activists construct tools for fighting against the pathologies of capitalism by, for example, occupying factories to prevent their owners moving production to lower wage countries; establishing new forms of money that put need above profitability; or taking land out of speculation through Community Land Trusts (CLTs), squatting, or land occupations. This is a Polanyian counter movement to the destructive capacity of a capitalism that reduces all relations to the profit nexus.

We argue that Latin American conceptions of the social and solidarity economy, and the diverse economies perspective associated with the work of J.K. Gibson-Graham and the Community Economies Collective, have opened up a new space for political action that has combined the search for alternative survival strategies with demands for popular participation and economic democracy and justice. This space offers work and, crucially, 'dignity', and provides people living under economic duress with ways in which they can cooperatively generate new forms of economic activity that meet their livelihood needs and build social connection, cooperation and solidarity. Such conceptions could be as much use in parts of those European cities blighted by austerity, and where the conventional solution is to entice an inward investor (who probably would not come, and if they did, would require significant bribes to do so, and then would not employ local people anyway) as it would in a Northern community looking to develop a localised, convivial economy in order to avoid dangerous climate change.

This book discusses the contribution of the SSE sector to building sustainable, liveable economies though which millions can meet their needs in ways that are embedded in, rather than exploitative of, the wider planetary ecosystem. To what extent is the SSE sector a tool for transition, part of the journey to a convivial low carbon economy that is seen as preferable to a low carbon version of exploitive capitalism? Or, as some critics would claim, should the SSE sector be seen as a Promethean force bringing into being a new world, as a Trojan Horse opening the way for darker, neoliberal forces, a Frankenstein that is transformed into something that its proponents never wanted, or a post-political panacea to deep-seated problems in which proponents can impose any reading they like (McMurtry, 2015). Is it a vehicle for neoliberalisation and austerity where myths of the benefits of self-management and self-actualisation are a cover for the withdrawal of state provision and their replacement with inadequate alternatives based on self-exploitation? Does the SSE sector challenge or reproduce market logic? As Ana Dinerstein discusses in this collection, if it attempts a challenge, will it be tamed? Alternatively, are conceptions of a unitary 'market logic' and a binary outcome (reproduction or challenge) misplaced? Both Samuel Smiles (1996 [1866]) and Kropotkin (1985 [1899]) argued for a society based on self-help and mutual aid. Neither saw management by a central state as necessary in a free society. There is as rich a tradition of small-is-beautiful ideas in the work of E.F. Schumacher (1973), now promoted by Greens and Transition Towns (Hopkins, 2008), or the mutualism of the cooperative movement as there is in de Tocquevillean liberalism or the traditional conservatism of societies' small battalions (Smith, 2011, p 27). In other words, can the SSE be a tool aiding a deeper transition to a democratic, inclusive, sustainable world? Can communities, through the generation of more robust SSE projects, start to generate more locally owned and democratically controlled businesses, social enterprises, and cooperatives that provide a viable alternative to unsustainable but highly dynamic capitalism?

A diversity of perspectives

The chapters that follow are organised into four sections. In Part I, we introduce the theoretical underpinnings to the discussion. José Luis Coraggio, our key partner from the Buenos Aires seminar, introduces a Polanyian perspective that argues that the SSE is an attempt by society to 'take back' and democratise the economy to prevent capitalism destroying society – or, we might say, the planet as whole. Penelope Ciancanelli and David Fasenfest take forward the Polanyian theme to ask to what extent the SSE sector, as part of the wider third sector, has been co-opted into global processes of dispossession. British-based Argentine academic Ana Cecilia Dinerstein's critical chapter looks at how, too often, the state co-opts and deflates SSE activities by 'translating out' discourses and proposals it cannot accept. Countering this, Ana calls for the SSE to be thought of as a 'hope movement', demanding what might not now be possible – the ability to live with dignity. Concluding the introductory section, and taking a more hopeful stance, Peter North's chapter discusses the role of the SSE in creating low carbon economies in the global North from a Diverse Economies perspective.

Part II, on the social and solidarity economy as a site of social innovation, includes four perspectives by Latin American authors that show how, with the support of universities, the SSE sector is developing forms of grassroots innovation (Seyfang and Smith, 2007). Lucas Becerra and Hernán Thomas (Argentina) open this section with a theoretical discussion about what a national innovation system to support the SSE sector could look like. Building on these theoretical contributions, Reinaldo Pacheco da Costa (Brazil), and Luiz Roberto Alvez and his colleagues (Brazil), show how Brazilian and Argentine universities have developed SSE 'incubators', mixed groups of students working with existing SSE organisations and communities to develop SSE activities to capture the process. On a different note, Erica Imbirussú and her collaborators show how researchers at the Universidade Federal do Bahia in north-east Brazil have been working with communities to understand and deepen the common grazing strategies conceptualised by Eleanor Ostrom as a response to Garret Hardin's famous (and misunderstood) theory of the 'tragedy of the commons', misused by the right to impose further strategies of dispossession from the land.

Part III, on the social and solidarity economy and the state, debates the extent to which the state can build capacity in, and facilitate, retard or oppose the development of, the SSE sector. Andrew Cumbers shows how, in Denmark, a supportive social democratic state has helped significantly to develop community-owned wind power. In contrasting chapters, Paul Singer, Brazil's Minister for the Social and Solidarity Economy, and Heloisa Primavera, a key Latin American local currency activist, discuss what they regard as a success story: how Singer's ministry worked with Primavera's local currency activists to import the best ideas from Argentine (and other) local currencies while avoiding bad examples. In contrast, Dario Azzellini looks at the mixed record of the Venezuelan state's attempts to support the solidarity, social, popular and communal economy as part of what it calls '21st century socialism'.

The final section discusses how ideas from Latin America have influenced activists fighting against dangerous climate change and austerity in the global North. Paul Chatterton discusses how his experiences working with the Zapatistas in Mexico inspired him to 'dig where he lived' in Leeds, UK, in ways that have translated into both his academic and activist practice. Author–activist Marina Sitrin has a wealth of experience working with social movements across Europe and the Americas. She recounts what experiences from Latin America can teach activists in the global North. Finally, Molly Scott Cato and Paola Raffaelli draw lessons from comparative experiences of developing social economy organisations in Argentina and the UK, arguing that these experiences converge.

As our seminar discussions evolved, new lines of enquiry were followed and these, in turn, are reflected in this collection. To reflect this fluid process, we have tried to avoid any artificial coherence that might stifle debate. We have tried to edit the chapters to produce a cohesive flow, but without trying to homogenise the message and do violence to the diverse voices emanating from continents as diverse as Latin America and Europe with their very different histories. We would ask the reader to respect this polyvocality, and allow the authors of these chapters to speak with their own voices.

Notes

[1] www.versobooks.com/blogs/736-slavoj-zizek-at-occupy-wall-street-we-are-not-dreamers-we-are-the-awakening-from-a-dream-which-is-turning-into-a-nightmare

[2] www.mtholyoke.edu/acad/intrel/interwar/keynes.htm (accessed 4/10/2016)

[3] In particular, we would like to acknowledge the contribution of Marcelo Lopez de Souza to this project.

References

Barkin, D. and Lemus, B. (2014) 'Rethinking the Social and Solidarity Society in Light of Community Practice', *Sustainability* 6: 6432-6445.

Dauncey, G. (1988) *Beyond the crash: the emerging rainbow economy.* London: Greenprint.

Fukuyama, F (1992) *The End of History and the Last Man.* Harmondsworth: Penguin.

Gibson-Graham, J.K. (2008) 'Diverse economies: performative practices for "other worlds"', *Progress in Human Geography* 32: 613-632.

Hopkins, R. (2008) *The Transition Handbook: from oil dependency to local resilience.* Totnes: Green Books.

Kay, C. (1989) *Latin American theories of development and underdevelopment.* London: Routledge.

Kropotkin, P. (1985 [1899]) *Fields, Factories and Workshops of Tomorrow.* London: Freedom Press.

Larner, W. (2003) 'Neoliberalism?', *Environment and Planning D: Society and Space* 21: 509-512.

Mason, P. (2012) *Why it's all kicking off everywhere: the new global revolutions*. London: Verso.

McMurtry, J (2015) 'Prometheus, Trojan horse or Frankenstein? Appraising the social and solidarity economy', in Utting, P (ed) *Social and Solidarity Economy Beyond the Fringe*. London: Zed Books/ UNRISD.

Mendell, M. (2009) 'The three pillars of the social economy: The Quebec Experience', in Amin, A. (ed) *The Social Economy*. London: Zed Books.

Munck, R. (2003) *Contemporary Latin America*. Basingstoke: Palgrave.

Norman, J. (2010) *The Big Society: the anatomy of the new politics*. Buckingham: University of Buckingham Press.

Pearce, J. (1993) *At the Heart of the Community Economy: community enterprise in a changing world*. London: Calouste Gulbenkian Foundation.

Santos, B. de S. and Rodríguez-Garavato, C. (2007) 'Introduction: Expanding the economic canaon and searching for alternatives to neoliberal globalisation', in Santos, B. de S. (ed) *Another Production is Possible: Beyond the Capitalist Canon*. London: Verso.

Schumacher, E. (1973) *Small is Beautiful: a study of economcs as if people mattered*. London: Vintage Books.

Seyfang, G. and Smith, A. (2007) 'Grassroots innovations for sustainable development: Towards a new research and policy agenda', *Environmental Politics* 16: 584-603.

Smiles, S. (1996 [1866]) *Self Help*. London: Institute of Economic Affairs.

Smith, M.J. (2011) 'The Intellectual Roots of Big Society', in Stott, M. (ed) *The Big Society Challenge*. Thetford: Keystone Development Trust Publications.

TFSSE (United Nations Inter-Agency Task Force on Social and Solidarity Economy) (2014) *Social and Solidarity Economy and the Challenge of Sustainable Development*. Geneva: TFSSE.

Utting, P. (ed) (2015) *Social and Solidarity Economy Beyond the Fringe*. London: Zed Books.

Wolch, J. (1990) *The Shadow State: Government and Voluntary Sector in Transition*. New York, NY: Foundation Center.

Part I
Theoretical perspectives on the social and solidarity economy

TWO

Towards a new economics: concepts and experiences from Latin America

José Luis Coraggio

Introduction

On the basis of a critique of the market economy advocated by neoliberal economic doctrine, this chapter presents the social and solidarity economy (SSE) both as an alternative theory and as a counter-hegemonic programme of political action framed within the substantivist economics current inspired by the works of Karl Polanyi and Karl Marx. The chapter identifies the ethical and economic principles, and the institutions, that contrast the practices of a market economy with those of the SSE. It considers how the 'New Left' in power in Bolivia, Ecuador, Venezuela and Argentina, and to some extent in Brazil, has institutionally supported the growth of the SSE. It discusses some of the concrete projects of economic transformation, and the new constitutional and/or public policy processes. Finally, the chapter discusses the advances and contradictions that the SSE sector faces in Latin America, and offers some generalisable lessons that have been learned so far in the 21st century.

The chapter aims to contribute to debates about the nature of the New Left or 'pink tide' Latin American governments with an analysis of the projects and transformations that have taken place since these governments came to power. The objective is not to present ideal models, but to discuss social and political projects involving contradictions and conflicts, even among themselves and their supporters, that are not always easily resolved. Specifically, the chapter aims to gain an understanding of how the New Left states have supported these economic processes, an issue that is not always adequately taken into account. From this, we focus on clarifying the conceptual framework on which it is proposed that further analyses of this issue can be based.

In terms of method, the starting point is the necessary critical analysis of the market economy, an obligatory reference given that it is the market that the neoconservative political project – with its economic ideology known as neoliberalism – seeks to impose on Latin America, exposing the relationships between society and economy to the interplay of forces of the real-world global market. Similarly, the question of how to move from an (admittedly historically incomplete) market economy to an **economy with a market** in a transformative process guided by the interests of popular sectors must also be subjected to critical thought.

This critique is founded on a conceptual and methodological proposal with paradigmatic claims that is inspired by Karl Polanyi. We develop this proposal by clarifying the relationship between ethics (without which there would be no effective transformative projects) and economics, and expanding the set of principles for the integration of economy and society by recovering the analytical priorities raised in the classical texts of Marx. Our analysis is made concrete through a discussion of the relationship between this conceptual framework and the theoretical and practical current of the SSE that is widespread in Latin America, in particular the new constitutional processes in Bolivia, Ecuador and Venezuela, and the major public policies associated with the SSE approach, particularly in Brazil. As data, we analyse both constitutional texts, and reflect on personal experiences assisting the design and/or the critique of laws aimed at regulating the development of the new economy in Ecuador.

Concepts and practices of the market economy

Conventional economics is both a discipline with scientific pretensions and a doctrine with hegemonic intentions that is dedicated to the formal development of models of a market system in which the laws of supply and demand reign supreme, following the rules of methodological individualism. Here, a general equilibrium and a socially optimal allocation of resources arises out of the utilitarian interaction of entrepreneurs and enterprises, guided by the maximisation of profits on the capital invested, and consumers aiming at the maximum satisfaction of their preferences, which are independent of the conditions of supply and the preferences of other consumers. Firms and consumers, it is assumed, have no other ties than those associated with the exchange of commodities. This presupposes the perfectly self-regulating operation of a system of interconnected markets characterised by perfect competition, where prices are formed by the matching tendencies of supply and demand.

This is a logically and empirically unattainable utopia. It is inconsistent, as Franz Hinkelammert and Henry Mora have shown (Hinkelammert, 2000; Hinkelammert and Mora, 2009), because it is not in fact a system of '[p]roduction of commodities by means of commodities' (Sraffa, 1960), that is, it is not an internally coherent system as is claimed, since it relies on the extraction of labour and nature that are not products of the system, because competition leads necessarily to monopoly; because if a condition of general equilibrium is reached, competition disappears; and because scarcity is not a natural condition, but produced by the market mechanism itself. All of these factors render the possibility of an equilibrium or a global optimum illusory. From an empirical point of view, there does not exist, and has never existed, a single case that fits this model or closely represents it. Economic agents do not possess the knowledge or computing capacity assumed by the model, nor do they display the assumed utilitarian, selfish and asocial morality. Moreover, whenever the dominant forces in society have sought to bring about this utopia by freeing up the economy to real-world market forces (economic liberalism at the beginning, and neoliberalism at the end of the 20th century), intrinsic self-destructive tendencies have manifested themselves. Neoliberal advocates have explained away the difficulty of rationally upholding their truth claims with the hypothesis that the natural evolution of societies *will* necessarily lead to a self-regulating market economy (the 'end of history').

On the other hand, its autopoietic character has not been corroborated, as from the emergence of the capitalist market system to the present day the role of the modern state in reproducing the 'external' conditions of the system has been decisive. Far from being a 'natural' development, the capitalist market system was built through violent methods (referred to as 'primitive accumulation' by Marx) that separated workers from the means of production and from free access to nature (Polanyi, 2001, 2012). This is how the markets in labour and land – treated as fictitious commodities – were formed. With present-day globalisation and the return of 'savage capitalism' in particular, the mode of accumulation, according to Harvey (2005), is no longer based on the classic mechanism of extracting surplus value from labour, but on the plunder of nature – treated as a reservoir of 'natural resources' (for example, Amazonia), the global overexploitation of hundreds of millions of politically repressed workers (for example, in China), or the gigantic levies on the wealth of the population mediated by the state (for example bailouts of the financial sector). Capital, which does not reproduce its labour power, nor its natural resources, launches into a speculative financialisation that, in addition to the crisis of its accumulation regime, provokes a series of social and ecological crises, the treatment of which is ultimately political.

Thus, economics, based on a theory of the market economy, does not present itself as a theory of a historically situated capitalism, nor does it acknowledge the characteristics just outlined. It barely admits a few 'mismatches' between abstract models and perverse reality. To protect itself dogmatically, it has developed a protective belt (Lakatos, 1993) made up of models that are complementary to, but not logically integrated with, the main theory (imperfect competition, macroeconomic cycles, asymmetric information, external diseconomies, transaction costs, markets in ecosystem services and technologies, theories of innovation and so on), the purpose of which is to protect the core of a theory that poses the perfect market as the objective and the benchmark of real economies. In the face of the evident 'failures' of the market, the explanation and diagnosis given by its professional advocates is that more markets are needed, and so the theory ideologically resists its rejection by existing evidence, contradicting its own falsificationist epistemological matrix.

During the recent historical period (which has clearly not ended) characterised by the hegemony of the neoconservative political project of capitalist globalisation, neoliberal doctrine has sought to justify the uncompromising implementation of this model in real-world societies. Like any utopia, attempts to adjust reality to the model have proved destructive of society and natural systems because of their extractivist postulates (regarding labour power and ecological systems) and its ethic of the irresponsibility of economic actors.

In the last three decades of the 20th century, beginning with the Pinochet dictatorship in 1973, the neoconservative project built another empirical economy in the countries of South America by means of the ruinous privatisation of the public sphere, the drastic reduction of the social and regulatory state, and the dismantling of the economic structures that development policies – however incomplete and contradictory – had attained (Amin, 1990). It has generated widespread *structural* social exclusion, and set in motion ecological imbalances that are irreversible within social timeframes. This process has put both life on the planet and the cohesion of societies – although weak, unfair and conflictive – at risk. Social resistance to this project has been met with the violence of civil-military dictatorships, blockades against international economic relations, demands for the payment of unpayable, illegitimate and odious external debts, and provocative actions aiming to destabilise societies and topple people-oriented governments.

The social and solidarity economy approach

In view of all the above, critical thinking requires a discourse distinct from conventional economic theory, and this differentiation has generally been achieved by adding the qualifier 'social' to 'economy'. Its theoretical implication is to reaffirm both that the relationship of embeddedness (Polanyi, 2012) between society, economy and nature is an inevitable feature of the socioecological metabolism (Hinkelammert and Mora, 2009), and that any attempts to make the real-world economy autonomous of social and political control will produce the above-mentioned destructive outcomes. Such processes of disembedding are always viewed as relative, as even in the most liberal of societies they involve the exertion of state power and concentrated corporate power, as well as the manufacture of a particular common sense that serves to legitimise regressive policies. In everyday life, economic liberalism proposes that the population should incorporate the logic of the market and the institutionalised patterns that it requires as second nature, accept that their social position is a function of market success, and that the 'good life' is defined by the possession of 'stuff' and by practices of consumerism. In conceptual terms, it implies assuming that it is inevitable that the organisation of economic processes (of production, distribution, circulation and consumption, and their coordination) is in the hands of a supposedly objective mechanism that necessarily generates cumulative inequalities, having no morals other than those of competition, utilitarianism and irresponsibility regarding the negative effects produced by the selfish behaviour of individuals and organisations.

In contrast, we affirm (on anthropological, historical and epistemological grounds) (Coraggio, 2011b; Polanyi, 2012; Oviedo Freire, 2013) the expanded reproduction of life as our ethical principle. Consequently, the objective of the organisation and institutionalisation of economic practices is to secure the livelihood of all human beings in accordance with historically situated definitions of what are legitimate needs and wants, or what society considers a 'dignified' life. This being the case, we recognise that the social division of labour is a feature of any complex society, resting on both material and symbolic foundations: the satisfying of wants is a social relation, not merely the consumption of a commodity. When these foundations are not well established, the viability of the system itself is in doubt, although under conditions of injustice it can nevertheless endure, as in the case of capitalism.

The theory of the 'social' economy allows the framing of alternatives to neoliberal proposals. Thus, the adjective 'solidary' or 'solidarity' – understood not in the philanthropic, but the consensual democratic sense (Laville, 2013), without asymmetries between the participants of this relationship – suggests that, to counteract the forces of the global market and avoid its unwanted effects, society (and politics) should affirm relations of reciprocity within the setting of a democratic system that legitimates the reconciliation of diverse interests. Recognising the plurality of motivations in real societies, the aim is to leave behind the prevalence of selfishness and to recognise that human beings are not merely functional agents of a market system that objectifies them by making them into an obstacle to – or a resource for – particular strategies of utility maximisation. Rather, the aim is to recognise that, in addition to competition, economies are constituted by relations that are intersubjective, communicative, reciprocal and cooperative, and based on complementarity. This solidarity also includes attention to the needs of future generations and the recognition of nature as an organic condition of human life in society, with its own laws and equilibria, and, for indigenous peoples, as subject. In particular, it acknowledges democratically guaranteed human rights and the responsibilities of community living, the values of social justice and a restorative relationship with nature as a condition of life – a relationship that, in present-day Latin America, finds its maximum discursive expression in the metaphor of *buen vivir* or *vivir bien*, meaning 'good living' or 'living well', a westernised translation of *sumak kawsay* (Quechua), *suma qamaña* (Aymara), *teko porâ* (Guarani) and other knowledges of indigenous peoples.

Understood by means of an analytical framework, empirical economic systems are theorised as multidimensional and historical, and, consequently, any explanation or comprehension of and intervention in 'the economic' must necessarily be transdisciplinary. This contradicts the proposition that 'the economy' is a societal sphere subject to its own laws, as supposedly universal as the laws of Newtonian mechanics, and that must be apprehended by that 'social science' known as economics as forming 'natural' limits to human action.

The alternative theoretical SSE framework, which is still under construction, includes, in a critical manner, elements of market theory to explain the tendencies of price (or terms of trade) formation according to notional laws of supply and demand. This inclusion is motivated by the fact that it is recognised that the 'market' both exists (although socially and politically regulated) and, moreover, is a *necessary* institution of modern economies, no less so than planning, community consensus or other modes of social coordination. Proposals for its elimination cannot be sustained. There is, however, a total confrontation with the dominant conception of the 'perfect' market, and with the treatment of human capabilities, nature, knowledge, money and the commons as fictitious commodities. The theory of the 'pure' market is rejected because the advocacy by neoliberal theorists of an all-pervading market principle, that is, the market as *the* economic institution subordinating all others through 'rational choice theory', postulates the commodification of all human activities constituting social life in the name of totalised instrumental rationality, as well as its own morals of utilitarian and irresponsible individualism. All of this implies a claim to universality that tends to homogenise cultures.

The substantive economy approach

The core of this body of theory (SSE) is the **substantive economy** approach, supported by the generalisations made by Polanyi on the basis of the historical and anthropological studies of concrete economies available at the time he undertook his research. It is also supported by Marx's theory of the modes of production (Assadourian et al, 1977), which states that, in any real-world society, the economic process is integrated into socioeconomic formations that combine a range of modes of production and reproduction. According to this approach, in any real-world economy, the principle of the market – when present – is **one among many**. It may be the dominant mode, or subsumed by others (householding, reciprocity or redistribution). On the other hand, it is affirmed (as is implicit in Polanyi's work) that the economy is and must be a moral system with rational ethical principles (Ulrich, 2008).

Thus, in one and the same economy, complementary or contradictory economic institutions and principles coexist, regulated by various moral rules and ethical principles, just as society is made up of a multiplicity of communities and cultures. This implies an understanding of contradictory practices or the ambiguous behaviour of individual actors (for example, cooperatives that behave like capitalist firms, or individuals who are competitive in the sphere of exchange but show solidarity with their family or community of reference). We suggest that these principles can be outlined in terms of broad categories (see Table 2.1).

Table 2.1: The principles of social integration of the economy: capitalism, social and solidarity economy, and socialism

	Capitalist economy	SSE	State socialism
Ethics			
	Accumulation to maximise capital – socially irresponsible.	Reproduction of life for all and to safeguard the natural environment – socially responsible.	Reproduction of collective/state capital – limited social responsibility.
Principles for the production of productive labour			
Possession or separation of workers from other factors of production – for example the natural world, scientific and practical knowledge	Capitalist direction. Work dependent on proprietors or possessors of the means of production. Concentration of the means of production in private hands.	Autogestión. Autonomy for workers, families or communities as possessors of the means of production: for household production (*oikos*); For exchange. Equitable access to the means of production.	State direction. Work dependent on the state as possessors of the means of production. Means of production as state property, or owned by a workers' cooperative.
Cooperation, complementarity	Heteronomous (owner, salaried).	Voluntary, according to custom.	Heteronomous (voluntary, workers' councils).
Relations between work and the natural environment	Extractive, unlimited growth.	Equal, respectful exchange.	Extractive, unlimited growth.
Typified by:	Privately owned company.	Pleural: families, communities, mutual aid networks, cooperatives, associations, public enterprises.	State-owned company.
Principles of appropriation and distribution			
	Indirect (by class and categories of monetary income, salary, unearned income, rent, interest).	Directly by the worker, the community, or a central authority.	Directly, through wages and surplus.
Principles of redistribution			
	Progressive-regressive according to the dynamics of capital flows and the balance of class forces. Limited public goods.	Progressive: paying attention to the needs of all. Investment, spending the surplus.	Conforming to the plan; creating the largest possible surplus of reinvestment.

	Capitalist economy	SSE	State socialism
Principles of circulation			
Reciprocity	Asymmetric.	Symmetric.	Symmetric (or a simulation of)/ asymmetric.
Exchange	Free market.	Market, barter network, social money.	Administration according to the plan.
Principles of consumption			
	Individual, according to unequal incomes, unlimited desires, irresponsible.	Individual, communal. Social, equal, sufficient, according to local custom and practice, responsible.	Enough to each according to the central plan.
Principles of coordination			
	Self-regulating market, with correction of 'market failure'.	By the community or society, participatory planning. Market limited and subordinate to society.	Central planning and regulation. Quasi markets.

Some of these principles are embodied both in individual practices and at the level of communities or entire societies through internalised norms and values. For example, the application of the *oikos* principle ranges from production for consumption at the household level to proposals for food sovereignty, countering the vulnerability of life that comes with the subjection of livelihoods to the vagaries and speculative movements of capital in global food markets. In this regard, guidelines for individual and collective decision making include acknowledging one's own abilities, not exposing oneself to unfairly competitive or exploitative labour conditions, toxic or unsustainable environments, and appreciating the benefits of the diversification of local production.

Thus in the SSE, the plurality of economic principles in an **economy with a market**, where there is room for everyone (individuals, groups, communities) to freely organise their lives to the extent that they do not interfere with social cohesion or with the principle of satisfaction of the legitimate needs and wants of each and all, is affirmed – on the basis of empirical evidence and rational arguments – by the programme for the construction, development and reproduction of an economic system guided by the ethical principles of life. In contrast, the dominant economic doctrine advocates a **market system** – and corresponding market society – tending to **commodify** all life and to impose utilitarian values, competition, inequality and irresponsibility regarding the consequences of individual actions on others and on nature. Rather than cultural diversity, this doctrine affirms the standardisation of values and the imposition of a Eurocentric culture that is none other than that of the countries that were the origin of the capitalist mode of social organisation (Quijano, 2008).

Given that they have historicity, generating varying combinations over time, the principles listed here should not be seen as static. There are different temporalities associated with the processes themselves, and with the cultures in which they take place. Finally, there are interdependencies and dialectical relations between categories. For example:

- the definition of nature as a resource influences the conditions for extractivism;
- the appropriation of a surplus can be achieved at the moment of distribution of the product according to the relations of ownership of the means of production and knowledge, and/or at the moment of redistribution or circulation;
- the structure of ownership of the means of production depends on historical legacies and the accumulation of surpluses; the capacities of appropriation through the processes of production and circulation are related to, and can be partially corrected through, the democratic application of the principle of redistribution;
- consumer desires and patterns of consumption are determined to varying degrees by the strategies of material and symbolic production and by the circulation of products, and in turn influence production;
- mechanisms of coordination affect the other categories of principles and institutions, and depend on the political regime and the structures of government.

Any diagnosis, prognosis or proposal for action that relies on these interrelated categories should acknowledge the particular and historical context of each real-world economy. This includes an understanding of the principles of feasibility, and of the social and political responsibility for the proposal. However, practices aiming to correct or modify certain unwanted situations do not always represent strategic programmes for the transformation of the particular circumstances or of the system that generates them, and their feasibility may be limited to actions that are functional to the reproduction of a system that does not correspond to declared ethical principles. Under the conditions determined by a hegemonic system, coherence and effectiveness are difficult to achieve, and the same is true for processes of transformation such as those discussed in this chapter.

The characteristics of SSE practices for transitioning from a capitalist market economy

A great variety of SSE practices, which together embody the ethical principle of the defence of the reproduction of life (albeit sometimes in contradictory ways), are guided both by this framework of critical thinking and by the conviction that 'another economy is possible'. This ethical principle is not based on *a priori* moral values, but on a judgement that is in fact universal: the economy of life is the ultimate end (Dussel, 2002; Hinkelammert and Mora, 2009).

Within the historical framework of material possibilities guided by this fundamental principle, mediated by the definition of specifically economic principles, the practices of the SSE incorporate moral elements of a non-universal nature: elements referring to human actions in the sphere of economic processes, and their consequences in specific situations. While acknowledging cultural diversity, it can nevertheless be postulated that these practices include, as common moral principles of action:

- promoting the inclusion of each and everyone in the system of social division of decent work, in particular community and/or self-managed associative work, recognising cooperative practices and the complementarity of individual jobs;
- ensuring that production is socially and ecologically responsible, managing processes of technological innovation with this in mind;
- safeguarding biodiversity and the diversity of economic forms and associated cultures, while respecting their dynamics and development;
- recognising that the economy cannot be disembedded from culture;
- promoting a fair distribution of the means of production and the wealth produced, and in particular recognising the state's responsibility in this area;
- advocating reciprocity, and in particular fair trade rather than utilitarian contracts;
- recovering the role of money as a public good, and encouraging the development of community currencies at local levels;
- ensuring the provision and distribution of the material means for satisfying the legitimate needs and wants of all, avoiding forms of consumerism that destroy nature and objectify social relations;

- promoting the fulfilment of needs by means of synergistic satisfactors;
- affirming awareness and critical-reflective practices as well as truly democratic participation, advancing towards the goal of human emancipation from objectifying structures.

More specifically, by SSE practices we mean non-capitalist economic experiences originating, first, in society towards a generation of material foundations and social ties aimed at achieving, at the individual or community level, the direct reproduction of a decent life and its corresponding moral values, and second, in the public sphere – whether or not of the state – ensuring the reproduction of the material foundations or general conditions directed at the improved reproduction of the life of individuals and communities. As a condition for sustainability and a goal of itself, these economic practices seek to establish a virtuous relationship with society guided by the ethical principle of ensuring the development and reproduction of life for everyone, in balance with the whole of nature. This implies the reinvention of the state in its relationship with civil society (Santos, 2005) and, of course, of the political system. Far from trying to implement a ready-made and agreed institutional system, these practices are part of an open-ended transition process with a timeframe corresponding to the structural transformations anticipated.

These transformative practices are situated within a socioeconomic system in which capitalism is hegemonic. In the face of this hegemony, actions towards the satisfaction of needs must engage in a cultural struggle for other values, other visions of the world, and other epistemologies.

Developing the SSE in Latin America

Two major categories of practice predominate in the SSE in Latin America, practices that are both very limited in terms of the programme of action suggested here. On the one hand, following the crisis of the mechanisms of inclusion provoked by neoliberalism, practices oriented at the reinsertion of the excluded and destitute through displays and practices of solidarity have emerged at the microeconomic level. Paradoxically, the aim of these practices is to achieve the insertion or reinsertion of individuals into the *same* markets from which they have been excluded, even though these markets will *keep* excluding masses of human beings, and continue to drive relentless processes of the destruction of natural equilibria. Instruments such as microcredit or subsidised small-scale seed capital accompany such programmes. On the other hand, through fiscal policy, the redistribution of monetary incomes (though not the means of production) is extended towards sectors of extreme poverty. Such efforts, however, can only be sustained by political will or moral principles, which can be difficult to uphold over long periods of time given the pressures of capitalist globalisation in both material and symbolic ways.

Both these sets of practices lack a totalising vision oriented at the construction of 'another economy', that is, another economic system characterised by social values and solidarity (as prescribed, for example, by the Ecuadorian constitution), even though it may not be possible to design an entire new institutional system. This level of thought and systemic action is essential for building another economy, rather than merely mitigating the social consequences of neoliberal globalisation that the powerful find undesirable or dangerous, thereby improving the governability of the peripheral capitalist system. It implies that all the communities that make up society should consider and practically engage with all the principles outlined here, countering the forces of the market and the processes of reproduction of capitalist culture. A firm foundation for this process is the 'popular' economy, with its potential to form a broad and organic sector of economic solidarity, making democratic demands on the state. The fact that SSE organisations are motivated by a desire to facilitate the expanded reproduction of the lives of their members, rather than capital accumulation, allows us to affirm the possibility of extending that logic to relationships with others, based on reciprocity (Coraggio, 2011a).

It is also important to note that there are relatively few of those collective agents that are indispensable for both sustaining this project of structural transformation, a project that involves a developing a different meaning of the 'economic', and injecting it into the logic of liberal democracy such that it becomes the basis for the constitution of people, articulating the interests and demands of various sectors (Laclau, 2005). Given the consequent difficulty of reconciling and articulating the practices of diverse agents at the centres of national authority with micro-level practices in what is a long transition, constructivist practices operating at the intermediate socioeconomic level as mediators between the two levels become significant. This involves creating or consolidating territories consisting of intersubjective relations of proximity, characterised by solidarity at the material and symbolic levels between individuals, communities and their natural environment, as foundations for the emergence of collective subjects with relative autonomy and a sufficient degree of detachment from the laws of the market. In the words of Alain Caillé, the goal is to 'revive, in the midst of secondary sociability, the cardinal values of primary sociability: loyalty, interdependence, trust, reciprocity' (Caillé, 2011, p 27).

This is important because, as Polanyi and Marx showed, the market was, and remains, a social construction made by forces relying on the violence of economic, political, symbolic and even military power, forces that currently progress the neoconservative project for world domination. The project for another economy, or SSE, faces opposition from these forces, and cannot ignore the need to radicalise democracy as an integral part of this alternative project (Gaiger, 2014).

Constitutional and legislative issues

The recent constitutional processes and the associated enactment of new laws in Venezuela, Ecuador and Bolivia explicitly embody and institutionalise forms of SSE.[1] In the case of Venezuela, we find an abundance of names used by the same government over a period of 12 years: social, communal, popular economy and so on (see Chapter Twelve of this volume). Among other things, this mirrors the rushed process of economic exploration, experimentation and learning that has taken place there. We can, however, also observe the evolution of the meaning of the social economy proposal in those countries, ranging from the democratisation of capital and the market – where the social economy based on associative companies and self-managed microenterprises is seen as an alternative and complementary to both the private and public economies – to the full blooded construction of a 'socialism of the 21st century'.

In Venezuela, Ecuador and Bolivia, laws have been enacted in support of a 'people's power' oriented at building a communal economic system, formed by communal (direct or indirect) social property enterprises, family production units (which are commercially oriented) and solidarity exchange groups. Faced with a bureaucratic state opposed to the new policies, and a society without organisations numerous or strong enough to put into practice autonomous initiatives or to take up the slogans of the government, an attempt was made to encourage cooperation by dedicating a great wealth of resource to the establishment of new social production enterprises, especially cooperatives, with results well below expectations. For similar reasons, a new institutional framework was set up to support practices aimed at building another economy, with new actors – the 'missions'. These are large mobilisations, particularly of young people, in parallel with the structures of the state, one of which (Vuelvan Caras, which translates as 'About-face') was responsible for mobilising resources and incentives for community-based economic initiatives.

In the case of Ecuador, the new Constitution recognises various forms of organisation of productive processes in the economy, such as public, private and mixed enterprises, as well as family, domestic, autonomous, community and associative enterprises, and cooperatives. The last six constitute the so-called popular economy, and the last three, the popular solidarity economy (PSE), to which the constitution assigns a prominent role. Similarly, the National Plan for Buen Vivir stresses the importance both of the PSE, and of participatory mechanisms for the formulation of public policy. With respect to the latter, no substantive progress has been achieved so far, which indicates the degree of resistance from existing institutions, including the state bureaucracy, civil society organisations, and the general citizenry. Article 283 of the new Constitution provides that 'the economic system is social and solidary and is comprised of the public, private, mixed, popular and solidarity forms of economic organisation, as well as those indicated by the Constitution', adding that 'the popular and solidarity economy will be regulated in accordance with the law and will include cooperative, associative and community sectors'.

In the case of Bolivia, the new Constitution requires the state to recognise, protect and promote cooperatives and the systems of production and reproduction of social life that are based on the principles and visions of indigenous peoples and nations as well as farmers. It also specifies that the state should prioritise support for the organisation of associative structures by small producers in urban and rural areas.

Public policy

In line with the general principle of redistribution that guides public practice in an SSE, a common feature of the politics of the new century in Latin America under the New Left governments has been the redistribution of both monetary incomes and public goods (education, health, housing programmes and so on) in favour of the poorest sectors of the economy, those neoliberalism has left behind. This has been facilitated by state appropriation (through renegotiation with multinationals, nationalisation, or heavy taxes on private exports) of international rents arising from price increases in the global market, and the application of high-productivity technologies in the raw material producing sectors. While social movement actors have been active in this regard (for example, Movimento dos Trabalhadores Rurais Sem

Terra (MST) in Brazil, the recovered factories of Argentina), progress in terms of the redistribution of the means of production, in particular of land and water, has been limited or non-existent at the macro level. Arguably this is due to a desire to avoid the heightened social conflict that would come with advances in this direction, and avoid the complicated web of legal actions that this would provoke when conducted within the rule of law. Public policies also respond to the SSE principle of guaranteeing labour market participation for everyone, and as such do not generate major conflicts with the propertied classes, with the exception of when elites argue that they are subjected to higher taxes to subsidise people who 'don't want to work'.

When viewed from a substantivist perspective, these elements of the SSE would be referred to as 'social policy', meaning compensatory social policies that address extreme poverty organised sectorally as 'education policy', 'healthcare policy', 'fiscal policy' and so on. The question of naming is no less important when disputing hegemony in the field of the 'economy'. In fact, the use of the new labels – social economy, solidarity economy, or social and solidarity economy – has generally been limited to the promotion of programmes for micro-entrepreneurship based on associative and self-managed labour. They have been understood as ways of integrating the excluded into paid work, that is, into the production of goods and services for the market, and as such typically do not manage to break away from the matrix of compensatory social policy. The main instruments are monetary subsidies conditional on the realisation of self-managed associative activities such as microcredits, which, while widespread, are a small part of the wider economy. Sometimes these projects are supported on communitarian grounds, and sometimes on business grounds. The usual training is provided. The sustainability of such micro-enterprises is, however, a recurring problem. The main causes of difficulty are competition in a market economy context, the incompleteness and uncertainties of public policy, and the absence of collective actors and organisations pursuing this strategy. It is well known that such programmes are unable to step out of the paradigm of the capitalist firm when assessing the actual and potential efficiency of popular enterprises.

In the Brazilian context, advances have been made in the context of the formalisation and recovery of workers' rights, including important improvements in wage levels, and the recognition of the status of the 'associated worker' with access to social security systems. In contrast, even in the cases of Bolivia and Ecuador where the existence of family and community economies has gained constitutional recognition, little or no attention has been paid to the development of household production for home consumption, except in the case of self-built homes.

The relationship between society and nature, which in SSE discourse is couched in the westernised terms of defending the 'rights of nature', has in all cases faced problems arising from its contradiction with the neo-developmentalist models that have re-emerged in the SSE processes discussed here. This contradiction has no easy solution because, on the one hand, Latin American economies, including the most industrialised, remain dominated by primary exports, while on the other hand, the preservation of the electoral legitimacy of the New Left governments requires continued improvement in the standards of living of the majority, in a context of economic stability. Given the political difficulties of advancing on other internal fronts, such improvements require a growing surplus, which in the short term depends on increasing exports. One possibility for reducing the impact of this contradiction, and the impact of unsustainable extractive activities that threaten the balance of nature, is to bring about an increase in societal self-sufficiency supported by regional integration, a project requiring a consensus about a shared project that goes beyond the proper and fair management of a peripheral market economy.

With regard to reciprocity, there is a notable recovery, development and coverage of social security, tending towards universality. In the case of Argentina, private saving schemes have been nationalised, although not the pre-paid health insurance companies. In terms of exchange, interventions in the system of prices of goods and services – aimed *inter alia* at directly limiting their variation, ensuring that education and healthcare services are free of charge, subsidising basic goods and services, and capping interest rates – have managed to reduce the cost of living for low-income sectors, but have equally benefited the middle class because of the difficulties of effective price discrimination. The multiplication of popular market fairs and popular credit systems constitutes another instrument, in this case for sharing responsibilities with producer and consumer organisations. Barter networks and the creation of community currencies have been left to grassroots initiatives, although in the case of Venezuela these institutions are expressly recognised by the Constitution. The fair trade path has also been left to civil society initiatives, except for its legal recognition in Brazil and the important case of ALBA (Bolivarian Alliance for the Peoples of Our America), led by Venezuela, which involves Central American countries as well as Bolivia and Ecuador. Its aim is to introduce reciprocity into the trade relations between the member economies (for example, the exchange of Venezuelan oil for education or healthcare services provided by Cuban professionals).

With regard to consumption, an issue obviously driven by other policies, there has been a return to models where stimulating demand is seen as the engine of economic growth, both through public spending as well as transfers of resources to the base of the income pyramid. Since the utilitarian perspective is that individual wellbeing is based on increased consumption, although the poor are not at risk of consumerism these policies can generate a certain 'trickle-up' effect leading to an exacerbation of consumerism. In all cases, the commercial, financial and industrial sectors and the media have generally enjoyed sharp increases in earnings and profits as a result of the application of this model. However, the response of the capitalist sectors in terms of greater productive investment has been limited, resulting in a growing gap in the current account balances of the above-mentioned countries (except for Brazil), which simultaneously find themselves blocked from obtaining resources on the international financial market. In fact, despite the gains obtained, the more concentrated sectors – especially the financial – use their capacity for action and their control of the media to harass and destabilise these processes.

Finally, in terms of system coordination, the three Andean processes have recovered the notion and the institutional framework for state planning, although without taking on board the criticism, raised before the neoliberal era, of its technocratic nature and the lack of civil society participation. This extends to the largely technocratic style in the design and management of public policy. This represents a failure to adhere to the democratic principles of SSE practices.

Conclusion: after the pink tide?

While there have been many advances, changes in government, particularly in Venezuela, Brazil and Argentina, suggest that progress on the implementation of another economy has been limited. SSE policy has continued to operate with the understanding that individuals and communities will continue to operate in utilitarian ways. There has been an increasing recognition that cooperation and reciprocity are difficult paths to follow given the persistence of the individualist culture that has been internalised as 'common sense' during the neoliberal period. Consequently, the main mechanism for the development of solidarity is not intersubjective, but superstructural, mediated by the state: and this does not facilitate the formation of collective agents capable of transforming the economic system. On the contrary, these processes, originating with autonomous popular mobilisations and the actions of social movements, have tended to deactivate such agents once government power is attained, as indicated by the predominant style of leader-mass politics[2] and it is not clear to what extent they will survive the passing of these leaders. In short, there is a concern that, being logically close to leftist programmes, the SSE approach may be limited to constituting a branch of social policy oriented at the poor, serving as valuable moral support for a neo-developmentalist model, with a tendency, for pragmatic reasons, to relapse into the reproduction of utilitarianism and extractivism.

Innovative practices falling under the umbrella of SSE may share the ethical horizon of the reproduction of dignified lives for each and all as the ultimate criterion, but may nevertheless differ in scope and form when translated into concrete public practices, and even be contradictory in the short term. Seen from the point of view of society, the problem is not easily resolved. Even though large social movements have driven or supported the process of change in favour of the popular economy, as well as more far-reaching attempts to create a new economic regime, these movements suffer from internal contradictions and should in any case defend the validity of their political mandate while they start to adapt economic practices to new proposals for their institutionalisation.

From an intergenerational point of view, as already stated, the popular economy and its forms of resistance or survival provide the socioeconomic and cultural foundations on which to build an SSE. The peasantry and its renewed organisations (MST in Brazil, Via Campesina and so on), the Argentine *piquetero* movement,[3] feminist movements, ethnic movements, currents of liberation theology and environmental movements, are organised social forces or forces that emerge in certain situations, that continue to have the potential to consolidate a political will able to take steps towards a social and solidary economic system, as a constituent part of a national and popular project that is regional in scope.[4]

Notes

[1] A more detailed treatment of this topic is in Coraggio (2011b).

[2] See Chapter Twelve in this volume.

[3] This refers to the popular mobilisations to defend jobs, initiated in areas affected by deindustrialisation caused by neoliberal policies at the end of the last century. The name derives from the form of protest – occupying public spaces and, especially, cutting transit. These mobilisations eventually gave rise to a national organisation.

[4] On this topic, see also José Luis Coraggio and Jean-Louis Laville (eds) *La economía social y solidaria en movimiento. Nuevas perspectivas teóricas y prácticas*, UNGS (forthcoming).

References

Amin, Samir (1990) *Delinking: towards a polycentric world*. London: Zed Books.

Assadourian, Carlos et al. (1977) 'Modos de producción en América Latina', *Cuadernos de Pasado y Presente*, Nro. 40, México.

Caillé, Alain (2011) 'Sobre los conceptos de economía en general y de economía solidaria en particular', in José Luis Coraggio (ed) *Qué es lo económico? Materiales para un debate necesario contra el fatalismo*. Quito: Abya Yala.

Coraggio, José Luis (2011a) *Economía Social y Solidaria. El trabajo antes que el capital*, Quito: Abya Yala/FLACSO.

Coraggio, José Luis (2011b) 'La economía popular solidaria en el Ecuador', in José Luis Coraggio, *Economía Social y Solidaria. El trabajo antes que el capital*, Quito: Abya Yala/FLACSO.

Coraggio, José Luis (2011c) 'Principios, instituciones y prácticas de la economía social y solidaria', in José Luis Coraggio, *Economía Social y Solidaria. El trabajo antes que el capital*, Quito: Abya Yala/FLACSO.

Dussel, Enrique (2002) *Ética de la liberación. En la edad de la globalización y de la exclusión*. México: Editorial Trotta.

Gaiger, Luiz Inácio (2014) 'La economía solidaria y el capitalismo en la perspectiva de las transiciones históricas', in José Luis Coraggio (ed) *La economía social desde la periferia. Contribuciones latinoamericanas*. Buenos Aires: UNGS.

Harvey, David (2005) 'El nuevo imperialismo: acumulación por desposesión', in Leo Panitch and Colin Leys (eds) *El nuevo desafío imperial – Socialist Register 2004*. Buenos Aires: CLACSO, pp 99-129.

Hinkelammert, Franz and Henry Mora (2009) *Economía, sociedad y vida humana. Preludio a una segunda crítica de la economía política*. Buenos Aires: UNGS/Altamira.

Hinkelammert, Franz, (2000) *Crítica a la razón utópica*. San José, Costa Rica: DEI.

Laclau, Ernesto (2005) *La razón populista*. Buenos Aires: Fondo de Cultura Económica.

Lakatos, Imre (1993) *La metodología de los Programas de investigación científica*. Madrid: Alianza.

Laville, Jean-Louis (2013) 'Solidaridad', in D. Cattani, J.L. Coraggio and J.-L. Laville (eds) *Diccionario de la Otra Economía*. Buenos Aires: UNGS.

Oviedo Freire, Atawallpa (2013) *Buen Vivir vs. Sumak Kaysay. Reforma capitalista y revolución alter-nativa. Una propuesta desde los Andres para salir de la crisis global.* Buenos Aires: Editorial CICCUS.

Polanyi, Karl (2001 [1944]) *The Great Transformation: The Political and Economic Origins of Our Time.* Boston, MA: Beacon Press.

Polanyi, Karl (2012) *Textos escogidos.* Buenos Aires: CLACSO, UNGS.

Quijano, Aníbal (2008) 'Des/colonialidad del poder: el horizonte alternativo', ALAI, América Latina en Movimiento (http://alainet.org/active/24123&lang=es).

Santos, Boaventura de Sousa (2005) *Reinventar la democracia. Reinventar el estado.* Buenos Aires: CLACSO.

Sraffa, Piero (1960) *Production of Commodities by Means of Commodities.* Cambridge: Cambridge University Press.

Ulrich, Peter (2008) *Ética económica integrativa. Fundamentos de una economía al servicio de la vida.* Quito: Abya Yala.

THREE

Monsieur le Capital and Madame la Terre on the brink

Penelope Ciancanelli and David Fasenfest

> It is an enchanted, perverted, topsy-turvy world, in which Monsieur le Capital and Madame la Terre do their ghost-walking as social characters and at the same time directly as things. (*Capital*, Vol III [Marx, 1967, p 830])

Introduction

The political weight of global capital, particularly finance capital and its reactionary side-kick, landed capital, can be measured by the new cities it has built in the global South where none existed before, by the rapidity with which it abandons emblematic zones of prosperity in the global North, and by the ferocity with which it destroys habitats, species and clean air everywhere. On the other side of the global ghost-walk by Monsieur le Capital and Madame la Terre, those marginalised and menaced by globalisation as well as those opposed to it in principle have been putting down the roots of social and solidarity enterprises (SSEs) in the thin soil of opposition, thereby asserting the existence of alternative ways of living in today's world. How do we assess these efforts and claims? Are they big enough? What is big? What is enough? In short, if we look to SSEs to challenge the hegemony of capital, how do we expect them to do this?

According to Marx's analysis, the Achilles heel of capital's hegemony is its successful mystification of how land and labour are commodified in the course of capitalist economic growth. One illustration of this idea will suffice. Marx in his discussion of the transformation of agriculture in Scotland wrote about the actions of a certain Duchess of Sutherland with respect to the communal lands adjoining her estates. He explained:

> From 1814 to 1820, all 15,000 inhabitants, about 3,000 families, were systematically hunted and rooted out. All their villages were destroyed and burnt, all their fields

> turned into pasturage. British soldiers enforced this eviction and thus this fine lady appropriated 794,000 acres of land that from time immemorial belonged to the clan. (Marx, 1887, p 682)

Violence, Marx argued, is the essential first step in the commodification of land and labour. Obscuring that violence is essential to defending capitalism; obscuring violence requires narratives that mystify how it comes to pass that people's lives are a plaything of market forces. Can such narratives fool people? Who would defend such actions, if they knew about them? Marx said, about the people of his own place and time, that many are fooled, many go along and some defend the indefensible because, in part, many lack the power to do otherwise and, in part, because some believe the alienation of land and labour is the natural order of things (Marx, 1967, p 831).

A century after Marx wrote, Polanyi reasserted the importance of the commodification of land and labour but focused not on how it comes about but its consequence: the subordination of both to market forces. In the *Great Transformation* and other writings, Polanyi challenged the view that free or self-regulating markets delivered prosperity. His shift from the commodification of land and labour to the treatment of land and labour *as if* they were commodities reflected the rejection of revolution as a political solution to the problems created by capitalism.

The intellectual basis for this shift lies in the academic debates of his youth in post-World War I Austria. All those studying economics in German-speaking countries studied Marx's assessment of capitalism and in particular its reliance on a labour theory of value. Much debated was the work of Bohm-Bawerk, who seemed to prove that Marx's dependence on this theory of value made his analysis of capitalism technically incoherent as well as the politics to which such a theory appeared to lead (Dobb, 1973; see Mason, 2015 for a discussion of contemporary versions of the labour theory of value).

Thus, Polanyi, along with many of his generation, abandoned Marx's emphasis on the violence of commodification in favour of a focus on the nation state and what governments could do to mitigate the effects of free market capitalism, including discussions of which markets to regulate and how to do so. In the course of the history of capitalism in Europe, Polanyi argued, the destructive effects of free markets led to opposition and to revolt, a double movement in which pressure for reform from below went hand in hand with institutional mitigation from above.

Over the past 30 years, capitalism has succeeded in commodifying perhaps more acres of land and more units of labour power than in the entire previous century. This unprecedented spurt of economic growth has been supported by national governments via efforts to rid themselves of regulations that supposedly reduced the efficiency of market operations. The result is a fragile global system with M le Capital on a financial knife-edge and the ecosystem of Mme la Terre on the brink of destruction. In short, the extraordinary scale and pace of economic growth has created a political economic mess, one that demands solutions; the question is how to evaluate the ones on offer in this book.

Theory is the lens through which we view the empirical world; differences in what theories enable us to see can arise, at least in part, because the focal length of interpretive schemes may differ. In the discussion that follows we reconsider the contrasting assessment of Marx and Polanyi in light of the effects of the 30-year, neoliberal crusade to instantiate global capitalism. We start with Marx's general law of capitalist accumulation, a lens whose focal length is the system as a whole and use it to construct a bird's-eye view of the consequences of that crusade for land and for labour.

Of course, the greater the focal length of any lens, the more detail is lost. To remedy that, the next part of the discussion looks at the same world through the lens of what we call the mitigation matrix – the composite of state-sponsored multilateral agencies, latter-day non-governmental organisations (NGOs) and civil society organisations (CSOs) that social democrats, following Polanyi, proposed as a means to mitigate the dystopian effects of market forces while at the same time encouraging capitalism as an engine of abundance.

This leads us in the third part to contrast the scale of the effects of global capitalism with the scale of the mitigation matrix, raising questions about the substantive orientation of SSEs and their capacity to 'scale up' politically. The conundrum we emphasise is how the scale of the environmental and the social destruction appears too great for them to overcome.

Economic growth: the general law of capital accumulation

> The greater the social wealth … the greater the industrial army … the greater the reserve army, the greater the mass of surplus population … the more extensive the working class, the greater official pauperisation. (Marx, 1887, p 603)

The general law of capital accumulation is the conclusion Marx drew regarding the effects of economic growth on the labouring classes. His highly detailed analysis of documents describing factory work, available economic statistics and reports from government enquiries revealed to him the destructive effects of industrial capitalism on the environment and on the labouring population in the parts of the United Kingdom where it had taken hold. Paramount among these effects was the creation of an ever-increasing 'surplus population', that is, people rendered surplus to the requirements of capital accumulation (Marx, 1887, p 603).

As we are now able to observe, once the geographical pathways of capital accumulation are globalised, the populations rendered surplus to requirements can be found in all parts of the world, from Glasgow to Soweto, from Detroit to Darfur. Far from providing the solution to poverty, Marx regarded economic growth as its engine. While in some parts of the world today, the central mechanism by which capitalism creates surplus populations is through the substitution of 'machines' for direct labour, in other parts of the world, the central mechanism is the expulsion of subsistence farmers from their lands, this time not by order of any duchess but through deals struck with government that give ownership of the land to multinational agribusiness firms (Sassen, 2014).

Throughout our discussion, we are aware that capitalism today renders obsolete concepts of a geographical core and periphery and that such concepts can lead to imprecision in how we think about social and solidarity projects. Thus, it is important to emphasise that such projects on the periphery of capital accumulation today are as likely to be found in the deindustrialised zones of US cities like Detroit as in remote rural estates in Argentina.

The reasons are clear: investment flows to all parts of the globe along with technical changes that have not merely transformed the locus of manufacturing but revolutionised the logistics underpinning market forces. This is made manifest in the globalisation of supply chains, which in turn has allowed unprecedented rates of economic growth in some places and accelerated rates of decline in others. The overall result is rapid increase in the numbers of people surplus to capital's requirements alongside lower production costs and higher profits. As more and more companies in a given production sector adopt changes initiated elsewhere, the average cost of production falls and creates incentives for more efficient producers to lower the market price to protect or increase their market share. This is one of the many, and sometimes quite complex ways, technical change can put downward pressure on market prices.

To forestall erosion of profit margins due to falling prices, one financial solution is to reduce the number of competitors through mergers or take-overs. The resulting production structure becomes an oligopoly such that fewer, larger firms compete on grounds other than price. Where legally allowed, cartels are formed that enable their members to fix the market price in spite of neoliberal claims that such an outcome is impossible in a free market system.

Obvious objections to Marx's narrative present themselves. Even if machines replace labourers, someone has to make the machines. As the demand for machines increases, so too does the demand for the labour to make them. Can this resolve the problem of surplus labour? Not always, and several reasons why come to mind immediately. First, the capitalists making the machines are under the same pressure to substitute machines for direct labour so the numbers of jobs lost may not equal the number of jobs created by the new machine-making sector. Second, workers made redundant in the sector using machines are not necessarily owners of the type of labour power required to produce machines. Third, the sector that is shedding labour may not be in the same geographical location as the expanding sector. Indeed, the globalisation of supply chains makes such a happy coincidence very unlikely. Seen through this lens, the big picture that Marx predicted was growing global wealth on the one side and growing surplus of labour on the other.

When we consider whether this picture can be substantiated by reference to economic data, we find ourselves having to make lemonade out of lemons. Data from official sources on the nature and on the scope of economic growth are not collected as a way to estimate surplus labour. They are, however, all we have (see also Hendrickson et al, 2008; ETC Group, 2013a, 2013b). Therefore, in spite of their many limitations, we draw on them to shed light on the connection between capitalist economic growth and the scale of surplus labour. We do this by making comparisons between changes in the reported size of capitalism and in the reported structure of the global population.

We begin with what is known about contemporary global employment, income and its distribution today. We then suggest there are perhaps 2 billion people in the world today who have no apparent means of subsistence. The question that presents itself is how great is their dependence on those in paid employment and on those engaged in subsistence farming? Given their numbers, how would social or solidarity enterprises affect their prospects?

Surplus people

In 1950, the global population was about 2.5 billion, with an estimated 70% living in rural areas, including many peasant households embedded in non-capitalist production relations and living, for the most part, outside the nexus of commodified land and labour. The long pulse of economic growth or capital accumulation from 1950 to 2015 increased global output approximately 20-fold (from about US$4 trillion to US$78 trillion) and the overall world population increased about three-fold. During that period, the rural population fell by 50%, but with important regional differences. In Asia and Africa, the rural population decreased from about 85% to about 60% of the total; in Latin America and the Caribbean from about 60% to 20%.

In 2015 the global population was estimated at 7.3 billion, with about 50% or 3.6 billion living in cities and largely reliant on money income for food, shelter and other necessities. The rest of the global population lives in rural areas comprising mainly villages, small towns and dispersed settlements with populations below the urban threshold of 2,000 residents.

To estimate the size of the global workforce, inferences are made from the known age structure of the global population along with some assumptions about those we may safely regard as either too young or too old to be economically active. In this fashion, some experts have estimated that 75-80% of the global population is economically active, that is between 5 and 6 billion people. Of this number, only 3.5 billion are recorded as employed, which leaves between 1.5 and 2.5 billion people working outside the formal labour force. If we subtract from that number those recorded as living in subsistence or peasant households (1 billion), we estimate that between 0.5 and 1.5 billion people are surplus to capital's requirements, half that number in Africa alone (Standing, 2011). Insight into how they survive can be derived from Table 3.1, which provides an overview of the global food supply.

Table 3.1: Food supplied by the industrial food chain and peasant food webs

Percentage of the total	Industrial food chain	Peasant food webs
Food consumed	30%	70%*
Arable land used	70%	20-30%
International traded	99%	?

* Inclusive of urban allotments (15-20%), hunting and gathering (15%), fishing (5-10%) and non-industrial farming establishments (35-50%).

Source: Authors' own summary of material found in poster published by ETC Group (2013b)

Most of the output of peasant food webs is consumed by its producers; some is shared with others connected to the producer household by kinship or other ties of solidarity. Any remaining surplus is sold in local markets. That 70% of all food consumed comes from peasant food webs provides an unexpected insight into the just how reliant on them is much of the world's population. Bearing in mind that much of the production in the web occurs on communal land of some type, one realises how much of the world's population is formally rather than substantively subsumed by global capitalism.

Alongside information about food consumption, Table 3.1 provides information on the extent to which arable land has been commodified. It is striking to note that 70% of this land has been appropriated by companies in the industrial food chain. By implication, this means, past and present, that the global population has been expelled from the majority of arable land. Equally important is the striking fact that in spite of its control of arable land, the industrial food chain feeds less than half the people fed by the peasant food web.

With respect to the global workforce, it is estimated that it generates an annual global money income of about US$87 trillion (PPP).[1] If this income were distributed equally, it would mean the every person receiving about US$20,000 in annual purchasing power. This fanciful statistic has only one merit: it helps to reveal the scale of social wealth worldwide, at least in monetary terms, and to place its distribution in stark relief because it is well known that global income is not distributed equally.

In reality, global income distribution is highly skewed. According to the estimate made by Davies and colleagues (2006, p 26), the global Gini coefficient is 0.892. This indicates that, *inter alia*, 45% of global income goes to 13% of the global population and that half of global households subsist on US$2161 or less per year. Concentrated in urban slums[2] and poor rural settlements, several billion people survive by virtue of non-capitalist links to peasant households, expelled from communal lands as surplus to the labour required by the land's new owners.

More than a century ago, Marx emphasised how capitalist economic growth rendered people surplus to the then emergent system's production requirements. The economic growth associated with the past three decades of globalisation bears out this diagnosis: rather than alleviating poverty, unregulated economic growth has been its engine.

The force of markets: Polanyi's double movement

Polanyi maintained that the social costs of economic growth derived from unregulated markets in land, labour and money because none of the three was a true commodity. Regulation of such markets emerged alongside the development of the modern state. The latter's monopoly of legitimate violence and of detailed legal structure went hand in glove with the evolution of modern markets. His view directly challenged claims by the neoliberals of his generation that the capitalist system was guided by self-regulating markets, which made them more efficient and endowed capitalism with evolutionary superiority. In today's parlance, such writers as Hayek insisted the freer the market, the greater the prospect for economic growth and prosperity.

Polanyi's contemporary importance lies in his detailed, empirically robust demonstration that such claims had no basis in the historical record. Furthermore, his work showed that until the state intervened to regulate them, markets had the capacity to entirely subordinate the moral and the aesthetic concerns of the whole of society. Moreover, unlike Marx, Polanyi did not lay the blame for social ills on capitalism but on the governance of the capitalist system. He accepted the idea that capitalist growth increased social wealth; the policy issue was how to ensure that it did so in the public interest.

However, he regarded the idea that such an economy could be independent of government and political institutions as mistaken. Such an idea constituted a 'stark utopia' – utopian because it is unrealisable and stark because the effort to bring it into being would inevitably produce dystopian consequences. Indeed, it was capitalism's need to treat land and labour *as if* each were a commodity that destroyed communities. It was the historical evidence of such past destruction that led Polanyi to argue how the state came to play a critical role in managing capitalism in the interest of society. Disruption arising from market forces in land and labour, he argued, puts pressure on the government of the day to respond to demands of those affected, if only to ensure its own legitimacy. Over time, interventions of mitigation sediment into institutions and these become integral to the functioning of capitalism itself.

For example, Mayhew (2000, p 3) emphasised the importance Polanyi attributed to state institutions in the relay between the economic and the social order, especially the self-regulating market (SRM). According to Polanyi, the SRM differed from pre-capitalist markets in that it was a society-wide system of markets in which 'all inputs into the substantive processes of production and distribution were for sale and in which output was distributed solely in exchange for earnings from sales of inputs' (Clough and Polanyi, 1944, pp 313-14).

Uniquely, Polanyi emphasised that political counter-movements to deregulation were decisively influenced by the composition of the class interests involved (Clough and Polanyi, 1944). Not only had members of the working class challenged the system, but also land owners, bankers and merchants. In effect all those whose interests were threatened by the effects unregulated markets would join forces to protect their various joint interests. Arguably, it is this possibility of cross-class alliances against free markets that many regard as the most politically salient of Polanyi's findings. It implies the possibility today of building counter-movements into coalitions with the latter able to influence governments to take measures that pre-empt or mitigate the negative effects of capitalist economic growth.

Many developments in the second half of the 20th century can be seen to substantiate the predictive power of Polanyi's double movement and to attribute to it the construction of a state-centred institutional matrix (the Bretton Woods system), whose overall remit was to encourage capitalist economic growth, on the one hand *and* to mitigate the negative effects of market forces on the other.

Mitigation

A new international order was in its infancy when *The Great Transformation* was first published (Polanyi, 1944). The ratification of the Bretton Woods system (inclusive of the World Bank and the International Monetary Fund) and the United Nations (a new global governance body) signalled the emergence of a state-centred institutional matrix whose overall remit was the regulation of international market forces (trade and tariffs) and the promotion of capitalist development. Thirteen years later (1957), the broad outlines of a public–private institutional matrix had taken shape, including international governmental and non-governmental agencies whose remit expanded to include publicly and privately funded mitigation efforts. Nearly 60 years later, the structure of this institutional matrix has hardly changed. However, its internal complexity has increased considerably even as the resources at its disposal have not kept pace with the social changes wrought by globalisation.

Reisen (2008a, 2008b) offered a rare empirical overview of the evolution and the current configuration of the mitigation matrix. An insider to these institutions, he nonetheless argued that its main characteristic is chaotic expansion and this expansive proliferation continues apace, on a largely unrecognised scale. He illustrated the point in various ways, including documenting the extraordinary increase in the number of organisations or agencies concerned *solely* with ways to finance organisations whose remit is poverty mitigation. There were about 10 of these in the immediate post-war period; the number increased to about 350 in 1994 and to about 1,000 in 2004. Over roughly the same period, he documented an increase in the number of Organisation for Economic Co-operation and Development aid projects from 10,327 in 1995 to 27,876 in 2003. Overall, the mitigation matrix now includes 47 United Nations agencies, funds and commissions, four European Commission public organisations, two International Monetary Fund (IMF) trusts, five World Bank Group organisations, 12 regional development banks and funds, 97 other multilateral institutions, 32 international NGOs and five main public-private partnerships (Reisen, 2008a).

The chaotic expansion of the matrix tracks the opening rounds of globalisation, especially the consequences of the various sovereign debt crises in the global South in the early the 1980s. It is well known, for example, that the structural adjustment reforms advocated by matrix heavyweights such as the IMF and World Bank created such a severe fiscal crisis in many of these countries that public service provision all but collapsed (OECD, 2008; Ciancanelli, 2010). This collapse provoked a variety of non-profit NGOs and CSOs to mitigate its effects by filling the service void. In many of these indebted developing countries, more money for public services is now managed by this 'third sector' than by government.

However efficiently an NGO may run local public services, there is not only an implied democratic deficit that warrants concern, but serious questions about the macro-social coordination problems arising from delivery of public services by a shifting set of mainly foreign, narrowly accountable NGOs, charitable or self-help organisations. These problems have attracted much deserved criticism even by important members of the matrix (OECD, 2008). To get an idea of the scale of the problem, we may consider Koch (2008, p 69), who noted that the then Tanzanian government had to deal every year with 1,000 incoming donor missions and in return for their support, find staff to write up the 2,400 quarterly reports of progress their sponsors demanded. Reisen (2008a) described the resulting alphabet soup of agencies as 'multilateral donor chaos'. The point is illustrated by the fact that 38 nations each hosted 25 or more development finance agencies associated with the mitigation matrix.

It should not be assumed that an increase in the number of separate organisations has meant an increase in the resources devoted to mitigation, whether measured as the costs funded by private donation or as some proportion of the taxes paid to governments or even as encouragement of self-help via social enterprises. There is no comprehensive source of information that would allow us to say with any certainty how much is spent on mitigation per se because there is no comprehensive audit that could distinguish the NGO costs of operating from the value of expenditures by them on the projects they undertake.

What we do have is information as to the spend of key actors in the international aid system and we can compare it to data on economic wealth, as measured by the global gross domestic product or Global World Product (GWP). Thus, for example, in 2010, after the global financial crash, the GWP was estimated by DeLong as US$62 trillion. Before the financial crash, the total spend by the key actors in the international aid system was about US$40 billion, or equivalent to seven-tenths of 1% (0.07%) of the global GWP. If we suppose private foundations, CSOs and NGOs were to have spent an additional US$40 billion, this would increase the total spend to US$80 billion, implying a global mitigation fund that is about one-tenth of 1% (0.12%) of GWP. Moreover, as Shah (2014) pointed out, even though high-income OECD nations pledged, in 1970, to give 0.7 % of their respective GDP as aid, they have not done so. Indeed, since the pledge, the accumulated shortfall is about US$5 trillion in 2012 prices.

Another way to measure the scale of mitigation is to consider how many people are paid to work in the industry. The core institutions report employment of about 50,000. If we assume the number working in specialist NGOs, CSOs and so on is an additional 50,000, we arrive at an estimated 100,000 people worldwide whose paid, full-time remit is to find ways to overcome the adverse consequences of capitalism on the roughly 2 billion people now rendered surplus to it.

It is important to add that none of the mitigation efforts discussed thus far, official, locally self-financed or philanthropic, includes the considerable scale and scope of the mitigation agencies operating within the governments of the global North. That aid is entirely domestic and includes such assistance as unemployment benefits, state pensions and so on. Nor does it include international associations, such as the European Union, whose agencies focus on member needs (for example, common agricultural policy). We estimate that these domestic-focused agencies provide some protection to perhaps as many as 50 million individuals (that is, 10% of the population of high-income countries).

Even if it turns out, on closer scrutiny, to be much more, say twice that number, or 100 million people, the overall effect does not change much. We can say with some confidence that roughly 1.9 billion people globally are without any sort of safety net and have to make do with a global mitigation spend that works out to be not much more than US$10–15 per capita per year.

Of course, it is possible to argue that the nation state system of the post-World War II/Cold War consensus (from 1945 to the dissolution of the Bretton Woods system in 1971) demonstrates the wisdom of Polanyi's views. Those years, they emphasise, provide ample evidence of the power of states to mitigate self-regulating markets (Block and Somers, 2014). However, demonstrating that modern states once worked that way is not the quite the same thing as demonstrating they do so now or that they can be made to do so again (Panitch and Gindin, 2013).

Position and movement in 21st-century civil society

For Marx, capitalist economic growth held few attractions; its expansion implied an extension of a type of social alienation that granted more important rights to things than to the people who laboured to produce them. This vision directs attention to the strategic importance of how land and other means of production are owned and managed.

For Polanyi, capitalism, properly governed and regulated, held out the promise of freedom from want as well as increased leisure time to allow individuals to cultivate cultural and aesthetic projects. His diagnosis directs attention to the democratic polity and how it structures governance to safeguard solidarity and social cohesion. Nonetheless, and in spite of these differences, both Marx and Polanyi accorded special status to land and labour, an agreement that prompts us to reflect on SSEs in the past few decades and the extent to which they concern themselves with them.

What is striking in the past few decades is the extent to which deindustrialisation in both the global North and South appears to provide fertile soil for SSEs as new forms of organising economic activity. How do we make sense of this phenomenon? Is it a harbinger of reforms to global capitalist governance or does it signal a decisive shift in political consciousness on the need for alternatives to the kinds of lives that capitalism appears to demand? Instead of trying to answer this question directly, we propose a way to consider it via a discussion of cooperatives, one of the oldest alternatives to private enterprise, and consider their long-standing exclusion from the post-World War II mitigation matrix. The reason is simple: if cooperatives were regarded as social/solidarity enterprise, the political weight of the SSE sector would be far greater than it appears to be now. Why they are not so regarded is something that requires thinking about.

Cooperatives

It is noteworthy that cooperatives have been and continue to be excluded from most official deliberations sponsored by the main multilateral organisations on the impacts of capitalist growth, including such impacts as unemployment, poverty, climate change and so forth. And of course, academic and other discussions of social and solidarity enterprises neither exclude nor include cooperatives in principle. In fact, there is very little discussion of whether the form itself recommends it as a social enterprise or whether it is the substantive use to which the form is put that is required to qualify as an SSE.

It is only recently that the exclusion of cooperatives from World Bank, IMF and other official discussions related to SSEs has attracted scholarly attention. It is noteworthy that in this rare, recent call for their inclusion (Utting, 2015) the burden of argument is not concerned with issues of accountability, democracy, organisational efficiency or purpose but with how many of them there are and how big many of them have become. Thus, Utting (2015) argues first that only if the SSE sector scales up (via aggregation, networking and so on) can it achieve the size required to take on the twin problems of climate change and destructive urbanisation. The question is how to scale up the sector. He proposes that the inclusion of cooperatives would turbo-charge the scaling-up process and result in a significant increase in the political weight of SSEs in finding solutions to climate change and destructive urbanisation.

To illustrate this point, Utting (2015) indicates how the size of the global SSE sector would increase if cooperatives were included, pointing to the size effect of bringing to bear their additional substantial assets of cooperatives (circa US$18.8 trillion), their additional substantial cash flow (US$24 trillion in combined annual revenue) and the substantial number of people advocating for change (worldwide about 800 million individuals are members of cooperatives). And it must be admitted that if such numbers did join in collective actions taken with other SSEs on such important problems as climate change, in size terms it would constitute a significant increase in opposition to business–as–usual capitalism (Utting, 2015, pp 3-5).

However, it is not obvious that a cooperative per se ought to be regarded as an SSE; certainly mainstream multilateral organisations such as the World Bank have never regarded them as social enterprises to be included in their remit, and of course many leading NGOs appear to regard cooperatives as distinct from social enterprises and consequently they have excluded them from their invitations to policy forums. However, this pattern of exclusion requires more critical thinking than is supplied by Utting (2015), especially in light of some of the facts he supplies.

For example, Utting (2015) pointed out there are more cooperatives than capitalist firms in the global North, making cooperatives the single most common way to organise economic activity; this is in itself suggestive. The question that he does not ask is why do the multilateral agencies and NGOs ignore them while at the same time maintaining frequent communication with those who follow the less common way to organise economic activity, for example as a capitalist firm?

Cooperatives also have other features that warrant consideration. According to Olsen (2014), the survival rates of workers' cooperatives, long assumed by economists at such places as the World Bank and IMF to be economically risky, are superior to the survival rates of conventional capitalist firms. Not to be overlooked is the evidence that cooperatives have proven themselves effective competitors in product and service markets, so much so that Jones and Kalmi (2009) argued that the cooperatives, as a type of organisation, manifest a similar size distribution to that of capitalist firms, and have proven to be a much more resilient and sustainable engines of enterprise than the joint stock company type of capitalist firm. In other words, research evidence regarding cooperatives challenges the presumption that corporations directed and controlled by a handful of top managers are more efficient. It is a direct challenge to the neoliberal claim that the capitalist firm has an evolutionary superiority to all ways of organising economic activity. In addition, one could argue that from a capitalist market standpoint, a cooperative per se is merely a competitor whose top managers are not bullied by either share price fluctuations or dividend decisions.

This brings us to a formal point about cooperatives. Legally, a cooperative is merely a type of association or undertaking that mandates *inter alia* members' ownership of surpluses generated by the cooperative's activities. However, how this distribution is carried out varies a great deal because the statutes of incorporation vary from one country, state or province to the next. As a result, there is considerable diversity in the commercial and managerial structure of cooperatives. It is this diversity that makes it difficult to classify them; some are substantively a type of business and others are closer in substance to a social enterprise or a solidarity enterprise.

For example, some cooperatives have highly focused business remits such as FrieslandCampina, a Dutch dairy cooperative with revenues of EUR9.6 billion in 2011. It functions as a pass-through vehicle for profit-making diary farms. Larg, an alliance of 14 insurance cooperatives and mutuals in Latin America, offers reinsurance and risk management services to cooperative and mutual insurers because few commercial providers offer these to the many small businesses operating there (McKinsey & Company, 2012). Both of these cooperatives contrast strongly with Mondragon, the highly successful, large (circa 80,000 employees) and much-studied worker cooperative that some argue offers an alternative path to prosperity (for a short summary, see Wolff, 2012).

Seen in this light, one can imagine why many of the very large joint stock corporations would prefer to exclude some of them from World Bank- or IMF-sponsored colloquia, seminars and other thought leadership events. They are larger, more efficient and more sustainable — features that the standard corporation might like ignored. Equally, many leading NGOs would find it difficult to include profit-focused pass-through agricultural cooperatives like FrieslandCampina in its deliberations on non-profit social enterprises whose remit is largely charitable in nature. It is this diversity and complexity that renders somewhat fanciful Utting's (2015) idea of including cooperatives in order to scale up the SSE sector. Few of the very largest cooperatives, particularly in agriculture, manifest any interest in eschewing the commodification of land or labour. Making things even more confusing is the fact that while the SSE sector already includes many cooperatives, it does not privilege this legal form as essential.

Conclusion

It seems more likely that scaling up the sector could occur through the self-organising, global networking made possible by the growth of the World Wide Web. This set of technologies has already scaled up the collective political weight of SSEs, in post-capitalist narratives, especially those emerging eco and social economy narratives that directly challenge the neoliberal narrative. Arguably, some sort of *entente cordiale* ought to be brokered that would encourage SSEs to identify common themes that form the basis of collective action. It may seems fanciful for us to suggest the sector can scale up via some high tech *entente cordiale* brokered over the World Wide Web but then a truly World Wide Web would itself have seemed highly implausible to most of us a couple of decades ago. In addition, we would advocate that a high priority be given to a focus on the commodification of land and labour along with political agendas that are highly specific, including concerted legal and other actions to prevent commodification of communal lands and the importance of alternatives to the 'self-commodification' of one's labour. Our view is that given the absence of an agreement on limits on the commodification of land and labour, it is very difficult to oppose pro-capitalist economic growth narratives. Moreover, we regard efforts by SSEs to prevent further commodification of land and further expulsion of labour as constituting an early warning system of immense importance in discussions of climate change and destructive urbanisation. Such early warning is essential for making others aware of the need to impose controls on at least these particular markets forces and provoke efforts to think about capitalist economic growth as a barrier to economic wellbeing.

Lacking agreement on the specifics of the commodification of land and labour should not mean rejection of the idea of agreeing a theme. Our central point is that construction of a common identity is an essential step in associating the sector with transformation rather than mitigation. Without a common social identity as transformative institutions, it is easy to characterise the decades-long increase in SSE formation as growth in the mitigation matrix rather than a movement to stop the engine that creates them.

Singer, the father of SSEs in Brazil and elsewhere in the global South, has proposed they be viewed as organisations operating in the tradition of utopian socialism, one in which individuals are encouraged to carve out opportunities for making a living within the existing social order but according to more communal, socialised property and work relations (Cibele et al, 2013). Vieta (2013) agreed with this perspective, adding the important argument that utopian imagining and the creation of alternatives to the factory system have grown in parallel with the growth of capitalism itself.

Another voice can supplement these observations. Gramsci argued issues of culture are at the heart of any challenge to the dominant discourse because culture is how class is lived (Crehan, 2002, p 71). This is what gives particular salience to SSEs: they offer to their participants an immersion in another way to live and to construct their livelihoods. They can build connections to the broader community and thereby to the creation of new forms of solidarity. It is, however, too early to say whether they can achieve the political weight required to challenge capitalist developments. What we documented in our earlier discussion of the past three decades of capitalist growth tries to make clear is that the scale of the destructive consequences of global capitalism requires a collective response of an order of magnitude beyond anything we might now imagine is possible for the SSE sector.

Notes

[1]   In this context Purchasing Power Parity (PPP) refers to a calculation that estimates the US dollar value of global output as if it were produced and sold in the US.

[2]   We are not engaging in the debate between Davis (2006), who saw little hope in these rapidly expanding slums on one hand, and Do Soto (2000), who, on the other hand, invoked the innovation and entrepreneurial potential that can emerge in those spaces.

References

Block, F. and Somers, M. (2014) *The Power of Market Fundamentalism: Karl Polanyi's Critique*. Cambridge, MA: Harvard University Press.

Cibele, J., da Costa, R.P. and Saraiva, A.F. (2013) 'Solidarity Economy in Brazil: Income Distribution in an Industrialized Services Cooperative', PPT Presentation, Production Engineering Department, University of São Paolo, Brazil.

Ciancanelli, P. (2010) 'Managing for Social Outcomes: Diverse Value Rationalities and Financial Control', *Critical Sociology*, vol. 36, no. 2, pp 1-18.

Clough, S.B. and Polanyi, K. (1944) 'Review of The Great Transformation', *The Journal of Modern History*, vol. 16, no. 4, pp 313-14.

Crehan, K. (2002) *Gramsci, Culture and Anthropology*. Berkeley, CA: University of California Press.

Davis, M. (2006) *Planet of Slums*. London: Verso.

Davies, J., Sandstrom, S., Shorrocks, A. and Wolff, E. (2006) *The World Distribution of Household Wealth*. World Institute for Development Economics Research of the United Nations University (UNI-WIDER).

Do Soto, H. (2000) *The Mystery of Capital: Why capitalism triumphs in the west and fails everywhere else*. New York, NY: Basic Books.

Dobb, M. (1973) *Theories of Value and Distribution Since Adam Smith: Ideology and Economic Theory*. London: Cambridge University Press.

ETC Group (2013a) 'The Cartel Before The Horse', *Communique No. 11*, 11 September, at www.etcgroup.org/putting_the_cartel_before_the_horse_2013 (accessed 15 August 2015).

ETC Group (2013b) 'Who Will Feed Us? Text and Poster: The Industrial Food Chain or the Peasant Food Webs?', 6 September, www.etcgroup.org/content/poster-who-will-feed-us-industrial-food-chain-or-peasant-food-webs (accessed 25 August 2015).

Hendrickson, M., Wilkinson, J., Heffernan W.D. and Gronski, R. (2008) 'The Global Food System and Nodes of Power', 2 August, http://ssrn.com/abstract=1337273 (accessed 15 August 2015).

Jones, D. and Kalmi, P. (2009) 'Trust, Inequality and the Size of the Cooperative Sector: Cross Country Evidence', *Annals of Public and Cooperative Economics*, vol 80, no 2, pp 165-195.

Koch, D.-J. (2008) 'A Paris declaration for NGOs', in *Financing Development: Whose Ownership?*), Paris: OECD, ch 3, www.oecd.org/dev/pgd/financingdevelopment2008whoseownership.htm

Marx, K. (1887) *Capital, Vol 1*. Original 1887 English edition reprinted by Progress Publishers, Moscow.

Marx, K. (1967) *Capital, Vol III*. New York: International Publishers.

Mason, P. (2015) *PostCapitalism: A guide to our future*. Milton Keynes: Allen Lane.

Mayhew, A. (2000) 'Review of Karl Polanyi's The Great Transformation', Net Economic History Services, June, http://eh.net/?s=Mayhew+2000 (accessed 15 August 2015).

McKinsey & Company (2012) 'International Summit of Cooperatives: How Cooperatives Grow', http://documents.mx/documents/mckinsey-on-cooperatives-how-cooperatives-grow.html (accessed 23 June 2016).

OECD (Organisation for Economic Co-operation and Development) (2008) *Financing Development: Whose Ownership?*, Paris: OECD, www.oecd.org/dev/pgd/financingdevelopment2008whoseownership.htm (accessed 15 August 2015).

Ohmae, K. (1990) *The Borderless World*. New York, NY: Harper Business.

Olsen, E.K. (2014) 'The Relative Survival of Worker Cooperatives and Barriers to Their Creation', in T. Kato (ed) *Advances in the Economic Analysis of Participatory & Labour-Managed Firms. Vol 14: Sharing Ownership, Profits, and Decision-Making in the 21st Century*, pp. 83-107, www.emeraldinsight.com/doi/abs/10.1108/S0885-3339%282013%290000014005 (accessed 15 August 2015).

Panitch, L. and Gindin, S. (2013) *The Making of Global Capitalism: The Political Economy of the American Empire*. London: Verso Books.

Polanyi, K. (1944) *The Great Transformation*. New York, NY: Farrar & Rhinehart.

Reisen, H. (2008a) 'The Multilateral Donor Chaos', OECD Development Centre, http://afd.fr/webdav/shared/PORTAILS/PAYS/EUROPE/Pdf (accessed 15 August 2015).

Reisen, H. (2008b) 'En route to Accra: The global development finance non-system', www.voxeu.org/article/development-aid-duplication-rivalry-and-mission-creep (accessed 15 August 2015).

Sassen, S. (2014) *Expulsions: Brutality and Complexity in the Global Economy*. Cambridge, MA: Belknap & Harvard University Press.

Shah, A. (2014) 'Official global foreign aid shortfall: $5 trillion', www.globalissues.org/article/593/official-global-foreign-aid-shortfall-5-trillion (accessed 29 August 2015).

Utting, P. (ed) (2015) 'Introduction: The challenge of scaling up social and solidarity economy' in *Social and Solidarity Economics: Beyond the Fringe*. London: Zed Books, pp. 1-37.

Vieta, M. (2013) *The emergence of the* empresas recuperadas por sus trabajadores*: A political economic and sociological appraisal of two decades of self-management in Argentina*, Euricse Working Paper No. 55|13, European Institute on Cooperative and Social Enterprises, www.euricse.eu/.

Wolff, R. (2012) 'Yes, there is an alternative to capitalism: Mondragon shows the way', www.theguardian.com/commentisfree/2012/jun/24/alternative-capitalism-mondragon_(accessed 23 June 2016).

FOUR

Co-construction or prefiguration? The problem of the 'translation' of social and solidarity economy practices into policy

Ana Cecilia Dinerstein

At the beginning of the 21st century, Latin America was characterised by a condition of political transformation. The social and labour mobilisations against neoliberalism that emerged during the 1990s facilitated the accession to power of new centre-left political forces and coalitions that took on board movement demands and cooperative practices and transformed state structures, legislation and institutions to the extent that they were collectively christened the 'pink tide'. The '21st century socialist' and 'neo-developmentalist strategy' under the leadership of Hugo Chávez, Evo Morales, Néstor Kirchner and Rafael Correa among other political leaders encouraged and supported grassroots movements financially and politically in many ways, especially via policy – and especially the social and solidarity economy (SSE). While these policies reflected the movements' political demands for state recognition and support for their SSE cooperative projects, the governmental strategy also responded to the growing pressure from international organisations towards obtaining the engagement, participation and support from social movements and SSE organisations for new public policies and laws in order to facilitate their access to the new policy schemes (Fonteneau et al, 2010; UNRISD, 2010). On the one hand, this underscores the growing importance of civil society actors (including social movements) in rethinking 'development' and the co-production of policy, particularly in the current period of global crisis. On the other hand, it 'translates' SSE practices as befitting neoliberal decentralisation. By translation, I mean the processes, mechanisms and dynamics through which the state incorporates the cooperative and solidarity ethos of SSE grassroots practices into policy.

This chapter presents three ideas.[1] The first is that, as autonomous practice, the SSE can be a tool for 'organising hope' (Dinerstein,

2015), that is, a practice that enables the anticipation of alternative reality/future practices, relations and horizons – in the present. Hope is not synonymous with the wish for a better future, dream or fantasy, but, following German philosopher Ernst Bloch (1986 [1959]), its utopian function allows us to engage with the unclosed nature of the world. To Bloch, there exists in the present a concrete possibility of prefiguring what he calls 'the-not-yet-become'. Hence, hope is not wishful, but wilful, that is, it guides concrete praxis (Levitas, 2013). Second, the integration of SSE practices into state policy requires the demarcation of a framework within which the 'institutionalisation of the SSE' (Coraggio, 2015) can take place, that is, the context of capitalist-coloniality. Vázquez (2011, p 36) suggests that the epistemic violence of modernity 'renders invisible everything that does not fit in the "parameters of legibility" of [its] epistemic territory'. Similarly, I suggest that the state renders invisible everything that does not fit in the parameters of the legibility of its policy territory. In this case, **neoliberal translation** subjugates the emancipatory dimension of SSE into capitalist-colonial logics of power, rather than enabling the transformative aspects of SSE to flourish. By so doing, it not only impoverishes the SSE, but is a barrier to SSE policy being as innovative and transformative as it could be. Is it possible to think of another form of translation? Third, I suggest that an adequate translation of the SSE into policy necessitates an engagement with the emancipatory call of social movements. We must explore and discuss the 'untranslatable' aspects of SSE, which contain the seeds for innovative alternative policy prescriptions.

The anti-/post-capitalist potential of the SSE

A thorough exploration of the emancipatory nature of the SSE goes well beyond the scope of this chapter (but see Chapters Two and Five of this volume). However, in light of my research with four social movements in Latin America, and the ideas presented here, I would like to problematise the idea that the co-construction of policy 'allows the SSE to realize its potential' (Mendell and Alain, 2015, p 168). Mendell and Alain (2015, p 167) argue that co-construction would help policymakers to understanding the process of 'learning by doing' that underpins SSE movements' collective action. It also necessitates 'permeable forms of governance' (Mendell and Alain, 2015, p 167) that allow work to be undertaken in more collaborative ways. Coraggio (2015, pp 136-7) uses the example of Brazil to highlight the country's experiment in the 'co-construction' of public SSE policy, which, according to the author, differs from the Argentinian model of populist social economy policy and the Ecuadorian creation of a social and solidarity economy system based on *buen vivir*.

I argue that, first, we must make sure that co-construction does not become a buzzword. Cornwall and Brock (2005, p 4) argue that new policy buzzwords such as participation, empowerment and poverty reduction (related to co-construction) are presently used for the reframing of World Bank policy discourse as feel-good terms, that is, as a policy rhetoric that demarcates the limits of what participation and empowerment mean. Insofar as it excludes dissident meanings, this rhetoric is inevitably realised through political processes that include co-option, coercion and, in many instances, direct state violence that is imposed on those who do not buy into this rhetoric.

Second, we must attend to the problematic nature of the capitalist state. The state is a state in a capitalist society, that is, it is not a neutral arena on which the common good is decided, but a *capitalist* state, that is, it is the political *form* of capital, the ultimate function of which is to preserve an order based on private property. The state facilitates the naturalisation of capitalism and sustains the separation between the social and the political. It does so by preventing socioeconomic practices from becoming political projects. But many social movements of the present are challenging this separation and see their prefigurative practices as political (Brissette, 2016).

Third, we must consider that for almost two decades now, and as the chapters in this collection show, civil society organisations and social movements – particularly in the global South – have been experimenting with non-profit forms of local and cooperative production, distribution, land occupation and use, driven by communal values, and organised through collective decision-making processes and direct participation of those involved in these endeavours. These are usually projects that involve the 'production of the commons in common' as a political activity around social reproduction understood as the reproduction of life (Gutiérrez Aguilar et al, 2017).

Many of these movements belong to national and transnational networks such as the Intercontinental Network for the Promotion of the Social and Solidarity Economy (RIPESS) that offer a critique of the alternative development (AD) paradigm. Under the AD paradigm, the SSE offers a critique of the liberal vision of development, embracing the principles of collective property, the distribution of wealth to meet the needs of people rather than capital, and freedom of association and autonomous decision making (Dacheaux and Goujon, 2012, pp 206 and 208). The AD discourse encourages associative forms of production, sustainable development, economic support for the marginalised through the provision of land and housing, women's empowerment and the revival of 'the local' (Escobar, 1992; Santos and Rodríguez Garavito, 2006).

However, while AD introduces elements of solidarity and proposes changes in the type and scope of growth, it challenges neither the market economy (Coraggio, 2010) nor 'the concept of economic growth *per se*' (Santos and Rodríguez Garavito, 2006, pp xxxix-xl). This is problematic for movements that repudiate the 'growth-based' development model and see themselves as articulating *alternatives to* development, with SSE being at the heart of these elaborations around the notion of *buen vivir* (living well).

Although the SSE can be seen in many ways – for example, as Marques (2014) suggests, 'a market oriented initiative', 'a method of local development' and a 'conscious project of social transformation' – these are not clearly discernible (on the later form of SSE, see also Lemus and Barkin, 2013). In Latin America, SSE movements and networks have tended to associate their communal projects with a diagnostic that regards capitalism as undergoing a multiple, interconnected and unparalleled crisis that combines ecological, energy, food, environmental, poverty and hunger crises, which are matched with an increase in the means of violence and social control by nation states and the free movement of global capital. When it is part of a broader process of social transformation SSE is inherently *political* and it is located at the centre of the present debate about the viability and desirability of capitalism and the shift to a 'post-capitalist' economy (see Gibson-Graham, 2006). Latin American scholars have explained the crisis of capitalism as a 'crisis of civilisation', that is, the impossibility of the (re)production of dignified human life on the planet (Lander, 2010). While important strands within the SSE movement actively support forms of social enterprise that fit comfortably within the AD paradigm, others embrace more radical paradigms that, as Utting (2012) suggests, 'call for very different growth, production and consumption patterns, and power relations'. Since the pressure for growth is embedded in capitalism (Smith, 2011), these radical strands of SSE argue for an engagement with 'alternative visions of democracy, economy and society' (Escobar, 1992, p 22) and non-capitalist political practices. They disagree with the idea that 'capitalist efficiency and resource allocation is the best we can come up with' (Smith, 2010, p 28), with SSE contributing to this by engaging with populations left out of society so as to police them, or by bringing business skills to solving social problems in the case of social entrepreneurship. As Smith highlights, 'this belief is incompatible with an ecological economy' (p 28). Conceived in this way, SSE 'seeks to change the whole social and economic system and put forward a different paradigm of development that upholds solidarity economy principles' (Kawano, 2013): SSE would be about 're-socialising economic relations' (Gibson-Graham 2006, p 79). Movements are putting their 'emancipatory energy' (Santos, 2001, p 78) at the service of the creation of alternatives to the present in the present. Thus, it seems that an adequate translation of SSE into policy necessitates a kind of 'co-construction of policy' (Mendell and Alain, 2015) that immerses itself in what I call the 'beyond zone' of SSE practices, towards a collective process of **prefiguration**. This is a prefigurative translation that entails an epistemological discussion (on this see Dash, 2014) and repositioning of the role of policy in the 21st-century radical transformation of the world.

The struggle over the meaning of the SSE

As one would expect, the process of translation of SSE practices into policy entails a struggle over the meaning of the SSE. Hence, SSE movements are compelled to 'navigate the tensions' between being integrated into the logics of power and development, and the possibility of moving beyond it (Böhm et al, 2010). This contention over the meaning of SSE practices is never direct but unfolds through struggles around different aspects of state policy such as the law, welfare provision, participatory processes and budgets, and other policies that might enable or deter the free development of the SSE.

The contentious politics between movements and the state that spread out during the neoliberal period, when mobilised citizens and movements openly confronted neoliberal reforms and policy, did not disappear with the political shift to the centre-left during the first decade of 2000s, but evolved into different forms. Unlike neoliberal governments, the centre-left pink tide administrations claimed to be determined to take on board movement demands and to expand the rights of indigenous and non-indigenous subaltern groups, facilitating self-determination, self-organisation and self-management (Seoane et al, 2011). Rather than a revolutionary process itself, this political shift to the left by new governments was unthinkable without the social mobilisations against neoliberalism that preceded it. Most of these governments brought about political innovation such as the creation of 'plurinational' states and the incorporation of the *buen vivir* indigenous cosmology into the state's agenda. Overall, they achieved economic growth, the decline of income inequality, and improvements in education, social and labour policy, and healthcare.

This notwithstanding, the governments did not always reflect the aspirations of the movements in their politics, and translate these aspirations into policy. The translation of grassroots mobilisations and broadly understood alternative and cooperative SSE practices into state policy did not always go smoothly. Their social and economic policy frequently contradicted their anti-neoliberal and bottom-up approach, therefore disappointing the aspirations of popular indigenous, peasant and social movements' collective dreams. The repression of the Movement of Rural Landless Workers under the government of Lula Da Silva illustrates this point. In practice, movement-created SSE alternatives were incorporated into state policy by virtue of their deradicalisation, thus remaining a utopian aspiration. The reality was that while mobilising against and also engaging in negotiation processes with governmental authorities at all levels, the movements *challenged* state policies and legislation that attempted to translate their collective practices into tools for neoliberal governance promoted by international development institutions. On some occasions, extreme state violence was used against the movements and such violence was a key factor in the process of paving the way for the process of translation of SSE into policy, as in the case of the repression of the Zapatistas – indigenous people in Chiapas who opposed the North American Free Trade Agreement in Mexico in the mid-1990s.

Deciphering SSE movements' action zones: the question of untranslatability

There has been a significant change in social mobilisation where movements are moving away from their claim-making role to perceive themselves as creators of new worlds (Dinerstein and Deneulin, 2012; Dinerstein, 2015). This means that much of social movement theory and its existing methods of enquiry are insufficient, deceiving, or obsolete. As argued elsewhere, SSE movements are new type of movement that are prefiguring concrete alternatives (concrete utopias) in the present:

> For the past two decades, we are witnessing a turning point
> in autonomous movement activity that, consequently,
> requires a shift in our approach to 'autonomy' in Latin
> America.... the new quality of Latin American movements
> is that autonomous organising is a tool for prefiguring

alternatives with political imagination. (Dinerstein, 2015,
p 2)

Autonomous (SSE) movements have shaped new territorial and
political realities where radical pedagogies, cooperative work, art and
entertainment, care, new forms of defending indigenous traditions
and customs, environmental awareness and territorialised resistance
develop in imaginative forms on a day-to-day basis. These allow for the
demarcation of new parameters other than those designated by the state,
global capital and the law. As an example, while many social scientists
continue trying to find the solution to 'unemployment', members
of the *piquetero* movement from the Argentine Movement of Solano
Unemployed Workers (Movimiento de Trabajadores Desocupados
Solano, or MTD Solano) define their struggle not as a working-class
struggle for job creation, social reform or even for a future revolution
in the traditional sense, but as a practice projected into the future and,
therefore, able to anticipate an alternative reality, the reality of 'dignity'
(MTD Solano and Colectivo Situaciones, 2002, cited in Dinerstein,
2014, p 19) in the present, which, according to them, cannot be
attained through capitalist work. In this, it is very different from social
economy practices in the UK and Europe that aim to insert those
excluded from the capitalist market into it, described in Chapter Five
of this collection. MTD Solano rejects a future of exploitation as wage
slaves in a capitalist system as a potential good life.

To understand this process, we can distinguish four dimensions
or SSE 'zones' (see Figure 4.1). First, the 'creative zone' is where
alternative practices unfold at an organisational level (through
collective practices and leadership structures, as co-operative practices
develop over time); at a socioeconomic level (sociabilities, relations
and values, economic possibilities, use of space); and at a politico-
institutional level (political engagement, non-representational politics,
direct democracy, autonomy). Second, the conflict zone is where
disagreements, negotiations and struggles between movements and
the state, corporate power and development discourses take place
within specific configurations of power, class relations, and forms of
capital accumulation, development and crises. Third, closely connected
to the conflict zone, is the translation zone, where mechanisms of
interpretation and rephrasing of SSE visions, aspirations and practices
by policymakers takes place in ways that might facilitate or deter
the development of the SSE. The fourth zone (the 'beyond zone')
emerges out of the breach between the realities prefigured by SSE
movements and the ways SSE-inspired policy is organised (Dinerstein

Figure 4.1: SSE zones

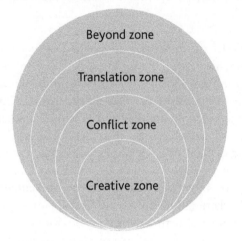

and Deneulin, 2012). This gap evokes both the impossibility of completely translating SSE practice that is led by movements into policy (programmes and legislation) and an 'epistemology of possibility' (Amsler, 2016) brought about by movements' cooperative collective actions. This means that SSE movements venture beyond the given reality, with little certainty about their praxis, which is facilitated by ongoing collective self-reflection and self-learning (*aprendizaje*). The fact that the law or policy demarcate the terrain of what exists and what does not exist (legibility) does not mean that SSE practices that are moving beyond those parameters do not exist at all. Following Vázquez (2011, p 36), the possibility of translation 'begs the question of untranslatability: so what is that which remains untranslatable, outside the scope of translation?' SSE practice is about creating alternative horizons, practices and relations that cannot be easily translated into policy without changing some fundamental features of the state and the economy. Although interesting policies have emerged to support some aspects of the claim for many areas in which the SSE sector is creating alternative visions and practices, for example food sovereignty or dignified work, the full realisation of these discourses and practices would entail a profound socioeconomic and political transformation that would frame policy differently. Policy has tended to fall into the category of food security or decent jobs or work.

To understand this more completely, let us develop the example of food sovereignty mentioned above. While food *security* is a tool for neoliberal governance and can provide a patchy and temporary solution to the problem of hunger, food *sovereignty* confronts agribusiness with hope in a democratic and autonomous agrarian project. As the *Nyéléni*

Newsletter (International Movement for Food Sovereignty, 2013, p 1)[2] suggests, unlike food security, food sovereignty is a concept that both 'challenges the corporate dominated, market driven model of globalised food, as well as offering a new paradigm to fight hunger and poverty by developing and strengthening local economies.... Where food security is a given, food sovereignty is a space of resistance.' Food sovereignty alludes to an inalienable right to food and requires a radical and more comprehensive process than 'securing' food to eliminate hunger in the world. Food sovereignty, therefore, goes well beyond land distribution and demands that governments respect, protect and implement people's *right* to food (Rosset, 2006), as well as other principles such as local development and agro-ecology as an alternative to agribusiness. As it is, food sovereignty (as well as indigenous autonomy and dignified work) has no representation in the grammar of state policy as it is and, therefore, remains untranslatable.[3]

Research on the SSE shows a complex relationship between movements and the state and how SSE movements can benefit from a certain degree of institutionalisation, and from the technical, legal and financial support offered by state. However, my contention is that despite its fundamental importance for SSE movements, the practices created within the beyond zone, which transcend the parameters of legibility demarcated by the state, have been made invisible and the SSE movements of Latin America and the world continue to express a desire to explore alternative realities. For example, in the statement of the SSE movement at the United Nations Conference on Sustainable Development (Rio+20), more than 370 social organisations defined the SSE as 'a social movement that together with others is contributing to the consolidation of a genuine economic and political democracy'. They scorn the creation of institutions of governance that are not 'structurally grounded in on-going consultation and participation of all sectors of society at local, regional and international levels', and are:

> dominated by those whose financial contributions are the greatest, or managed by 'experts' ... people's sovereignty must be respected, as well as that of communities who are the only ones to have the legitimate right and the capacity to implement the solidarity development that can guarantee the preservation of the Commons. (RIPESS, 2012)[4]

Likewise, the declaration of the Convergence Assembly on Economic Alternatives at the RIPESS World Social Forum, 2013, declared that:

social solidarity economy in its various forms throughout the world represents the alternative to the global capitalist system ... the Assembly calls upon all civil society actors to network their actions at global level in order to enable people all over the world to assert their rights, and to replace the current system that is based on individual selfishness, over-consumption of resources, competition, male hegemony and war, by a peaceful, fraternal, sober economy of cooperation and peace between all humankind. (Participants in the Assembly of Convergence, Another World Already Exists Here and Now, World Social Forum 2013, Tunis)[5]

Towards a prefigurative translation

Social movements have posed new epistemological, theoretical and methodological questions that should enable us to rethink our methodological and theoretical assumptions, in order to offer a critique *with* the movements in question. An example. Unemployment is a fact of the present world economy. And yet, it is only so if we are discussing unemployment in a capitalist society. Were such a society not naturalised as it is, we should state that unemployment is only a fact in a capitalist society. In a different society where wage labour does not exist, the concept of unemployment would not make any sense at all. We could talk of lack of an occupation or contribution to the work of the common, but not of unemployment. This relativisation of the term unemployment opens a space to discuss not just the problem of labour in capitalism, but the type of society that produces such a situation. Thus, the *piquetero*'s critique can be understood not as a critique of unemployment, but as a critique of capitalist society that produces a situation where people need to work in order to live. The *piquetero*'s critique is a critique of capitalist work.

In light of this, how do these transformations change the question of policy? What theory is needed for a SSE-informed policy? My argument is that an *adequate translation* via co-construction can only be achieved by a *method of translation* that engages with the processes of prefiguration, or it cannot be considered a co-construction of policy at all. That is, without an engagement with the concrete processes of anticipating the future in the present in heterotopic spaces created to that end, with a concomitant and commensurate consideration of the significance of the struggles surrounding the process of prefiguration, co-construction pf policy would remain a constraining factor – or just a buzzword. Prefiguration is not simply a fashionable idea, but the reality of many movements today. Carlos Marentes, the co-coordinator of the North America Region of La Via Campesina (LVC) recently put it like this: "We not only believe that another world is necessary, the members of La Via Campesina are already building a better world."[6] Evidence shows that examples of everyday life resistance are not castles in the air: they are struggles for the production and reproduction of life. Collective actors such as LVC are undergoing an 'experiential critique' of the hegemonic project, a critique that, far from being ideological, is rooted in everyday life, in the body, in social relations, in communal practices (Dinerstein, 2017).

Our methodological and epistemological assumptions tend to 'naturalise' capitalism, thus contradicting the creative and forceful spirit of the movements' anti-/post-development or capitalist practices, and dispossessing SSE from one of its main qualities – the capacity to prefigure alternative realities to the present ones. Ironically, the universe of 'surplus possibilities' (Gibson-Graham, 2006) offered by movement-led SSE practices is usually made invisible by the same law or policy that claims to enable them to develop and expand. But as already argued, translation 'by erasure' (Vázquez, 2011) inevitably *removes* the surplus possibility, thus impoverishing SSE-inspired policy.

I argue that prefigurative translation (PT) can both enable the emancipatory ethos of SSE movements and enrich SSE policy. It can simultaneously problematise 'reality', engage with the open-ended and process-like quality of reality, and recognise the movements' alternative-creating capacity. PT postulates that insofar as hope guides contemporary social mobilisation, as previously discussed, policy needs also to be prefigurative, that is, it must be directed to render visible what is already being proposed and experienced by SSE movements. Prefigurative translation does not only learn from the movements' alternatives to development, but also facilitates the emergence of a 'collective intelligence' (RIPESS, 2012).[7] Far from being naïve, utopian, romantic or unfeasible, the engagement of the beyond zone of SSE movements only requires the intellectual effort to critique political economy and transcend its capitalist realism. We must render visible 'what has been and is actively being produced as non-existent' and, as a result, 'reality is reduced to what exists' (Santos, 2007, p 8). Prefigurative translation does not classify or measure SSE practices with ossified concepts of a reality, but constitutes an open process that uses co-production as a form of learning from the practices that are developed in the beyond zone of SSE practices.

Finally, to be sure, to immerse ourselves into the dimension of the 'not-yet' is challenging, and requires us to admit, at the least, that we can 'tolerate not knowing' (Gibson-Graham, 2006, p xxxi). Any policy that results from the movements' alternative-creating capacity can only reflect the prefigurative programme that corresponds to the SSE movements' practices of an open and unclosed reality. Our key questions are whether the SSE opens new horizons and practices, that is, opens spaces for prefiguring other realities not yet materialised that contest capitalist reality, and whether they elicit expansive waves of ideas, feelings and actions that open the horizons of the mind more widely. There is a tension that lives within prefigurative translation that cannot and must not be ignored, which emanates from the very nature of capitalist society: state policy can be an enabling practice but it is *also* a tool for regulating and deradicalising movements for change. But policy is not a given: it is a contradictory and contentious process. It is not guided by technical rationality: it is political. As the state seeks to achieve order and stability, and a certain degree of consensus is formed, policy reforms are only the temporary resolution of ongoing conflicts or, better, their crystallisation in time. A prefigurative translation can push policy further, to its limits, and become part of the process of 'organising hope'. It can try to escape the contours of the given reality to allow itself to venture with the SSE movements into their beyond zone: 'What if we ...?'

Notes

[1] This chapter evolved from a paper presented at the symposium Potential and Limits of Social and Solidarity Economy, convened by the United Nations Institute for Research in Social Development (UNRISD) and sponsored by the International Labour Organization on 6-8 May 2013 in Geneva. It was subsequently published as an UNRISD Occasional Paper No. 9, *The Hidden Side of Social and Solidarity Economy: Social movements and the 'translation' of SSE into policy (Latin America)*. I am grateful to Nadin Van Dijk, Peter Utting, Marguerite Mendell and Andrés Spognardi, who commented on previous versions of the paper, and to Peter North for his insightful suggestions that have helped to improve this chapter. The chapter has benefited from the insightful comments from participants of the Social Movement and Policy panel at the symposium Evidence and the Politics of Policymaking: Where Next?, convened by the Institute for Policy Research and the Centre for Development Studies at the University of Bath, 14-15 September 2016.

[2] *Nyéléni* is the newsletter of a broader food sovereignty movement that considers the Nyéléni 2007 declaration as its political platform.

[3] On grassroots women and SSE, see also Muñoz Cabrera (2013, p 12).

[4] This declaration, written in 2012 by the board of RIPESS, was based on the discussions at Rio+20 of the 5th Latin American and Caribbean Conference on Solidarity Economy and Fair Trade, and input from the delegates from the other

continents. More than 370 organisations and networks from all over the world expressed their support for the declaration between 16 and 25 June 2012 (http://rio20.net/en/propuestas/the-economy-we-need-declaration-of-the-social-and-solidarity-economy-movement-at-rio20).

[5] www.ripess.org/wp-content/uploads/2013/04/Declaration_Assembly_of_Convergence_SSE_WSF_2013_EN.pdf (accessed 18 July 2014).

[6] Declaration of LVC's delegation to the 2016 World Social Forum, Montreal, Quebec, 14 August 2016.

[7] www.ripesseu.net/en/presentation.html

References

Amsler, S. (2016) 'Learning Hope: An Epistemology of Possibility for Advanced Capitalist Society', in A.C. Dinerstein (ed) *Social Sciences for An Other Politics. Women Theorising without parachutes*. Basingstoke: Palgrave Macmillan.

Bloch, E. (1986 [1959]) *The Principle of Hope*. Cambridge, MA: MIT Press.

Böhm, S., Dinerstein, A.C. and Spicer, A. (2010) '(Im)possibilities of autonomy: Social movements in and beyond the state, capital and development', *Social Movement Studies*, 1(9): 17-32.

Brissette, E. (2016) 'The Prefigurative is Political: On Politics beyond "the State"', in A.C. Dinerstein (ed) *Social Sciences for An Other Politics. Women Theorising without parachutes*. Basingstoke: Palgrave Macmillan.

Coraggio, J.L. (2010) 'Economía Social y Solidaria', Portal de Economía Solidaria, 12 November, www.economiasolidaria.org/documentos/economia_social_y_solidaria_jose_luis_coraggio (a)

Coraggio, J.L. (2015) 'Institutionalising the social and solidarity economy in Latin America', in P. Utting (ed) *Social and Solidarity Economy. Beyond the fringe*. London: UNRISD/Zed Books, pp 130-149.

Cornwall, A. and Brock, K. (2005) *Beyond Buzzwords: 'Poverty reduction', 'Participation' and 'Empowerment' in Development Policy*, Programme Overarching Concerns, Programme Paper No. 10. Geneva: UNRISD.

Dacheaux, E. and Goujon, D. (2012) *The Solidarity Economy: An Alternative Development Strategy?*, Open Forum, UNESCO. Oxford: Blackwell.

Dash, A. (2014) 'Towards an epistemological foundation for social and solidarity economy' UNRISD Occasional Paper No. 3, Potential and Limits of SSE, www.unrisd.org/dash.

Dinerstein, A.C. (2014) 'The Dream of Dignified Work. Legacies of the Movement of Unemployed Workers in Argentina', *Development and Change*, Forum 2014, 45(5): 1037-1058.

Dinerstein, A.C. (2015) *The Politics of Autonomy in Latin America. The Art of Organising hope*. Basingstoke: Palgrave Macmillan.

Dinerstein, A.C. (2017) 'The critical subject and its theory', in A.C. Dinerstein (ed) *Social Sciences for An Other Politics. Women Theorising without Parachutes*. Basingstoke: Palgrave Macmillan.

Dinerstein, A.C. and Deneulin, S. (2012) 'Hope Movements: Naming Mobilization in a Post-development World', *Development and Change*, 43(2): 585-602.

Escobar, A. (1992) 'Imagining a Post-development Era? Critical Thought, Development and Social Movements', *Social Text*, 31/32, 20-56.

Fonteneau, B., Wanyama, F., Pereira Morais, L. and de Poorter, M. (2010) *Social and Solidarity Economy: Building a Common Understanding*. Turin: International Training Centre, International Labour Organization.

Gibson-Graham, J.K. (2006) *Postcapitalist Politics*. Minneapolis, MS: University of Minnesota Press.

Gutiérrez Aguilar, R., Linsalata, L. and Navarro Trujillo, M.L. (2017) 'Producing the Common and Re-producing Life: Keys towards Rethinking "the political"', in A.C. Dinerstein (ed) *Social Sciences for An Other Politics. Women Theorising without Parachutes*. Basingstoke: Palgrave Macmillan.

International Movement for Food Sovereignty (2013) *Nyéléni Newsletter 13*, www.nyeleni.org/DOWNLOADS/newsletters/Nyeleni_ Newsletter_Num_13_EN.pdf (accessed 25 July 2014).

Kawano, E. (2013) 'Social Solidarity Economy: Toward Convergence across Continental Divides', UNRISD, www.unrisd.org/unrisd/ website/newsview.nsf/%28httpNews%29/F1E9214CF8EA21A8C 1257B1E003B4F65?OpenDocument (accessed 10 April 2013).

Lander, E. (2010) 'Estamos viviendo una profunda crisis civilizatoria', América Latina en Movimiento 452, http://alainet.org/publica/452. phtml (accessed 15 April 2013).

Lemus, B. and Barkin, D. (2013) 'Rethinking the Social and Solidarity Economy in light of Community Practice', Paper presented at UNRISD Conference Potential and Limits of SSE, Geneva, 6-8 May, www.unrisd.org/sse-draft-lemus-barkin.

Levitas, R. (2013) *Utopia as Method*. Basingstoke: Palgrave Macmillan.

Marques, J. (2014) 'Social and Solidarity Economy. Between emancipation and reproduction' UNRISD Occasional Paper No. 2, Potential and Limits of SSE, www.unrisd.org/marques.

Mendell, M. and Alain, B. (2015) 'Enabling the social and solidarity economy through the co-construction of public policy', in P. Utting (ed) *Social and Solidarity Economy. Beyond the fringe.* London: UNRISD/Zed Books, pp 166-184.

Muños Cabrera, P. (2012) 'Economic alternatives for gender and social justice: Voices and Visions from Latin America', *Policy & Practice: A Development Education Review*, vol. 14, Spring: 64-84.

RIPESS (Réseau Intercontinental de Promotion de L'économie Sociale Solidaire) (2012) 'Declaration of the Social and Solidarity Economy Movement', Rio+20, Rio de Janeiro, June, www.ripess. org/declaration-ripess-rio20 (accessed 15 April 2013).

Rosset, P. (2006) 'Conclusion: Moving Forward: Agrarian Reform as Part of Food Sovereignty', in (eds) *Promised Land. Competing Visions of Agrarian Reform.* Oakland: Food First Books, pp 301-322.

Santos, B. de S. (2001) 'Los Nuevos Movimientos Sociales', *Observatorio Social de América Latina*, 5: 177-84.

Santos, B. de S. (2007) (ed) 'Reinventing Social Emancipation: Towards New Manifestos', in *Democratising Democracy. Beyond the Liberal Democratic Canon.* London: Verso, pp xvii-xxxiii.

Santos, B. de S. and Rodríguez Garavito, C. (2006) 'Introduction: Expanding the Economic Canon and Searching for Alternatives to Neoliberal Globalisation', in B. de S. Santos (ed) *Another Production is Possible: Beyond the Capitalist Canon.* London: Verso, pp xvii-lxii.

Seoane, J., Taddei, E. and Algranati, C. (2011) 'Balance de una Década de Luchas y Cambios', Centre Tricontinental (CETRI), 30 December, www.cetri.be/spip?page=imprimer&id_article=2454 (accessed 5 April 2013).

Smith, R. (2010) 'Beyond Growth or Beyond Capitalism?, *Real-world Economics Review*, Issue No. 53, 26 June, pp 28-42, www.paecon. net/PAEReview/issue53/Smith53.pdf

UNRISD (United Research Institute for Social Development) (2010) *Development in an Uncertain World*, Social Research Agenda 2010-2014. Geneva: UNRISD.

Utting, P. (2012) 'Intervention at the UN Human Rights Council Social Forum 2012', http://communityforge.net/UN_Human_Rights_Council_Social_Forum_Transcripts (accessed 15 April 2013).

Vázquez, R. (2011) 'Translation as Erasure: Thoughts on Modernity's Epistemic Violence', *Journal of Historical Sociology*, 24: 27-44.

FIVE

Transitioning towards low carbon solidarity economies?

Peter North

Introduction

We can perhaps now more easily imagine the end of the world through climate catastrophe than we can envisage the end of capitalism (Žižek, 2011). After 200 years of capitalist exploitation, we have ignored the depletion of the Earth's resources for too long. Not only is capitalism exploitative and unequal, but as a species we are consuming more than we are replenishing, not sharing the wealth we have with future generations and distant others, and destroying other species (Klein, 2014). We need to turn things around. We now, according to some theorists, need an 'economic ethics for the Anthropocene' – that geological period in which human activity is changing the physical nature of the planet in ways that will remain in the geological record (Gibson-Graham and Roelvink, 2010). Through this economic ethics, we need to think about ways in which we can meet the needs of all for a dignified life in a climate- and resource-constrained world. We will need to create an economy that enables all of us to make decisions on how we produce what we need, distribute surpluses and maintain a commons in ways that respect the rights of other humans and non-humans. In doing this, Gibson-Graham and Roelvink (2010) argue that we need to ask ourselves the following questions:

- How do we live well?
- How shall we produce what we need?
- What shall we do with any surplus?
- How shall we share with others?
- What should we consume?
- How do we create a world worth living in, and invest in the future?

This chapter discusses the contribution of the social and solidarity economy (SSE) sector to building sustainable, liveable economies though which millions can meet their needs in ways that are embedded in, rather than exploitative of, the wider planetary ecosystem. It examines the extent to which the SSE generates a *vision* of a just and sustainable economy and enables it to be *performed*. Is there dignity, self-management and a lack of hierarchy in the everyday experience of life in the SSE sector? If not, does this suggests that capitalist market logic is ultimately dominant and that the SSE is a form of utopian socialism (Engels, 1968 [1892]); or does it mean that that 'not yet' does not mean 'never' (Gibson-Graham, 2006) and that recognising that there are formidable ideological forces in the form of neoliberalism does not mean either that these forces are all powerful, or that developing alternative perspectives is fruitless? This vision of a just and sustainable SSE sector needs to be developed through the hard work of local experimentation that focuses on what could be, rather than what currently is.

The chapter asks what a Polanyian, substantive or diverse economies approach might add to conceptions of the SSE in the UK, and how we might learn from past experiences in both the UK and Latin America. It understands that, following Žižek, we are at the very early stages of movement building in that respect, but, contra Žižek, it rejects the idea that conceptions of sustainable and egalitarian economies are post-political, that is to say, are warm fuzzy words that no one could object to and that fail to recognise that there are power relations in society that need to be countered.

Social and solidarity economies

The broad 'social economy' includes a range of market-based activities that have economic, social and often environmental objectives and involve varying degrees and forms of cooperative, associative and solidarity relations between workers, producers and consumers (Amin, 2009). Social economy organisations generate their income through trade. The SSE sector collectively looks to meld values of economic efficiency with social inclusion and environmental sustainability. The sector holds that an economic enterprise should be viable, in terms of its income covering its costs, but that success or failure should be gauged in terms of the social value created and the livelihoods supported through that economic activity, not the amount of profit created for the entrepreneur, for senior management, and/or for shareholders. Auinger (2009) argues that in SSE discourse decisions about what to produce and how much to pay people should not be made by a small economic elite with an eye on short-term profit.

Utting (2015) argues that the SSE sector has considerable potential for promoting sustainable development as an alternative to uncritical conceptions of growth that assume that the fruits of growth will trickle down – a potential that is not yet realised. With a focus on the triple economic, social and environmental bottom line, the SSE has the potential to address a deficit in ethics in conceptions of the economy, and to democratise economic and governance systems, and should up its game, scaling up, to maximise its potential. In particular, for the United Nations, the SSE sector has great potential for transitioning from informal to decent work; greening the economy and society; facilitating local economic development in sustainable cities and settlements; promoting women's empowerment, food security and smallholder empowerment, good health and transformative finance.

For SSE activists, the social and economic inequality characterised by capitalism is not an innocent result of the outcome of competition between individuals with different abilities and different opportunities in a more or less free market. Rather, the SSE sector is associated with democracy, with the argument that people should be able to shape their lives rather than only have the opportunity to sell their labour power in return for low wages and poor working conditions in a disadvantageous relationship to the owner of capital who appropriates the surplus value. The sector argues for the democratisation of the economy as populations seek to participate in decisions about what forms of economy suit them and the places in which they live. At its heart the SSE critique is of the naturalised neoliberal argument that economics is competition over scare resources given unlimited needs, and the best way to decide how allocation should be made is through competition. SSE discourse argues that the best way to decide is through democratic debate in public spaces involving as many people as possible (Kerlin, 2009). Laville (2013), Dash (2014), Hillenkamp et al (2013), Lemaître and Helmsing (2012) and Coraggio (Chapter Two of this volume) all locate the SSE sector within Polanyian and Mausian conceptualisations of economies as embedded, pleural institutions that include economic relations based on market exchange, but also redistribution, householding and reciprocity as substantive alternatives to the utopia of the self-regulating free market promoted by neoliberals.

While large, the sector is often inappropriately homogenised by analysts (Kerlin, 2009), and takes different forms in different places (Dacheux and Goujon, 2011). Inspired by Esping-Andersen's (1990) models of welfare, Salamon et al (2000) argue that the local and regional differentiations in the form and nature of the SSE can be explained by social, economic and political contexts, with the size and vibrancy of civil society and levels of welfare spending as the two key variables, with the relative importance given to the state or to the market by policymakers a third. Are citizens expected to help themselves and each other when in difficulty, perhaps with a high priority given to self-help and philanthropy or individual insurance provided through a market, or is the state expected to secure welfare? If the state did not provide welfare, could civil society or market provision step up, or would people effectively be abandoned? To this end, the Johns Hopkins Comparative Nonprofit Sector Project conceptualised four models of the SSE sector (or in US terms, the non-profit sector):

- liberal, in which there are low levels of public spending on welfare and a large independent and SSE sector, perhaps (we would argue) with a focus on social entrepreneurship – bringing business skills to solve problems (as in the US, for example, and the Big Society vision for the UK);
- social democratic, where state provision of welfare is high and where the SSE sector is correspondingly small (as in Finland, for example);
- statist, where a bureaucratic state that acts in defence of elite interests is combined with low levels of SSE activity (for example, Colombia); and
- corporatist, where the state supports a large but incorporated SSE sector that delivers its policies (as in the Netherlands and in the UK under New Labour).

These models can be summarised in Table 5.1.

Table 5.1: The four models of the SSE sector

State welfare spending	SSE sector scale	
	Small	Large
Low	Statist	Liberal
High	Social democratic	Corporatist

Source: Salamon et al, 2000, p 16

This model is a good place to start, but what matters is what is *not* included: a social democratic state with a strong SSE sector that is not incorporated, but facilitated to do things that the state cannot do (see Chapters Ten and Eleven in this volume). It also fails to differentiate between models of the social economy in Catholic societies (Western Europe, Canada) where the social economy aims to include those capitalism has left behind, and more resistant conceptions of the solidarity economy that start with how we want to live, sustainably, with dignity (see Chapter Four in this volume).

The relationship between the state, the market and the SSE sector also needs to be conceptualised dynamically across time as well as geographically across space (Moulaert and Ailenei, 2005), given that levels of welfare spending, different emphases on the role of state and market, and levels of SSE mobilisation and/or state repression or facilitation change over time. In the UK, for example, since 1945 we have seen a move from social democracy, where state provision was high and the SSE sector was minimal, through Thatcherism (a liberal model) to corporatism under New Labour, where the SSE sector was expected to deliver central government welfare objectives and a large SSE sector had little independence (North, 2000), and back to a liberal model with the Big Society (North, 2011).

In this vein, Kerlin (2009, p 172) identifies four drivers of the SSE sector: market, state, civil society and international aid. She argues that the rise of social entrepreneurship in the US came from the cuts in grants to non-profits from the late 1970s, while in the UK a similar growth in social entrepreneurship and social enterprise emerged from the retrenchment of the welfare state, and as a response to unemployment and inner-city decline. In Eastern and Central Europe, civil society arose from the fall of the Berlin Wall. In Argentina, structural adjustment and crisis saw the withdrawal of corporatist Peronist state provision associated with the crisis of clientelism after the 2001 crisis (see Chapter Fifteen, this volume). In Brazil, a Catholic commitment to social inclusion and the coming to power of the Workers' Party saw a massive increase in state welfare provision and support for the SSE sector (Chapter Eleven, this volume). Kerlin sees state-funded civil society as the driver of the SSE sector in Western Europe through a commitment to socially inclusive and sustainable development, and Catholic Quebec talks about an inclusive social economy in a European vein. In contrast, Putin's Russia is suspicious of all autonomous forms of political organisation. In Francophone Africa, the social and solidarity economy looks to give new life to traditional village economies.

This diversity belies accusations that in attempting to build an economy based on solidarity, equality and sustainability the SSE is in some ways 'post-political'. Erik Swyngedouw (2010) argues that the need to avoid future climate calamity is framed as being so obvious that no one of goodwill would refute it. We are 'all in it together'. He, and others (see Kenis and Mathijs, 2014a, 2914b; Raco, 2015) argue that in this context sustainability strategies are often characterised by technocratic, bland, vague commitments to 'sustainable development' that do not challenge the underlying logic of neoliberalisation, or longstanding inequalities and forms of dominance and oppression. 'Post-politics' means the 'political' – a space of antagonism – is replaced by 'politics'– based on consensus, technocratic management, and participation in which the parameters of possible outcomes are defined in advance within an uncontested paradigm of representative democracy, and free market neoliberalism.

Swyngedouw argues that the post-political forecloses more radical visions of socio-environmental futures that envisage fundamental challenges to neoliberal accumulation strategies delivered by technocratic experts removed from democratic control and scrutiny. Challenges to the inherent unsustainability of neoliberal capitalism are neutered. Alternatives to a paradigm of 'growth' such as 'degrowth', localisation, the need to consider the needs of other species and future generations, or even the need for a fundamental change of course to a simpler, more low-tech economy lack credibility. As a result, Inglofur Blüdorn (2015) argues that what purport to be policies to avoid dangerous climate change are actually locked into a paradigm of fundamental *un*sustainability, in which a bland commitment to sustainable development has neutered the challenges of the environmental new social movements of the 1970s and 1980s. Growth is not challenged, but, it is claimed, delinked from greenhouse gas emissions. Thus the priority for elites is to protect and police consumer capitalism and unsustainable levels of consumption, with the result that the radical action necessary to avoid calamitous climate change is not taken, and discourse of the simulation of sustainability obscures an unsustainable reality (Blühdorn, 2007). The radical changes necessary to avoid catastrophe are not taken, and we are running out of time (Anderson and Bows, 2011). While radical critics argue for an alternative, socially just conception of the economy (Featherstone et al, 2012) founded on an economic ethics for the Anthropocene (Gibson-Graham and Roelvink, 2010), the post-political thesis argues that such visions are off limits, and that antagonisms are repressed. Is this the case?

In contrast, a number of authors (see North, 2011; Mason and Whitehead, 2012; Chatterton et al, 2013; Featherstone, 2013; Larner, 2015; Van Puymbroeck and Oosterlynck, 2015) argue that the pessimistic and politically disempowering post-political perspective both oversimplifies and overestimates the extent that neoliberalisation is being rolled out in uncontested, monolithic ways across space. It underplays the extent that, as the chapters of this book show, activists are arguing for, mobilising in favour of and constructing alternatives to current economic and societal organisational norms that entail an implicit rejection of neoliberalisation that goes beyond technocratic demands for policy reform. Swyngedouw comes dangerously close to reproducing 'denialist' tropes about climate change in potentially counter-productive and unintended ways and overestimates the extent that the need to avoid dangerous climate change *is* so uncritically accepted, as an immediate priority for which action should be taken (Blühdorn, 2015). The post-political arbitrarily sets the bar for what counts as real 'politics' too high, demanding total societal transformations such as those achieved in the classical revolutions (1789, 1917), and a commitment to equality or to 'communism' in ways that fail to recognise the political status of many of the grassroots challenges that might form the germ of an alternative to neoliberalism (Larner, 2015; see also the chapters in this volume).

I argue that a more productive set of engagements with the project of transitioning to a convivial low carbon economy through the SSE is through the more hopeful ontologies of the diverse economies perspective of J.K. Gibson-Graham. Working from feminist accounts of the economy in what they call a 'poststructural vein', J.K. Gibson-Graham argue for the production of a non-capitalocentric discourse of economic difference, for a conceptualisation of the economy as 'heterospace' of profit-orientated and political, ideological, emotional and affective (rather than strictly economic) forms of economic motivation (Gibson-Graham, 2006, 2008; Gibson-Graham et al, 2013). They argue that a 'language of the diverse economy can be used to explore the multi-dimensional nature of economic existence and the possibilities this creates for political acts of economic transformation' (Gibson-Graham, 2006, p 77) and that economies are 'contingent outcomes of ethical decisions, political projects and sedimented localised practices, continually pushed and pulled by other determinations' (Gibson-Graham, 2006, p 3).

Gibson-Graham and their colleagues from the Community Economies Collective explore diverse performances and practices for a better world (Gibson-Graham, 2008) to examine the conditions of rather than the fundamental limits of what could be. They see themselves as 'dancing, participating in creating a reality in which we are implicated and involved', disrupting 'the great clanking gears of capital' (Gibson-Graham, 2003, p 35). Their work has focused on developing a richer language of economic possibility where none previously existed; cultivating new economic subjects able to engage in debates about how we want to live, rather than being the passive carriers of exploitative practices; and exploring living examples of alternative and diverse economic practices. In particular, they echo Eve Sedgewick's (2003) call for 'non-paranoid' ontologies that do not assume a world of oppression, exploitation and the inevitable victory of capital over all challenges, preferring to focus on more hopeful stories about what 'could be', but which is 'not yet', and on a reparative reading of how we can make things better than they are. That is not to argue that we should not be interested in learning from past struggles, avoiding past failings and learning lessons, but it does not mean assuming that capital will always win – the paranoid stance. With that in mind, the next section of this chapter reviews the experience of UK social economy practice, drawing lessons for an understanding of what the possible contribution of the SSE sector to building just and sustainable economies could be.

The practices of the UK social economy sector: liberation or abandonment?

Non-state centred visions of how to create socially inclusive, cooperative economies – the good life in the UK – go back at least to working-class self-organisation in the 19th century (Thompson, 1981) and to the cooperatives and intentional communities supported by Robert Owen (Cole, 1925; Donnachie, 2000). The consumer cooperatives developed by the Rochdale Pioneers from 1844 continue to exist today in the UK in the form of the Co-operative Group. Between World Wars I and II in the UK, Guild Socialists argued for workers control of production through their guilds, running industry democratically and providing their own welfare services, as a direct challenge to state socialism (Cole, 1921). The seeming success of the statist model of socialism in the USSR and the rise of the Keynesian mixed economy in the years between 1917 and the mid-1970s saw a reduced interest in cooperatives in the UK until the late 1960s and early 1970s. The capitalist crisis associated with the oil shock saw a rise in community activism in Britain's inner cities as students radicalised by the student movement of the late 1960s set up squats in run-down streets, tenants engaged in rent strikes, and activists developed a range of community-run services such as adventure playgrounds, childcare centres, welfare rights centres and trade union resource centres in places that lacked state provision (Hain, 1975; Curno, 1978). A number of cooperatives were established, and Co-operative Development Agencies were established to support their development.

Further, workers responded to the crisis that decimated manufacturing in the UK with a wave of factory occupations. During the 1970s, some 200 enterprises were occupied by their workers (Coates, 2003; Sherry, 2010, pp 119-28). The Alternative Production movement in the 1970s looked to help workers in threatened factories diversify, moving away from military production to manufacturing more peaceable products (Wainwright and Elliott, 1982). Both inspired the development of a new cooperative sector in the UK (Cornforth, 1983; Tuckman, 2011) that was supported by many radical local authorities (Boddy and Fudge, 1984; Alcock et al, 1989; Wainwright, 2003). While this movement provided a fightback against the restructuring that we now call neoliberalisation, perhaps it was unequal to the task of confronting the forces it opposed. Studies in the 1980s (Cornforth, 1983) suggested that worker buy-outs and defensive cooperatives formed to fight job losses generally struggled with a lack of capital and a lack of custom, as they were often formed in declining industries or in crisis conditions (so the problem was not what Sitrin – in Chapter Fourteen of this volume – calls a 'boss problem' for an otherwise viable enterprise). The workers lacked commercial expertise and found it difficult to manage their way out of the crisis. As a result, while things could have been different had an interventionist state supported them, these so-called 'Benn cooperatives'[1] were labelled by rightwing critics as Luddite attempts to resist inevitable forces. Cooperatives formed in crisis conditions often struggle. Against this, it must also be noted that the survival of conventional SMEs is also poor (Cornforth, 1983, p 164) and the success or failure of cooperatives needs to be assessed in that light. Difficult economic conditions can pass, and state support can help a worker-owned enterprise through hard times. As we discuss below, Latin American experiences point to worker-run cooperatives that *have* survived in the long term (see Chapter Fourteen, this volume).

Not all 1970s and 1980s cooperatives were formed in such inauspicious circumstances. Endowed cooperatives were successful businesses given away by their owners, and many of them continued to trade profitably, with perhaps the best examples being the John Lewis Partnership and the Scott Bader Commonwealth in the UK. Here the downside was that there was no attempt at developing and deepening cooperative principles beyond the shallowest forms of consultation and employee share ownership. In contrast, the alternative cooperative sector, for example radical bookshops or wholefood shops, were good at maintaining their cooperative principles, but struggled to be profitable. They could last many years if located in places where they had a large enough customer base, but many struggled in the long run. Few radical bookshops remained in business by the end of the century.[2]

The neoliberalisation of the UK social economy

The election of the Thatcher government and the rise of neoliberalism made the environment for workers' self-management much more difficult (Smith, 2014). During the 1980s and 1990s, as part of the 'entrepreneurial' turn in British urban policy (Harvey, 1989), policymakers began to see community-based economic development as a tool for revitalising inner-city areas unlikely to be attractive to inward investors (DETR, 1998; Haughton, 1999). A number of community businesses were set up in inner-city areas to deliver services to local residents, with perhaps disappointing results (McArthur, 1993; Leeming, 2002). The emphasis on cooperation and workers' control was replaced in the UK by the concept of the social enterprise and the social economy (Moulaert and Ailenei, 2005). The new emphasis was on meeting needs through business methods by creating enterprises that combined business values and organisational methods with a social agenda – social enterprises – run by a new class of dynamic individuals called social entrepreneurs (Southern, 2011). Hegemonic neoliberalism at the level of discourse and the Thatcherite prejudice in favour of the ability of private sector 'movers and shakers' (Peck, 1995) to solve problems that continued to shape the policies of the Blair and Brown New Labour administrations meant a renewed focus on the power of social enterprise and social entrepreneurship, now seen as a mainstream and accepted part of inner-city policy in the UK (Morrin et al, 2004). Community Interest Companies (CICs) that traded for community benefit, rather than for the benefit of the owners or workers, were introduced as a new institutional form in 2008. By 2010 David Cameron saw the social enterprise sector as the motor of his Big Society (North, 2011).

Thus, for the UK social enterprise movement in both the New Labour and Big Society eras, entrepreneurial values were, and remain, the vehicle for the creation of a more just and socially inclusive society. Today's social enterprises raise income through trade and do not rely on grants as do voluntary or third sector organisations. They often contract with local authorities through competitive tendering to deliver services previously provided in-house, in which case they may have only one source of income (from the local authority to provide a service), so the extent that these are bona fide trading organisations is debatable. Critics of this approach argue that it is a process of neoliberalisation through which capitalist, profit-making logic is extended into new areas of life that emerge in times of capitalist crisis and can be seen as little more than inadequate example of self-help (Auinger, 2009) to which the 'surplus, dispossessed proletariat' is abandoned (Harvey, 2004). Have today's UK social enterprises become creatures of market forces, deflected away from their progressive origins through mission creep (Cornforth, 2014)? Thus Marques (2013) wants to understand the extent to which the social economy reproduces or challenges market logics. Is it an alternative to neoliberalism, or part of variegated capitalism in which welfare is provided by companies claiming philanthropic aims? Can goods and services produced by the social and solidarity economy complete with those produced conventionally without the introduction of (self-)exploitative practices to get the price down?

Sustainable localised economies

A more hopeful, non-paranoid reading might be to examine the extent to which social enterprises can help us rethink markets and what it means to be entrepreneurial or an entrepreneur, in democratic or inclusive ways. Here, the emergence of climate crisis and of looming resource constraint has led to the emergence of a new social economic sector aimed at ecolocalisation (North, 2009). Transition Initiatives and low carbon communities work at a city, town or grassroots level to develop community-based strategies to avoid dangerous climate change and problems associated with resource depletion (Hopkins, 2008; Bailey and Wilson, 2009; Aiken, 2012; Barr and Pollard, 2016). They focus on practical solutions, creating examples of the sort of society their participants want to see, where food and power are produced locally, where life has a more relaxed pace, and where more people are employed in locally owned businesses than at present. They focus on developing the power of local communities to solve problems, believing that developing the power of grassroots acts to act, to 'do', is a more fruitful course of action than protesting 'against' issues. Here they definitely echo the voices of the Picqueteros, the Zapatistas and other 'hope' movements (see Chapter Four, this volume), which focus more on creating and deepening alternatives than protesting against neoliberalism or taking state power (Holloway, 2002). Some Transition Initiatives have developed local currency networks, local food and power projects, community transport, community cafes and housing cooperatives that are quite robust (for example, the Bristol and Brixton Pound, Incredible Edible Todmorden's local food project, and innumerable local community power cooperatives and self-build housing initiatives). These provide examples of spaces where alternative projects for transitioning the city onto a sustainable path via SSE practices are being developed (Hodson et al, 2016).

While the climate crisis and the recognition that there might be limits to economic growth is problematic for some, Transition Initiatives do not see this as an unwelcome adjustment to a new life of austerity, a process of self-regulation of docile bodies in response to neoliberal politics of limits and constraint. Rather, the Transition movement argues that the triple crisis (of climate, carbon and capitalism) is an opportunity to transition to ways of life that are seen as more connected and enriching than those provided by globalised neoliberal capitalism, and more cognisant of the limits of the planetary ecosystem on which all life depends. Thus the key claim of the Transition movement is that:

> ... we used immense amounts of creativity, ingenuity and adaptability on the way up the energy upslope, and that there's no reason for us not to do the same on the downslope.... if we collectively plan and act early enough there's every likelihood that *we can create a way of living that's significantly more connected, more vibrant and more in touch with our environment than the oil-addicted treadmill that we find ourselves on today.* (Hopkins, 2008, emphasis added)

A key element in the repertoire of some of the more mature transition initiatives is the generation of what they call 'transition orientated enterprises', 'financially viable trading entities that fulfil a real community need, deliver social benefits and which has beneficial, or at least neutral, environmental impacts'.[3] Transition's 'reconomy' programme looks to support the development of a wide range of locally owned businesses, cooperatives and social enterprises producing enjoyable work, rather than alienated toil for capitalist business for the sake of generating growth. A key driver of these locally owned businesses would be minimising emissions and fossil fuel use and maximising opportunities for local employment and the use of local inputs, financed by local money and other locally-owned financial institutions. Local economic welfare would focus more on quality of life, the provision of good, wholesome food, and time for family and friends, rather than on economic growth per se. Thus the Transition approach focuses on a politics of experimentation and prefiguration through community-led, bottom-up institution building that resonates strongly with the values of SSE sector. It is also the latest iteration in a more longstanding economic localisation movement that arose out of counter-cultural and alternative movements as a reaction against large-scale technocratic industrial society captured by E.F. Schumacher's philosophy of 'small is beautiful' (Schumacher, 1973) that led to the rise of the Green movement. In turn, this movement led to a huge rise in cooperative economic activity, and through the 1980s and 1990s a new wave of green activists developed a range of local examples of what they called the 'community economy' (Dauncey, 1988; Pearce, 1993).

While the concrete success of the transition movement has been examined elsewhere (Mason and Whitehead, 2012; North and Longhurst, 2013; Kenis and Mathijs, 2014b) and is not the key focus of this chapter, we do know that place-based studies of alternative networks in some of the towns where alternative green networks are dense and longstanding reveal a palimpsest of initiatives built on each other over time that does achieve some form of sustainability that reflects the diversity of 'actually existing', practical substantive economies, and the rejection of Marxist criticisms of such practices as 'dwarfish co-operatism' (Amin et al, 2002; Longhurst, 2013). In such places, the sustainable social economy has some local depth, providing spaces in which considerable innovation in refining what works in the SE sector can be progressed, as opposed to the breadth and reach advocated by advocates of scaling up the SSE sector (see Utting, 2015). Seyfang and Smith (2007) call these spaces 'grassroots innovation niches'.

Just and inclusive social economies – into austerity

While the Transition movement has been active in developing convivial, localised community-based economies, combating poverty has been another strong driver of the social economy in the UK. In the 1980s in the UK, many cooperatives were developed to provide opportunities for unemployed people, and supported in this by Co-operative Development Agencies. In time, many of these morphed into social enterprises or CICs. Many have become very successful at delivering programmes for the public good, for example, furniture recycling, community media, skills training, and support for healthy lifestyles. The 1997–2010 New Labour government in the UK funded a large number of such social enterprises, ideologically preferring them to the delivery of services by local authorities. Some have prospered, while others have remained over-reliant on ever-reducing public funding and have struggled to move from a public sector or non-profit mentality to one where they are expected to compete with perhaps more aggressive competitors for the delivery of public services.

In a climate of austerity since 2010 in the UK, social enterprises have struggled with competing pressures of service delivery competition, and maintaining their ethos, and as a result have suffered from 'mission drift' (Cornforth, 2014). Business logic may take over from an emphasis on social value, or too much of a public sector ethos may limit competitiveness. There are doubts about the ability of smaller social enterprises to deal with a commercial environment, and recognise opportunities they are able to capitalise on, and when they are being set up to fail. When are assets resources from which social enterprises can grow, and when are they liabilities or assets to be conserved, and which soak up time and money? Some have coped with this by prioritising one set of values over another (Cornforth, 2014), or by 'compartmentalising' (Hillenkamp et al, 2013), accepting the need to operate with business values to get the wherewithal to meet social and environmental demands. This might be by the creation of a trading arm or CIC to complement or support other non-profit focused activities. More recently, in response to this concern some UK local authorities have established municipally-owned enterprises to run services 'in house', rather than contract with either the private or social enterprise sector although there continues to be an appetite for contracting with social enterprises as a response to austerity (Munby, 2015).

There has, however, been widespread scepticism of the ability of the social enterprise sector to replace government spending through the transition of the UK from a still (if rather battered) social democratic welfare regime to a neoliberal one in which a small state is complemented by an active civil society – such as is observable in Latin America (North, 2011). More hopeful has been the introduction of the Public Services (Social Value) Act 2012, which places a responsibility on all public sector organisations to consider wider social value in issuing service contracts, not just having to accept the lowest tender. While a capitalocentric reading will obviously see this as the latest element of progressive neoliberalisation accompanied by the rise of the shadow state, a diverse economies reading suggests that it also has the potential to open up local service delivery to organisations able to meet the needs of local people in more diverse ways.

A pessimistic reading would suggest that the trajectory of the UK social economy experience from the cooperative hopes of the 19th and 20th centuries represents a retreat from the conception that a solidaristic economy can be built within an overall framework of capitalism such that it replaces it. The replacement of the worker-managed cooperative of the 19th and 20th centuries with the social or transition-orientated enterprise, CIC and the social entrepreneur using business skills for community, social benefit can, in one reading, be seen as the process of colonisation or taming of the UK SSE sector identified in the Latin American context by Dinerstein (Chapter 4, this volume). This is, to some extent, because hegemonic conceptions of neoliberalisation have naturalised the idea at a discursive level that cooperatives 'fail' and/or are 'inefficient', while social enterprises bring 'business vigour' to solving problems. Social entrepreneurs bring 'get up and go'. In the 19th century, critics of cooperatives argued that working people not only did not have the skills to run a business, but could not be trusted to do so without managerial discipline. They argued that cooperatives would focus on internal democracy and not on the wider marketplace, and as a result would become stagnant. The workers would resist necessary changes to their jobs, and struggle to think less like workers, and more like business owners. This, they argued, was the reason for the relative success of the consumers' as opposed to producers' cooperative movement in the UK (Webb and Webb, 1921). This rather paranoid reading might be changing. In 2016, the shadow Chancellor of the Exchequer, John McDonnell, announced that a future Labour government would look to double the size of the UK cooperative sector, arguing that evidence shows that when workers own and manage their companies they last longer and are more productive than privately owned companies.

Conclusion: towards low carbon solidarity economies

The aim of the discussions from which this book emerged was to understand how social economy practitioners in the UK could learn from Latin America, and vice versa. For this author, the attractiveness of the Latin American concept of the solidarity economy is, first, its emphasis on working to develop the power to act to control our lives on the part of those who do not have such power at present, or who need to develop their ability to self-manage (Holloway, 2002). Second, the solidarity economy looks first at how people want to live well, and then helps them to develop economic models and practices that enable them to do so – rather than, in the social economy model, helping those excluded from the market to become wage slaves. Third, like the Latin American solidarity economies perspective, Northern Transition initiatives embody a collective, progressive politics of responsibility for climate change and resource crises that is hopeful, optimistic and generative of possibilities rather than focused on structural barriers to change, or conceptualising the SSE as the latest configuration of a wider neoliberal politics of regulation and privatisation. That globally privileged actors are taking responsibility for their 'geographies of responsibility' (Massey, 2004) for historic carbon emissions is to be welcomed, and is a useful corrective to Southern voices that argue that the North caused the climate crisis and the North should fix it. Transition, and the SSE sector, offer a more hopeful vision that goes beyond the provision of services that the state previously delivered, perhaps less effectively, the neoliberal valorisation of the social entrepreneur as a 'hero' who can solve problems that eluded the state, or the disciplining of recalcitrant unemployed bodies into the work rhythms of the market.

However, notwithstanding this positive stance, community-based agents like Transition initiatives face real barriers to implementing their visions of a low carbon future. There are longstanding and well-understood problems around the capacities of subaltern groups to remake growth-based capitalist market economies in the face of opposition, centred mainly on their exclusion from the control of the forces of material and energy production, which are in private sector hands. The poor success rate and lack of ability to scale up of many cooperatives (and 'normal' SMEs) needs to temper over-optimistic conceptions of local economies brought into being by transition-orientated enterprises.

Of course, from a diverse economies perspective, it is perfectly possible to develop larger, robust SSE institutions that last some time. But given the radical and utopian nature of the visions the Transition movement generates, its capacity to persuade mainstream actors to abandon growth as a policy objective is limited. Consequently, questions remain surrounding the extent to which a local politics of transition can provide the motive power for a fundamental reorganisation of carbon-intensive economies, especially in small places far away from major sources of emissions and from the control centres of the system that generates them. For a substantive transition to a sustainable, low carbon economy operating within the limits of the planet to provide the inputs the economy needs and absorb its wastes, Transition initiatives in the North need to develop closer alliances with the social economy sector, and with the wider global SSE sector, to create a global change movement that will develop a wider SSE sector that millions can participate in. In Latin America, we see links between universities, the SSE sector and the state that are lacking in more thoroughly neoliberalised countries like the UK.

In understanding the transformational potential of the SSE, Egan (1990) and Baldacchino (1990) argue that the balance of class forces matters: how much of a cooperative ethos is there to facilitate survival in a hostile environment, so people support each other and stick together? In this context, 'counter-institutional' support can be provided to strengthen these counter-hegemonic organisational forms, and to help the cooperatives survive in a wider sphere of circulation in which they buy inputs, sell their products, and provide the means to secure livelihoods for their families, a sphere based on cooperation not competition. As da Costa shows in Chapter Seven of this volume, universities can be vital sources of such support, a sector that was more prevalent in the 1970s and 1980s, and even in the New Labour period (1997–2010), than in the current neoliberalised UK university system driven by elite metrics like the Research Assessment Framework. This is a strategic question: can a counter-hegemonic, Gramscian or Polanyian strategy strengthen this sector (Baldacchino 1990)? For McMurtry (2013), context matters. The social and solidarity economies can be a liberating Prometheus *or* a neoliberal Trojan Horse trumpeted as a panacea, introducing market mechanisms and competition into the delivery of inadequate levels of welfare by state-created Frankenstein social economy organisations masquerading as part of civil society. What matters is not the alterity of the social or solidarity economy, but the capabilities, assets and support of those the social or solidarity economy aims to help, both in providing dignified livelihoods, democratic self-management, and a sustainable future for humans and the other species we share the planet with. Here, the SSE should be seen not as post-political, but as part of a Polanyian counter-movement to a neoliberalism that, left unchecked, would destroy society. As Polanyi wrote:

> Robbed of the protective covering of cultural institutions, human beings would perish from the effects of social exposure; they would die as the victims of acute social dislocation through vice, perversion, crime and starvation. Nature would be reduced to its elements, neighbourhoods and landscapes defiled, rivers polluted, military safety jeopardized, the power to produce food and raw materials destroyed. Finally, the market administration of purchasing power would periodically liquidate business enterprises, for shortages and surfeits of money would prove as disastrous to business as floods and droughts in primitive society. (Polanyi, 1944/1980, p 4)

We now see how prescient Polanyi was in making this statement. The SSE is more than bringing business skills to solving social problems, important though that is: it is society's response to the inability of neoliberalism to provide the ability of millions to live prosperous, sustainable lives with dignity.

Notes

1   Named after their sponsoring, and widely felt to be left wing, minister Tony Benn.
2   Liverpool's News from Nowhere radical bookshop is a women's cooperative. It recently celebrated its 40th anniversary as a result of the commitment of the radical community in Liverpool to supporting it, the sweat equity at minimum wage, and – crucially – the fact that it had bought its building at the time when Liverpool's economic fortunes were at their nadir. It is now a viable co-operative located in a central part of town.
3   www.reconomy.org/inspiring-enterprises/whats-a-transition-enterprise

References

Aiken, G (2012) 'Community Transitions to Low Carbon Futures in the Transition Towns Network (TTN)', *Geography Compass*, 6: 89-99.

Alcock, P, Gamble, A, Gough, I, and Walker, A (1989) *The Social Economy and the Democratic State*, London: Lawrence and Wishart.

Amin, A (ed) (2009) *The Social Economy: International Perspectives on Economic Solidarity*, London: Zed Books.

Amin, A, Cameron, A and Hudson, R (2002) *Placing the Social Economy*, London: Routledge.

Anderson, K and Bows, A (2011) 'Beyond "dangerous" climate change: emission scenarios for a new world', *Philosophical Transactions of the Royal Society A: Mathematical, Physical and Engineering Sciences*, 369: 20-44.

Auinger, M (2009) 'Introduction: Solidarity Economics – emancipatory social change or self-help?', *Journal für Entwicklungspolitik*, XXV: 4-21.

Bailey, I and Wilson, GA (2009) 'Theorising transitional pathways in response to climate change: technocentrism, ecocentrism, and the carbon economy', *Environment and Planning A*, 41: 2324-2341.

Baldacchino, G (1990) 'A War of Position: Ideas on a Strategy for Worker Cooperative Development', *Economic and Industrial Democracy*, 11: 463-482.

Barr, S and Pollard, J (2016) 'Geographies of Transition: Narrating environmental activism in an age of climate change and "Peak Oil"', *Environment and Planning A*, 49(1), 47–64.

Blühdorn, I (2007) 'Sustaining the Unsustainable: Symbolic Politics and the Politics of Simulation', *Environmental Politics*, 16: 251-275.

Blühdorn, I (2015) 'Post-Ecologist Governmentality: Post Democracy, Post Politics and the Politics of Unsustainability', in J Wilson and E Swyngedouw (eds) *The Post-Political and its Discontents*, Edinburgh: Edinburgh University Press, pp 146-168.

Boddy, M and Fudge, C (eds) (1984) *Local Socialism*, London: Macmillan.

Chatterton, P, Featherstone, D and Routledge, P (2013) 'Articulating Climate Justice in Copenhagen: Antagonism, the Commons, and Solidarity', *Antipode*, 45: 602-620.

Coates, K (2003) *Workers Control: Another World is Possible*, Nottingham: Spokesman Books.

Cole, G (1921) *Guild Socialism: A Plan for Economic Democracy*, New York: Frederick A. Stokes.

Cole, G (1925) *Robert Owen*, London: Benn.

Cornforth, C (1983) 'Some Factors Affecting the Success or Failure of Worker Co-operatives: A Review of Empirical Research in the United Kingdom', *Economic and Industrial Democracy*, 4: 163-190.

Cornforth, C (2014) 'Understanding and combating mission drift in social enterprises', *Social Enterprise Journal*, 10: 3-20.

Curno, P (ed.) (1978) *Political Issues and Community Work*, London: Routledge and Kegan Paul.

Dacheux, E and Goujon, D (2011) 'The solidarity economy: an alternative development strategy?', *International Social Science Journal*, 62: 205-215.

Dash, A (2014) *Towards an Epistomological Foundation for Social and Solidarity Economy*, Geneva: UNRISD.

Dauncey, G (1988) *Beyond the crash: The emerging rainbow economy*, London: Greenprint.

DETR (Department of the Environment, Transport and the Regions) (1998) *Community-Based Regeneration Initiatives: A Working Paper*. London: DETR.

Donnachie, I (2000) *Robert Owen: Owen of New Lanark and New Harmony*. Phantassie, East Lothian: The Tuckwell Press.

Egan, D (1990) 'Toward a Marxist Theory of Labor-Managed Firms: Breaking the Degeneration Thesis', *Review of Radical Political Economics*, 22: 67-86.

Engels, F (1892/1968) *Socialism: Utopian and Scientific*, London: Lawrence and Wishart.

Esping-Andersen, G (1990) *The Three Worlds of Welfare Capitalism*, Princeton: Princeton University Press.

Featherstone, D (2013) 'The Contested Politics of Climate Change and the Crisis of Neo-liberalism', *ACME: An International E-Journal for Critical Geographies*, 12: 44-64.

Featherstone, D, Ince, A, Mackinnon, D, Strauss, K & Cumbers, A (2012) 'Progressive localism and the construction of political alternatives', *Transactions of the Institute of British Geographers*, 37(2), 177-182.

Gibson-Graham, JK (2003) 'The Impatience of Familiarity: a commentary on Michael Watts' "Development and Governmentality"', *Singapore Journal of Tropical Geography*, 24(1), 35-37.

Gibson-Graham, JK (2006) *A Post Capitalist Politics*, Minneapolis, MS: University of Minnesota Press.

Gibson-Graham, JK (2008) 'Diverse economies: performative practices for "other worlds"', *Progress in Human Geography*, 32: 613-632.

Gibson-Graham, JK and Roelvink, G (2010) 'An Economic Ethics for the Anthropocene', *Antipode*, 41: 320-346.

Gibson-Graham, JK, Cameron, J and Healy, S (2013) *Take Back the Economy*. Minneapolis: University of Minnesota Press.

Hain, P (1975) *Radical Regeneration: Protest, Direct Action and Community Politics*, London: Quartet Books.

Harvey, D (1989) 'From Managerialism to Entrepreneurialism: The Transformation in Urban Governance in Late Capitalism', *Geografiska Annaler. Series B, Human Geography*, 71: 3-17.

Harvey, D (2004) 'The "New" Imperialism: Accumulation by Dispossession', *Socialist Register 2004: The New Imperial Challenge*, 40: 63-87.

Haughton, G (ed) (1999) *Community Economic Development*, London: The Stationery Office.

Hillenkamp, I, Lapeyre, F and Lemaître, A (2013) *Solidarity Economy and part of Popular Security Enhancing Practices*, Geneva: UNRISD.

Hodson, M, Burrai, E and Barlow, C (2016) 'Remaking the material fabric of the city: "Alternative" low carbon spaces of transformation or continuity?', *Environmental Innovation and Societal Transitions*, 18: 128-146.

Holloway, J (2002) *Change the world without taking power: The meaning of revolution today*, London: Pluto.

Hopkins, R (2008) *The Transition Handbook: From oil dependency to local resilience*, Totnes: Green Books.

Kenis, A and Mathijs, E (2014a) 'Climate change and post-politics: Repoliticizing the present by imagining the future?', *Geoforum*, 52: 148-156.

Kenis, A and Mathijs, E (2014b) '(De)politicising the local: The case of the Transition Towns movement in Flanders (Belgium)', *Journal of Rural Studies*, 34: 172-183.

Kerlin, J (ed) (2009) *Social Enterprise: A Global Comparison*, Hannover, NH: University Press.

Klein, N (2014) *This Changes Everything: Capitalism vs. the Climate*, London: Allen Lane.

Larner, W (2015) 'The Limits of Post Politics: Rethionking Radical Social Enterprise', in J Wilson and E Swyngedouw (eds) *The Post-Poliitcal and its Discontents*, Edinburgh: Edinburg University Press, pp 189-207.

Laville, J (2013) *The Social and Solidarity Economy: a theoretical and plural framework*, Geneva: UNRSID.

Leeming, K (2002) 'Community businesses - lessons from Liverpool, UK', *Community Development Journal*, 37: 260-267.

Lemaître, A and Helmsing, AHJ (2012) 'Solidarity Economy in Brazil: Movement, Discourse and Practice Analysis through a Polanyian Understanding of the Economy', *Journal of International Development*, 24: 745-762.

Longhurst, N (2013) 'The emergence of an alternative milieu: conceptualising the nature of alternative places', *Environment and Planning A*, 45: 2100-2119.

Marques, J (2013) *Social and Solidarity Economy: Between Emancipation and Reproduction*, Geneva: UNRISD.

Mason, K and Whitehead, M (2012) 'Transition Urbanism and the Contested Politics of Ethical Place Making', *Antipode*, 44: 493-516.

Massey, D (2004) 'Geographies of Responsibility', *Geografiska Annaler*, 86B: 5-18.

McArthur, A (1993) 'An exploration of Community Business failure', *Policy & Politics*, 21: 219-230.

McMurtry, J-J (2013) *Prometheus, Trojan Horse or Frankenstein? The Social and Solidarity Economy as Community Creation, Market Wedge, or State Monster*, Geneva: UNIRSD.

Morrin, M, Simmonds, D and Somerville, W (2004) 'Social Enterprise: mainstreamed from the margins?', *Local Economy*, 19: 69-84.

Moulaert, F and Ailenei, O (2005) 'Social Economy, Third Sector and Solidarity Relations: A Conceptual Synthesis from History to Present', *Urban Studies*, 42: 2037-2053.

Munby, S (2015) 'Miracles can happen ...', *Soundings*, 61, pp 35-48.

North, P (2000) 'Is there space for organisation from below within the UK Government's Action Zones? A test of "collaborative planning"', *Urban Studies*, 37: 1261-1278.

North, P (2009) 'Ecolocalisation as an urban strategy in the context of resource constraint and climate change: a (dangerous) new protectionism?', *People, Policy and Place Online*, 3: 28-38.

North, P (2011) 'The politics of climate activism in the UK: A social movement analysis', *Environment and Planning A*, 43(7): 1581-1598.

North, P and Longhurst, N (2013) 'Grassroots Localisation? The Scalar Potential of and Limits of the "Transition" Approach to Climate Change and Resource Constraint', *Urban Studies*, 50: 1423-1438.

Pearce, J (1993) *At the Heart of the Community Economy: Community enterprise in a changing world*, London: Calouste Gulbenkian Foundation.

Peck, J (1995) 'Moving and shaking: business elites, state localism and urban privatism', *Progress in Human Geography*, 19: 16-46.

Polanyi, K (1944/1980) *The Great Transformation*, New York, Octagon.

Raco, M (2015) 'The Post-Politics of Sustainability Planning: Privatisation and the Demise of Democratic Government', in J Wilson and E Swyngedouw (eds) *The Post-Political and Its Discontents*, Edinburgh: Edinburgh University Press, pp 25-47.

Salamon, LM, Sokolowski, W and Anheier, HK (2000) *Social Origins of Civil Society: an Overview*. Baltimore: Working Papers of the Johns Hopkins Comparative Nonprofit Sector Project, no. 38, The Johns Hopkins Center for Civil Society Studies.

Schumacher, E (1973) *Small is Beautiful: A study of economcs as if people mattered*, London: Vintage Books.

Sedgewick, EK (2003) *Touching Feeling: Affect, Pedagogy, Performativity*, London: Duke University Press.

Seyfang, G and Smith, A (2007) 'Grassroots innovations for sustainable development: Towards a new research and policy agenda', *Environmental Politics*, 16: 584-603.

Sherry, D (2010) *Occupy! A short history of workers occupations*, London: Bookmarks.

Smith, A (2014) *Socially Useful Production*,STEPS Working Paper 58. Brighton: STEPS Centre.

Southern, A (ed) (2011) *Enterprise, Deprivation and Social Exclusion: The Role of Small Business in Addressing Social and Economic Inequalities*, London: Routledge.

Swyngedouw, E. 2010. 'Apocalypse Forever?: Post-political Populism and the Spectre of Climate Change', *Theory, Culture & Society*, 27(2-3), 213-232.

Thompson, E (1981) *The Making of the English Working Class*, London: Penguin.

Tuckman, A (2011) 'Worker's Control and the Politics of Factory Occupations', in Ness, I and Azzellini, D (eds) *Ours to Master and to Own: Workers Control from the Commune to the Present*, Chacago: Heymarket, pp 284-301.

Utting, P (ed) (2015) *Social and Solidarity Economy Beyond the Fringe*, London: Zed Books

Van Puymbroeck, N and Oosterlynck, S (2015) 'Opening Up the Post-Political Condition: Multiculturalism and the Matrix of Depoliticisation', in J Wilson and E Swyngedouw (eds) *The Post-Political and its Discontents*, Edinburgh: Edinburgh University Press, pp 86-108.

Wainwright, H (2003) *Beyond the State: Experiments in participatory democracy*, London: Verso.

Wainwright, H and Elliott, D (1982) *The Lucas Plan: A new trade unionism in the making?*, Allison and Busby.

Webb, S and Webb, B (1921) *The Consumers' Co-operative Movement*, Self-published.

Žižek, S (2011) *Living in the End of Times*, London: Verso.

Part II
The social and solidarity economy as a site of social innovation

Innovation, cooperatives and inclusive development: rethinking technological change and social inclusion

Lucas Becerra and Hernán Thomas

Introduction

In South America, during the past 10 years, the relations between technological innovation and inclusive development have been stabilised into research and policy agendas. However, our conventional understandings of what constitutes innovation still guide the ideas and practices that are embedded in science and technology public policy. This chapter aims to provide a reconceptualisation of the notion of the innovation and production system in order to foster the social and solidarity economy as a pathway to social and inclusive development.

In particular, the chapter utilises theoretical perspectives to position worker cooperatives as actors providing dynamism to innovation and social development processes. In particular, the goal is to highlight the role of these productive units in the context of science, technology and innovation (STI) public policy. The working hypothesis is that a shift in focus towards worker cooperatives could have the potential to set in motion a series of dynamics of learning, knowledge sharing, and techno-productive capability generation that would entail new socio-technical alliances oriented to more democratic processes of knowledge acquisition and generation of the associated value.

In that sense, the chapter presents a brief review of the economic literature on the role of the company in terms of innovation, followed by a critical analysis of those principles. From a methodological point of view, the work deploys a conceptual approach that combines theories of the sociology of technology, particularly socio-technical analyses (Thomas, 2008a, 2008b, 2009) and learning economy (Lundvall, 1992). From this framework, the chapter provides an explanation of the systemic implications of an innovation and production system focused on the profit-maximising company *vis-à-vis* a system focused on worker cooperatives. Finally, the chapter closes with a series of reflections on STI public policies aimed at inclusive development.

Economy, technology, and development: from theory to the implications for analysis

Various schools of economic thought, at different points in history, have assigned a diverse set of meanings and signifiers to the technological dimension of economic development: 'technical progress', the 'development of productive forces', 'modification of technique', 'technological change' and 'innovation', among others. In this chapter, technology is understood as artefacts, processes and methods of organisation. Technology, in its various manifestations, has been a key aspect in the development of economic theory. From the classic works by Adam Smith and Karl Marx, the way in which technology, capital and labour relate to each other has been of particular interest in describing the factors that determine the generation of exchange values and wealth generation–accumulation (MacKenzei, 1984). These drivers were codified and stylised (setting off a long theoretical journey) by Robert Solow (1956 and 1962) in the following argument: in the long run (with full resource utilisation), a particular economy's rate of growth equals its rate of technical progress. At the company level (that is, in microeconomic terms), the neoclassical approach was oriented to the analysis of the relative prices of factors and changes in the production function.

This school of thought works on the assumption that capital is a homogeneous unit that can adopt different shapes in terms of artefacts (machinery) and processes (techniques) that enable full flexibility in the shares capital and labour factors present in the production process. In that sense, if capital-labour relations are altered through modifications in wage and profit rates, businesspeople can choose from a set of available techniques, or develop new ones, to increase efficiency in terms of savings in the use of productions factors. Ontologically speaking, full exchangeability between factors enabling a choice among different techniques is formalised in the development of a 'production function'. Considering a given production function, technology is thus reduced to a set of codified and available data that can be ordered continually based on different capital-labour relations. However, in the debate that gave rise to the 'Cambridge capital controversy', Sraffa (1960), Pasinetti (1969) and Robinson (1953) inverted the neoclassical argument. For these authors, the causal relationship does not move from the wage and profit rate vector towards the choice of technique, but the other way around. Neo-Ricardians argue that it is the choice of technique that determines the distribution of income, rather than the latter determining the former.

This shift in focus enables 'technique reswitching'. The value of a given capital good at a given point in time is the sum of the cumulative value of labour (labour time multiplied by mean wage) in different periods and the relevant profit rate. Thus, as the profit rate increases (which, by extension, implies a decrease in the wage rate), the value of a given merchandise (or in this case a given capital good) will experience tensions: there will be an increase in the relative value of the labour from prior periods and a relative reduction in the value of the terms referring to more recent labour. Then, considering that capital is a heterogeneous category (and not homogeneous, as posited by the neoclassical tradition), it is possible to use the same capital–intensive technique, chosen when the wage rate was high, after wages diminish (a development that would suggest, according to the neoclassical view, a switch towards a labour-intensive technique). This is what neo-Ricardian economics classifies as 'technique reswitching'.

Briefly, the debate of neoclassic economists and neo-Ricardians has attempted to shed light on the dynamics of economic growth, increased efficiency, and wealth distribution stemming from different technological configurations of capital-labour relations. However, the epistemological tool of developing production functions to analyse these dynamics has created at least three analytical problems:

- On the one hand, a 'black box' of sorts is configured regarding how technological change processes occur, in particular as regards the visibility of the dynamics of learning, the creation of knowledge and capabilities, worker-machinery relations, and the role played by different types of knowledge (technical, scientific, social).
- These analyses assume production-circulation relations that are necessarily in a situation of equilibrium, thus ignoring the disruptive implications of innovative processes.
- The focus on individual and homogeneous companies' production functions fails to take into account the role played by other actors (universities, government bodies, regulations, the end users of the merchandise) in the shape and the trajectory of technological change.

In that line, the approach proposed by the economics of technical change and evolutionary economics (Schumpeter, 1928; Usher,

1955; Freeman, 1987; Nelson, 1995, among others) represents a way of thinking about these socioeconomic processes ignored by the aforementioned approaches, inasmuch as it attempts to pry the 'black box' of technology open (Rosenberg, 1982). In this approach, technological change is understood both as a modification in technique (aimed at increasing efficiency) and as a development of new products that enable the creation of new markets that provide extraordinary profits through 'natural monopolies'. Thus, companies no longer compete only through price, but also in dynamic terms, trying not to 'fall behind' as regards technological development. In that sense, inasmuch as the companies' activity takes place in competitive contexts, there is an incentive to innovation, as companies secure their survival over time by means of accumulating capital through growing profits. In other words, innovation is inherent to a system in which competition determines the social rules by which companies coexist. However, which are the processes or mechanisms enabling innovation?

Evolutionary economics posits that innovation hinges on self-organised processes involving not only technological factors, but also the 'context or environment' in which innovation processes take place. The introduction of the concept of a self-organised process enables us to include in the conceptual-analytical corpus the possibility of change in the behaviour of agents, incentives to adopt new technologies and the capabilities to make an efficient use of a given innovation (Yoguel, 2000). Innovation and diffusion are constituents of the same process. In that sense, innovations can change based on incremental improvements or their own diffusion.

Along the same lines, it is useful to think of processes at the system level in terms of the National Innovation System (NIS). An NIS is developed on two basic structures: a production structure, and an institutional structure. A given NIS contains 'all the elements contributing to the development, introduction, diffusion and use of innovations, including not only universities, technical institutes and research and development labs, but also elements and relations seemingly unrelated to science and technology' (Johnson and Lundvall, 1994, pp 696-7).

The approach in Lundvall (1992) focuses on analysing society as a collective actor for the innovative process, showing constant, diverse and complex learning actions associated with routine production, distribution and consumption activities that become inputs in the innovation process. Said activities include various types of learning: learning-by-doing (Arrow, 1962), learning-by-using (Rosenberg, 1982), and learning-by-interacting (Lundvall, 1988). Thus, Lundvall identifies a new model to explain the innovation-production dynamics, based on the concepts of a learning society and a learning economy (Christensen and Lundvall, 2004).

Lundvall's (1992) approach to understanding an NIS is based essentially on the fact that innovative activity lies within the system and cannot be reduced to its constituents: 'The important thing about the NIS is not each component's individual feature, but the relation and the type and degree of interaction between components' (Thomas and Gianella, 2008, p 44). However, if competition drives corporate innovation and capitalist companies need legal-normative instruments to secure the wealth generated through innovation, would that dynamic not contradict the broader collective process, in which the creation and diffusion of knowledge takes place at a societal level?

The socio-cognitive interactive model: inclusive innovation and a learning society

When the focus of analysis is moved from companies to other types of organisations, it is possible to identify new ways of innovation in new contexts: research and development (R&D) institutions (both public and private), government bodies, socially based institutions, non-governmental organisations (NGO) and cooperatives. Normally, organisations of this type are not considered in case studies or in economists' theoretical discussions of innovation and technological change.

Considered in the context of an analytical-explanatory model, this heterogeneous set of organisations can be thought of in terms of a complex system of socio-cognitive interactions showing dynamics of generation and circulation of learning, knowledge, problem-solution relations and capabilities. A systemic model of this type requires combining theoretical inputs from the learning economy and the sociology of technology. Works on the dynamics and mechanisms of learning (Lundvall, 1992; Johnson and Lundvall, 1994) focus their attention on the learning-by-doing, learning-by-using and learning-by-interacting processes. These three 'ways' of learning are related to different types of interaction: in the case of learning by doing, learning stems from the interaction between an actor (with the relevant set of knowledge, information and practices) in relation with new technological, institutional and social practices on the one hand, and knowledge codified and tacit relative to an artefact, productive activity and/or social use, on the other; in the case of learning by using, learning stems from the interaction between actors and things, which dynamically creates the capability of the actor to fully use, transform and resort to the artefact in question; and, finally, learning by interacting tries to explain learning processes stemming from interactions between the actors (institutions) in a national innovation and production system.

Similarly, the sociology of technology focuses on that interaction rather than on accumulation (Callon, 1992; Thomas, 2008a, 2008b), and, in particular, considers phenomena in which societies and their technological endowments are co-constructed (Bijker, 1995; Thomas, 2008a). Artefacts are co-constructed by producers and users, societies with the technologies they use: the very socio-technical process by which technologies are designed, produced and used creates social relations of production, work, communication and coexistence.

The 'hybrid' combination of both inputs is what this chapter classifies as the 'interactive socio-cognitive model' (see Figure 6.1). This model attempts to explain, from a systemic perspective, the interactions between heterogeneous actors (universities, firms, cooperatives, R&D institutions, NGOs, government bodies and end users), processes (problem-solution relations and learning) and practices (knowledge and capabilities). From a constructivist approach, processes and practices are the result of the actors' interactions, but said actors also create their identities, give shape to ideologies, and activate or hinder innovation and socio-technical processes based on the activation of particular processes and the production, reproduction and circulation of concrete practices.

The general model assumes that knowledge moves freely and interactions between the different actors in the system are fluid, which in ideal terms boosts the generation of learning and capabilities based

Figure 6.1: Interactive socio-cognitive model: general case

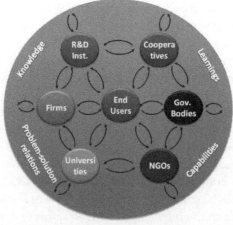

on broad and open participation in the construction of problems and the democratisation of solutions. In its ideal version, the maximisation of interaction processes ensures the creation of new learning and, by extension, innovative and technological change processes that are sustainable over time, aimed at meeting the techno-cognitive needs and requirements of societies.

However, in practice, systems can have key nodes or elements defining a systemic 'style'. In this sense, a system can develop around a particular set of institutions, such as profit-maximising companies. What does this mean? It means that the configuration of problem-solution relations, the generation of knowledge, the increase in capabilities and the direction of learning are aimed almost exclusively at boosting the role of the company as an 'innovative agent'. Borrowing from Therborn, the material matrix configuring the mesh of institutional relations provides the needed support for the ideology rooted in public policy (in this case, science and technology public policy aimed at the creation of new products and markets), the activities of research groups (assuming the 'progress of science and technology' and the neutrality of scientific 'truth') and legislation (ensuring with no restriction the private appropriation of the benefits of learning) to reproduce in the long run a systemic style in which socio-cognitive production is individually acquired.

More importantly, this style restricts rather than drives the possibility of learning and, by extension, the creation of new innovative dynamics. This is possible because the knowledge management dynamics in a standard profit-maximising company leads to attempts by the company to appropriate such knowledge and keep it for itself, either via intellectual property or trade secret (see Figure 6.2). For the capitalist company, this situation is inevitable: in its systemic environment, knowledge and learning are a way to obtain dynamic competitive advantages. Companies are forced to appropriate that 'learning income', because that is the way to survive in an environment defined by the principle of competition. Thus, in the context of a systemic style focused on the profit-maximising company, the innovative result expected from interactions is lower than the result expected from styles ensuring more fluid interactions.

That said, the realm of cooperatives is ruled by a principle contrary to that of competition. The same rationality that organises each cooperative productive unit can be deployed between different cooperatives (as happens in practice with federations or associated cooperatives, as in the case of Mondragón and SanCor). Cooperatives can (and in fact tend to) interact more among themselves than standard capitalist companies. Thus, if shared knowledge lies at the root of innovation, worker cooperatives can be better generators of local innovation than standard capitalist companies.

The common idea behind worker and service cooperatives is instead the socialisation of knowledge. This is due to the fact that the organisational constitution favours rationalities in which cooperation

Figure 6.2: Interactive socio-cognitive model: focus on profit-maximising companies

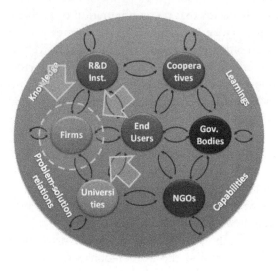

Figure 6.3: Interactive socio-cognitive model: focus on worker and production cooperatives

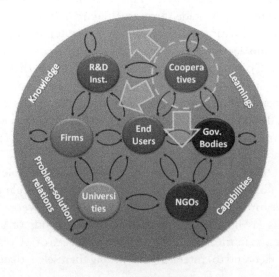

is the normal situation for a cooperative. The systemic style changes as a whole if the focus is placed on worker cooperatives rather than on profit-maximising companies.

From that starting point, it is possible to imagine (and develop) a new way of cognitive development, in which other institutions – much more fluid than profit-maximising companies – are linked with different public institutions and, besides, exchange knowledge in different dynamics, like universities, R&D institutions, cooperatives, users, NGOs and government institutions. This model of knowledge circulation is viable as long as no productive unit appropriates the knowledge generated by the system to the exclusion of the rest. That is the only way to consider these dynamics. At this level, cooperatives are able to socialise knowledge better than other companies focused solely on profit.

From the analytical model to the explanatory dimensions

Now that the model has been described, it is possible to present supplementary analyses by explanatory dimension. Four concepts are used for the comparison between profit-maximising companies and cooperatives: co-construction, problem-solution relations, working/non-working, and socio-technical alliance (Thomas, 2008a, 2008b).

The idea of co-construction posits that society is technologically constructed, just as technology is socially constructed. Both a system's material configuration and the allocation of the idea of the 'working' of a given technology (artefact, organisation or productive process) are constructed as a contingent derivation of disputes, pressures, resistances, negotiations and convergences that give shape to the heterogeneous set of actors, knowledge and material artefacts. The dynamics of innovation and technological change are processes of socio-technical co-construction, which means that changes in any of the elements produce new changes both in the meaning and working of a technology and in the associated social relations. In this sense, 'problems' and the corresponding 'problem-solution' relations are socio-technical constructions. In socio-technical co-construction processes, the relative participation of the problem-solution dynamic becomes dominant enough to condition the whole spectrum of socio-institutional practices and, in particular, the dynamics of learning and generation of organisational instruments. Knowledge generated through these problem-solution processes is partly codified and partly tacit (only partially explicit, featuring routine practices, developed in the context of decision making).

The 'working' or 'non-working' of an artefact is the result of a process of socio-technical construction in which heterogeneous elements play a role, generally in a self-organised fashion: material conditions, systems, knowledge, regulations, financing, features and so on. The 'working' (Bijker, 1995) of artefacts is not a given aspect, 'inherent to the artifact's features', but a contingency constructed socially, technologically and culturally. It assumes complex adequacy processes of technological responses/solutions to concrete and specific socio-technical articulations, set in a particular historical frame. The 'working' or 'non-working' of a given technology is an interactive relationship: the result of a process of socio-technical construction in which several heterogeneous elements play a role: systems, knowledge, regulations, materials, financing, features and so on. It is possible to posit that the idea that 'working' status is constructed in the context of socio-technical adequacy processes: self-organised and interactive processes of integration of a given knowledge, artefact or technological system in a socio-technical trajectory, within a socio-historical framework. The technology's working/non-working status comes from the meaning constructed in these self-organised socio-technical adequacy/inadequacy processes: adequacy leads to a 'working' artifact (Thomas and Buch, 2008).

The notion of 'alliance' complements as a mechanism for analysis the articulation between artefacts, materials, knowledge and actors that gives shape to the network that enables or restricts the possibility of a given technology's being considered working/non-working. Thus it is possible to define a socio-technical alliance as a coalition of heterogeneous elements implied in the process by which a technology's working/non-working status is constructed. Alliances are created dynamically, in terms of the movement or alignment and coordination of artefacts, ideologies, regulations, knowledge, institutions, social actors, economic resources, environmental conditions, materials and so on that enable or prevent the stabilisation of the technology's socio-technical adequacy and the meaning behind the ideas of working/non-working. Thus, socio-technical alliances make it possible to describe and analyse the relations between actors and technological systems, between relevant social groups and artefacts.

Now, it is possible to use these concepts to explain the systemic implications of an innovation and production system that is focused on the profit-maximising company *vis-à-vis* one that is focused on worker cooperatives.

Co-construction

What does a profit-maximising company co-construct? In principle, it selects and promotes standards related to the reinforcement of the appropriation of the benefit and, thus, the appropriation of knowledge. As a result, it promotes an accumulation model based on the notion of capitalist profit and income concentration, and on the competition between companies. In the case of cooperatives, the idea is that through sharing and socialising, the situation will improve for all in terms of solidarity, equality and fairness, and in terms of cooperation and coordination between institutions, and that this will lead to a social network capable of accommodating all of us.

Problem-solution relations

Additionally, problem-solution relations change depending on whether we deal with profit-maximising companies or cooperatives. In principle, in the case of the former, problem-solution relations (and, in particular, valid solutions to all types of problems) are those related to maximising profits.

First, there is the issue of how problems are constructed. What constitutes a problem? A problem is anything preventing an increase of productivity and/or competitiveness and making it impossible to increase the profit rate. That is a problem in the eyes of capitalist companies. Problems are not constructed based on the type or the quality of employment, the needs of the families that are part of the company's community, or the generation of the goods (in enough quantity or with enough quality) needed to improve a community's quality of life. In order to solve those types of problems, it would be necessary to have a share of the power of the unit constructing the problem. A capitalist company tries to keep as few entities as possible involved in the construction of the problem, and even fewer in the design of the relevant solution. In the case of cooperatives, those who construct the problem and those who benefit from the solution are the same people. The process is much more open and democratic; at the same time, it is much more efficient in techno-productive terms, and much more open as a learning process.

Working/non-working

In practice, when a technology 'works', it means that it is compatible not only with other technologies, but also with its initial endowment of factors, the workers' capacity to operate that technology, and the users' taste and their level of knowledge to use it, among other aspects. That is, something 'works' or 'does not work' not because it is constructed 'correctly' or 'incorrectly', but because it connects well with everything that existed previously, and because some decision groups are part of the process by which its working is constructed (Thomas, 2008a, 2008b, 2009). The question then is, in what respect are technologies generated by profit-maximising companies 'adequate'? These companies create socio-technical dynamics in which, metaphorically speaking, anything 'plugged' to the rest of the system creates a profit.

For a capitalist company, what works is anything that maximises the income from capital. Anything not conducive to that end is not useful, and therefore does not 'work'. For that reason, in practice, some technologies 'evolve' faster than others: companies focus on some, not all. That is the reason why some strategies are promoted by some companies in terms of clinical therapies, while others are not explored as much. Cooperatives, instead, construct – or at least should construct – problems differently, based on the problems of the people working on process technologies, or the problems of the recipients or end users of product technologies, at any rate.

Socio-technical alliances

Finally, according to the constructivist theory of technology, technologies (in their artefact, organisation and process dimensions) function in complex and heterogeneous alliances, alliances between actors and actants. For instance, a regulation is passed that favours a certain techno-productive sector using a certain type of technology, with engineers capable of developing certain machineries, which, in turn, give meaning to certain workers with certain capabilities – machines and workers that make products consumed by certain consumers. Behind internal-combustion cars, there is a huge international alliance encompassing the people who change Pirelli or Goodyear tyres, the fuel provision network, the steel mills providing plates, the cars' consumers, the need to cover long and medium distances, and even the foreign energy policy of the United States. This is defined as a 'socio-technical alliance'.

This is why creating an alternative alliance is so difficult: in order to make a new alternative-technology vehicle work – remember that 'working' is a socio-technical construction – a new alliance is needed. Developing an electrical engine and lithium batteries is not enough. When we think of public strategies in which techno-productive and social development is associated with the participation of large transnational companies via foreign direct investment (following the aforementioned traditional rationale of the economics of technological change), the implications stemming from the socio-technical alliances they are already a part of are made invisible.

In this sense, worker cooperatives are privileged actors in a technological change, local development and social inclusion strategy: they can enable different types of alliances, which are impossible if based on profit-maximising companies. Clearly, this begs the question about the resources needed to make these new alliances strong enough to compete for power with existing alliances.

On observation of current political and economic dynamics, it can be seen that regional governments currently favour investments and subsidies aimed at the entry of transnational companies, at the survival of large national companies, and to a very small degree, at the creation of new local dynamics. Large local companies exist because the government creates conditions adequate for their existence and permanence. In other words, active policies are developed to promote the use of profit-maximising technologies. Therefore, it is possible to think of alternative policies aimed at creating inclusive development processes, redirecting public resources that currently enable the operation of large capitalist companies.

Conclusion: science and technology policy for inclusive development

First of all, we should avoid being naïve. Science and technology policy for inclusive development does not refer to a particular technology, such as making a car, a computer, a piece of software or a drug. It is about creating comprehensive social technological systems – the material base for new socio-technical alliances – with a new orientation, with mutual feedback and mutual compatibility. These social technological systems are understood as heterogeneous socio-technical systems (of actors and artefacts, of communities and technological systems) aimed at bringing about social and economic inclusion dynamics, a democratisation of technological decision-making processes, and sustainable development. They imply product design actions, productive process and organisation technologies focused on inclusive problem-solution relations, fit for:

- the socialisation of goods and services;
- the democratisation of control and decisions;
- the empowering of communities of producers and users.

A single technology is not enough to change a socio-technical dynamics.

The idea of a socio-technical alliance enables us to think in strategic terms, with questions such as: What will be accepted? How will it be deployed? Which technologies will be taken into account in their present state and which will be modified? How will we operate on them? All these are actionable notions, they are not ideal rationalisations. For instance, a first step could be to make locally generated scientific and technological knowledge socially useful. Most of the knowledge produced in the region is 'not-applied applicable knowledge', or NAAK, according to Kreimer and Thomas (2002). At best, it is 'applied' elsewhere, used by other actors, in other regions, but it is not used to solve local social issues.

Second, it is necessary to consider, in terms of public policies in the socio-cognitive sphere, that there is a contradiction between the appropriation and the socialisation of knowledge. This does not imply a naïve socialisation of knowledge: to think of knowledge as a public good is not equal to declare it 'free to use'. There are different ways to license knowledge and choose which users are acceptable, which companies are acceptable. The only thing needed is a government slightly more subtle in terms of choices and legislation.

In this sense, worker cooperatives can be the new loci of innovation or, at least, one of the privileged loci of innovation. To that end, new means of financing should be developed: loans for development and learning, subsidies for innovation. Rather than analysing the university-firm relation in unspecific terms, the university-cooperative relation should be analysed strategically. Indeed, such inter-institutional links already exist.

Broadening public space

In socioeconomic terms, it is necessary to think of learning economy dynamics and the possibility of opening up new public spaces. In terms of technological innovation, the realm of the public could be expanded. There is potential to develop public health and public education technologies. The infrastructure of public transport, public housing and public food policy can – and should – be improved. In the socio-political sphere, this broadening of public space links governance in the region's countries with the production of common goods: goods shared by all and capable of being governed by all.

Broadening the public space would make it possible to improve our quality of life: access to goods and services, knowledge and cultures, the deployment of new ways to exist and coexist. So far, someone is making the choices, and those choices are, in general, not in the best interest of society as a whole: expensive rather than cheap, for a few rather than for many, exclusive rather than inclusive. At any rate, broadening public space amounts to recovering spheres in which to exercise our citizenship.

Socio-technical citizenship

When we think of socio-technical citizenship, it is mandatory to reflect about the people who make technological decisions in our countries, about the people who benefit from those decisions, about the interests they further, and about the levels of risk they pose. At that level, socialising the appropriation of technology is a non-secondary, non-trivial matter. It is not just an environmental or productive, local or corporate issue. It is a matter of survival.

Social technological systems could be the most democratic way of designing, developing, producing, implementing, managing and assessing the future material matrix. That is, after all, the goal of technology: it is the material matrix that keeps human societies alive. At this level, worker cooperatives and other social articulations (like state-owned and public companies, universities and R&D units) – not focused on maximising profit – could prove to be the best place to design and produce those social technological systems. The fate of future societies in terms of equality of rights, creation of spaces of freedom, population quality of life, deepening of democracies and protection of the environment, depends on the material base on which they will develop.

References

Arrow, K. (1962) 'The Economic Implications of Learning by Doing', *Review of Economic Studies*, vol 49, no 80, pp. 155-173.

Bijker, W. (1995) *Of Bicycles, Bakelites and Bulbs. Toward a Theory of Sociotechnical Change*, Cambridge, MA: MIT Press.

Callon, M. (1992) 'The dynamics of techno-economic networks', in R. Coombs, P. Saviotti and V. Walsh (eds) *Technological Changes and Company Strategies: Economical and sociological perspectives*, London: Harcourt Brace Jovanovich.

Christensen, J.L. and Lundvall, B.-Å. (eds) (2004) *Product Innovation, Interactive Learning and Economic Performance*, Amsterdam: Elsevier.

Freeman, C. (1987) *Technology and Economic Performance: Lessons from Japan*, London: Pinter.

Johnson, B. and Lundvall, B.-Å. (1994) 'Sistemas nacionales de innovación y aprendizaje institucional', *Comercio Exterior*, vol 44, no 8, pp 695-704.

Kreimer, P. and Thomas, H. (2002) 'The Social Appropriability of Scientific and Technological Knowledge as a Theoretic-Methodological Problem', in R. Arvanitis (ed) *Section 1.30 Science and technology policy of the EOLSS*, London: EOLSS.

Lundvall, B.-Å. (1988) 'Innovation as an interactive process: from user-producer interaction to the national system of innovation', in G. Dosi, C. Freeman, R. Nelson, G. Silverberg and L. Soete (eds) *Technical Change and Economic Theory*, London: Pinter.

Lundvall, B.-Å. (1992) *National systems of innovation: towards a theory of innovation and interactive learning*, London: Pinter.

MacKenzei, D. (1984) 'Marx and the Machine', *Technology and Culture*, vol 25, no 3, pp 473-502.

Nelson, R. (1988) 'Institutions Supporting Technical Change in the United States', in G. Dosi, C. Freeman, R. Nelson, G. Silverberg and L. Soete (eds) *Technical Change and Economic Theory*, London: Pinter.

Nelson, R. (1995) 'Recent evolutionary theorizing about economic change', *Journal of Economic Literature*, vol 33, pp 48-90.

Pasinetti, L. L. (1969) 'Switches of Technique and the "Rate of Return" in Capital Theory', *The Economic Journal*, vol 79, no 315, pp 508-531.

Robinson, J. (1953) 'The Production Function and the Theory of Capital', *Review of Economic Studies*, vol 21, no 2, pp 81-106.

Rosenberg, N. (1982) *Inside the Black Box: Technology and Economics*, Cambridge: Cambridge University Press.

Schumpeter, J. (1928) 'The instability of capitalism', *Economic Journal*, no 38, pp 361-386.

Solow, R. (1956) 'A contribution to the Theory of Economic Growth', *The Quarterly Journal of Economics*, vol 70, no 1, pp 65-64.

Solow, R. (1962) 'Technical Progress, Capital Formation, and Economic Growth', *The American Economic Review*, vol 52, no 2, pp 76-86.

Sraffa, P. (1960) *Production of Commodities by Means of Commodities: Prelude to a Critique of Economic Theory*. Cambridge, Cambridge University Press.

Thomas, H. (2008a) 'Estructuras cerradas vs. Procesos dinámicos: trayectorias y estilos de innovación y cambio tecnológico', in H. Thomas and A. Buch (eds) with M. Fressoli and A. Lalouf *Actos, actores y artefactos. Sociología de la Tecnología*, Bernal: Editorial UNQ.

Thomas, H. (2008b) 'En búsqueda de una metodología para investigar Tecnologías Sociales', Paper presented at the 'Tecnologías para la inclusión social y políticas públicas en América Latina' workshop, organised by the Campinas State University, National University of Quilmes, Financiadora de Estudos e Projetos and the Canadian International Development Research Center, 24–25 November.

Thomas, H. (2009) 'De las tecnologías apropiadas a las tecnologías sociales: conceptos/estrategias/diseños/acciones', Paper presented at the First Conference on Social Technologies, Ministry of Science, Technology and Production Innovation, Buenos Aires, 14 May.

Thomas, H. and Buch, A. (eds) (2008) *Actos, actores y artefactos. Sociología de la Tecnología*, Buenos Aires: Prometeo Editorial.

Thomas, H. and Gianella, C. (2008) 'Procesos socio-técnicos de construcción de perfiles productivos y capacidades tecnológicas en el Mercosur', in G. Rosenwurzel, C. Gianella, G. Bezchinsky and H. Thomas (eds) *Innovación a escala Mercosur*, Buenos Aires: Prometeo.

Usher, A.P. (1955) 'Technical change and capital formation', in National Bureau of Economic Research *Capital Formation and Economic Growth*, Princeton, NJ: Princeton University Press.

Yoguel, G. (2000) *Economía de la Tecnología y de la Innovación*, Bernal: National University of Quilmes.

SEVEN

Brazil's social economic incubators

Reinaldo Pacheco da Costa

Introduction: the Brazilian solidarity economy

The solidarity economy movement emerged in the 1980s during the struggle for re-democratisation of the country in response to the government's neoliberal economic plan guided by the Washington Consensus. Neoliberalism in Brazil was characterised by the restructuring of the world of work, the reconfiguration of the international process of capital accumulation, an extraordinary increase in foreign debt, economic stagnation and growing unemployment. In this context, many companies were bankrupted, and their workers became unemployed. Brazilian workers reacted to this crisis by recovering insolvent factories and creating productive organisations based on self-management, first as an alternative to unemployment, and later as part of a wider economic, political and social movement known as the 'solidarity economy', which amplified calls for democracy to be transmitted from the political to the economic sphere. For Cruz (2006, p 58), the term solidarity economy is a disputed concept. He argues that:

> those advocating the use of the expression do not coincide with its meaning, and those criticising it, obviously do not coincide with their criticism, either.… One of the landmarks of this contextualisation was [the work of] Chilean sociologist Luis Razeto (1982) entitled *Empresas de Trabajadores y Mercado Democrático*, in which the terms the economy of solidary/solidarity economy is presumed to have first emerged in Latin America.

The solidarity economy that has emerged in Brazil represents an upsurge of political and social contestation against neoliberalism. It is composed of different political, social and religious streams, such as liberation theology, adopted by the progressive wing of the Catholic Church in the 1980s and its ecclesiastical base communities; Cáritas Brasileira and its alternative community projects; the Landless Workers' Movement (Movimento dos Trabalhadores Sem Terra, or MST); and the Pastoral Land Commission created in 1975 during a pastoral meeting of the Amazonian Catholic Church.

A number of associations emerged during this upsurge such as the Brazilian Association of Solidarity Cooperatives, which today includes the Brazilian Confederation of Agrarian Reform Cooperatives, created in 1992, which gathered cooperatives and associations of rural workers settled by agrarian reform in Brazil; the Brazilian Association of Family Agriculture and Solidarity Economy Cooperatives; and the Union of Cooperatives and Solidarity Ventures. Another institution instrumental in the foundation of the solidarity economy in Brazil was the World Social Forum, which, at a roundtable event on the solidarity economy held in 2001 in Porto Alegre, coined the phrase 'another world is possible'. Another important actor is the Social Development Agency, which is connected to the Workers' Unitary Central, the National Association of Workers' Self-managed Companies, and two incubator networks, the Technological Incubators of Popular Cooperatives and the Unitrabalho Foundation.

The Brazilian solidarity economy now consists of over 20,000 solidarity economic ventures (SEVs), which create work and income beyond conceptions of employment that involves a bond with an employer. The SEVs have the following basic principles: cooperative work, self-management, internal democracy, consensual distribution of economic surpluses (in contrast with the distribution of profit in capitalist ventures) and sustainability. In this way, SEVs bring together social, economic and environmental concerns. There are different forms of formal or informal SEVs: producers' associations, production cooperatives, self-managed ventures, production groups, bartering clubs, purchase and sale networks, central cooperatives, community banks, self-managed ventures, and industries that come from bankrupted companies whose assets were exchanged with the workers as an alternative for redundancy payments.

Paul Singer, unequivocally the inspiration for, and catalyst of, much of the academic study of the solidarity economy in Brazil, defines the solidarity economy as a different 'production mode', an alternative to capitalism, and an alternative political project of Brazilian society (Singer, 2002). Paul Singer himself, in the video available at EM CONSTRUÇÃO (2006), argues that:

Solidarity Economy is a reformulation of the socialist idea that somehow incorporates the original utopian socialism. This 'utopian' socialism from Owen, Fourier and Proudhon – utopian in quotation marks – was a socialism that bet on the free association of producers. Proudhon became a revolutionary assembly deputy of 1848, but was deeply disappointed with parliamentarism. So he is the father of anarchism and was interested in organising the people directly, changing society from bottom up. The experience of both Communist Russia and Eastern Europe etc. and the social democratic experiences of the most advanced capitalist countries, who followed, so to speak, Marxist doctrine, have failed to change society through state action.

For Singer there is not one consolidated theory of the solidarity economy. Given its focus on cooperation and self-management, its fundamentals are based on similar models in the history of human societies. Solidarity economy is a broader name for a wider social, economic and political movement that is widespread in Brazil, in Latin America, and in other countries. There are several other denominations and meanings, such as *économie sociale et solidaire* (France), *sociedades laborales* (Spain), and *economia solidária* in Brazil and the countries of South America (Argentina, Chile, Paraguay, and Uruguay) (Singer and Machado, 2000). Today over 1.6 million people are involved in cooperative ventures in the Brazilian solidarity economy.

This chapter describes the contributions of the university incubators to the construction of the solidarity economy sector in Brazil. The picture presented here is already historical, since a legislative coup unseated President Dilma Rouseff in September 2016 (we would argue illegitimately), and left the country in a state of political uncertainty. It is a situation we have seen before in Latin America, whereby a one-dimensional neoliberal policy framework is being (re)imposed on the country. Readers are requested to consider this text, therefore, as a framework for understanding the solidary economy movement that has emerged over the past 12 years in Brazil. We do not yet know what public policies aimed at the solidarity economy will (or will not) be constructed over the coming next years, or whether we will have to fight old battles again.

Social economic incubators

The emergence of the solidarity economy has been facilitated by the Technological Incubators of Popular Cooperatives (TIPCs) network and, since 1996, social economic incubators (SEIs). These TIPCs/ SEIs (forthwith SEIs) emerged to support the creation of solidarity economic ventures (SEVs) in low-income communities through an incubation process conducted by academics to help generate income and jobs. While SEIs exist in several states in Brazil, and have different working methods and names, all of them seek to link economics and social responsibility. Parra (1999, p 159) explained the rationale for the name TIPCs:

> They are called Incubators because, like maternity units, they aim to provide a favourable environment for the self-development of the groups assisted, combining an external focus with support for the development of the group's own internal capabilities. They are Technological as they provide not only an intervention methodology and support for continuous improvement, but also the state of the art to improve the cooperatives. The word Cooperatives defines a collective work alternative as a form of social organisation that can promote more effectively social inclusion. The Popular adjective has been added to identify ordinary people.

In this chapter, we use the term social economic incubator to refer to a wide variety of incubators connected to the solidarity economy movement that now operate in over a hundred Brazilian universities, technical institutes and municipal governments, and in the private sector. The chapter introduces the innovative social technology adopted by SEIs. It begins with a discussion of their historical evolution and the political scene that shaped the movement, before moving on to a discussion of the political and pedagogical process adopted within the incubators and their methodologies in order to help the reader to understand how the solidarity economy movement is supported by the incubators. Finally, the results and benefits of the incubation process are discussed, not only in economic terms, but also in terms of education, culture and politics.

The SEIs had their roots in the Citizenship Action (Ação da Cidadania) movement, led by the sociologist Herbert de Souza, which established the Committee of Public Ventures to Alleviate Hunger and for Life (Comitê de Empresas Públicas no Combate à Fome e Pela vida; or COEP). As a reaction to the unemployment and economic recession in Brazil in the late 1980s, the Oswaldo Cruz Foundation, connected to the National Faculty of Public Health, built the first popular cooperative in Manguinhos, a dense favela area in Rio de Janeiro. During the first COEP meeting in 1995, the Oswaldo Cruz Foundation proposed a discussion of the problems of the Manguinhos favela in which the meeting was taking place. From these discussions an idea emerged: 'Why not incubate cooperatives in the community in order to promote social inclusion as work and income generation and a reduction of violence?' (Pateo, 2008, p 42). This inspired the Coordination of Engineering Graduate Programs (COPPE) at the Federal University of Rio de Janeiro (UFRJ) to create the first technological incubator of popular cooperatives, the TIPC-COPPE-UFRJ, in Brazil, financed by Funding Authority for Studies and Projects (FINEP) (Pateo, 2008).

In 1997, the Unitrabalho Foundation, which aims to integrate academic knowledge with social practice, hosted a solidarity economic working group, coordinated by Professors Paul Singer, Candido Vieitez and Newton Briand. From these discussions, academic debates on the theme emerged. In 1998, five other social economic incubators were created with the financial support of FINEP at Ceará Federal University, University of São Paulo, Juiz de Fora Federal University, Pernambuco Rural Federal University, and Bahia State University (IADH, 2011). The SEI model was taken up abroad by the Universidad de la Republica (Uruguay) as the 'University Incubator Program of Popular Economic Societies' (INCOOP / UEC). The Universidad de la Republica (Uruguay) participates in the Association of Universities Grupo Montevideo (AUGM) – a network of 32 public and autonomous universities in Argentina, Bolivia, Brazil, Chile, Paraguay and Uruguay – where it coordinates the Academic Committee of Cooperative and Associative Processes.

University-based SEIs support the creation of SEVs in low-income communities through an incubation process that supports the generation of work and income. They develop the capacity of workers, students and professionals to embed processes and conceptions of self-management into the work process, identify new research themes within the universities, and support the participation of solidarity economy activists in the international social/solidarity economy movement. SEIs create spaces of democracy, equality and freedom to produce knowledge and income for SEVs. They facilitate new connections between universities and society and between social movements and university outreach programmes; for universities and students, the incubators foster an environment for the exchange of scientific and popular knowledge.

The incubators show the inseparability of teaching, research and outreach programmes by providing students with an investigative attitude (learning to learn), and opportunities to intervene in the world outside the university to (re)build or reconfigure knowledge, instead of merely transmitting or copying it. Besides being a technical partner, the SEIs also understand the social problems of the people involved in the formation of the cooperatives. More concretely, the incubators follow and collaborate in several specific SEVs in areas including the collection and selection of recyclable and solid residues, food/food safety, clothes making/sewing, urban/rural ecological agriculture, manufacturing of cleaning/hygiene products, technical advisories, popular handcraft and community finances, among others. Of particular note are the municipal social centres that use solidarity economy principles to help people recently released from prison, and those with disabilities.

SEIs are composed of multidisciplinary teams of professors, non-teaching staff, technicians, undergraduate and graduate students. They are characterised by interdisciplinary activities, but also by innovative theoretical and more practical research for popular ventures. Public policies aim to design and finance innovation systems directed at the solidarity economy, and as a result many different social technology projects are being developed by SEIs with other participants in the solidarity economy. In economically peripheral areas in particular, a proactive stance is taken towards the social realities outside of the university, especially when unexpected developments demand creative and ethical responses from the incubators. The social incubators have also participated in the municipal and regional forums contributing to the discussions of the Brazilian Forum of the Solidarity Economy since 2003, which has organised five national plenaries. They interact with each other through two national networks, and work collaboratively to give assistance to constitute new incubators, both in and outside universities, with governmental entities such as municipal governments and civil society.

Two important reports provide a solid basis for understanding the performance of the SEIs in Brazil. The first is a report on the national programme for TIPCS and SEVs from the Institute for the Assessment of Human Development (Instituto de Assessoria para o Desenvolvimento Humano [IADH, 2011]). This is a broad survey of SEIs and their institutional financing that examines the performance of over 50 SEIs and hundreds of SEVs. The second is a report on a project also financed by FINEP that systematised the experiences of the TIPCs. In this project, five university incubators in São Paulo state undertook a longitudinal analysis of their experiences (USP, 2013). These two reports form the basis of the following discussion.

Pedagogy, technology and incubation

This section examines processes of self-management, social technology and incubation methodology as fundamental categories of analysis in order to gain an understanding of the effectiveness of processes of capacity-building SEVs, the main objective of the SEIs.

Self-management

Social economic ventures aim to foster self-management in which workers take over the operation of the productive venture under a direct democratic regime. Owners or associates do not exist; the workers participate democratically in administrative and operational decision making. While conceptions of self-management vary according to local political or social conditions and the needs and preferences of different groups, what matters is distinguishing 'self-management' in the context of the solidarity economy with the 'Toyota' or 'Keizen' model of continuous improvement in which the owner concedes autonomy to the workers, but with the objective of increasing profits that are then retained by the owners and/or shareholders. In this sense, as Ana Luiza Laporte argues in the USP report

> Self-management is a form of workers organisation experienced by the popular councils that emerged from different political contexts (be they revolutionary or not), and is characterized by the direct action of their members through egalitarian structures that contest social relations characterised by hierarchy and exploration. Historical experiences of self-management can be identified in the Spanish Revolution (1936-9), the Portuguese Carnation Revolution (1974), the Paris Commune (1879), etc. when workers self-organized and developed structures opposed to the vertical hierarchy normally supported by the left such as unions, political parties and the State. (Laporte, 2013, p 43)

With their focus on self-management, SEIs are part of a wider political project of the solidarity economy, which develops counter-hegemonic production processes. The solidarity economy modifies the ownership of the means of production, opening up new possibilities. It facilitates the collective distribution of the surplus and improves economic, social and cultural relations. In particular, the IADH study (IADH, 2011) argued that solidaristic practices within SEVs increases their members' participation, solidarity and self-esteem.

Solidarity economic ventures have their own logics and specific problems, so traditional business planning and management methods cannot be used uncritically. SEVs are often undercapitalised, their members lack formal qualifications, and they often lack technical skills. As a result, SEVs require a democratic and participative management model, guided towards both economic feasibility *and* the (re)appropriation of citizen rights so that these defects are addressed by developing the capacity of SEVs to self-manage these issues. We discuss specifically how this is done later in this section.

Social technology

SEVs are often fragile organisations that frequently lack access to knowledge and to technologies that could strengthen their economic feasibility. To address this, a social-economic perspective is adopted that presupposes that technology developed by SEVs considers, and contributes to developing, ways that the local cultures and knowledge of SEV members contribute to the development of work processes that improve health and safety at work, and to sustainability (IADH, 2011). Social technology in management, production and marketing has to be developed for excluded populations as an alternative and counterpoint to conventional technology. Technology can be expensive. New social technologies need technologists and access to tools. Appropriate technological solutions require engagement with the whole production process, with the distribution of surpluses, and with decision making.

Technology is a term that involves tacit, short-term and practical, strategic, technical and scientific knowledge, as well as tools, processes and materials. How technology is produced and used is mediated by culturally differentiated practices. In the solidarity economy context, it is necessary to expand debates about how to understand, use and perhaps appropriate technologies, and how different technologies should be understood and validated within the solidarity economy field. SEVs cannot do this alone: university participation is very important for the development of *appropriate* social technology (Dagnino, 2016). The following two examples illustrate the issues:

(1) A Social Technology Fair allowed workers to talk about the process whereby the equipment used by SEVs is developed. It was made clear that technology is always constructed from the identification of a problem, but the exchanges among people about how to solve the problem can be more important in the process of identifying technological solutions than the solution itself. For example, a technician from an incubator learned how to manufacture one of the machines exhibited (a large mixer for producing soap bars), and took this knowledge to his neighborhood SEV, which was having difficulty in meeting orders, as they needed a larger mixer. (USP, 2013, p 77).

(2) In the fourth Seminar, a notable contribution was made by the Cirandeiros team, who spoke about solidaristic ways of providing childcare called 'Ciranda'. Ciranda is a dance in which participants are arranged in a circle which is regularly used by the MST to entertain children collectively while the adults are at work. A team of TIPC-Unicamp instructors organised this activity, which they called Ciranda, as a way of helping the children have fun and be occupied in ways that helped their educational and political development. It was crucial in helping many women, especially mothers, get involved who would otherwise not be able to participate if they had to look after their children on their own. The TIPC-Unicamp Cirandeiros team met the need for childcare in ways that gave the children a rich experience of spontaneous, creative and educational play. (USP, 2013, p 14)

The modus operandi of the incubators

The incubators' *modus operandi* promotes self-management. A common model in university-based SEIs is the use of multidisciplinary teams of both graduate and undergraduate students that bring together insights from economics, social sciences, psychology, accountancy, agronomics, biology, engineering and so on. The students earn income from public funds, and the projects are publically financed; but, while the student teams are helpful, it is equally important to ensure that the capacity of the SEVs for self-management is maintained, especially in the context of policy formation and decision making. Thus the teams work collectively through consensus-building processes such as the identification of the scientific state of the art in which team members share the challenges faced (projects, processes, events, management) and the development of themes and collective practices such as the organisation of the physical space of the SEI, and through professors' talks and workshops. Collective planning is carried out in ways that aim to strengthen the team's identity and the working process. Internal management issues are usually tackled by a coordinating committee comprising elected students and/or recent graduates.

Coordination of the process as a whole, which can involve students, non-teaching staff and professors, is usually rotated, with established term periods. At each rotation, an election changes the composition of the coordinating committee. Equality between the different members of a usually hierarchical university system is highly valued, with work relations not directly based on the function an individual has at the university, but rather on the accumulated contribution that has been made over time to the incubator's development, as well the individual member's involvement with specific tasks. New people join the team periodically, by means of an induction that aims to facilitate the formation of a group process and strengthen its collective identity, which is reconfigured with the introduction of new participants. The induction aims to get new members to be part of a team and think about the collective task in hand rather than their individual perspective.

It should be noted that this type of incubation is a recent form of interdisciplinary working and outreach for the universities. The methodological experiences of the pioneers were passed on to those who later joined the process, and these experiences have gradually enriched the conceptual base on which the principles of the universities outreach programmes were built:

> The 'Self-Management Methodology' should facilitate the radical participation of all those involved in the decision processes regarding the planning, execution, assessment and systematisation of activities. The self-managed methodology is not restricted to economic education; it is rather the founding nature of the economic and political relations of those practicing Solidarity Economy. It should foster participation and cooperation, facilitate the production of better goods and services delivered by the ventures, and support the quest for active citizenship. (USP, 2013, p 9)

SEIs are designed to promote the study of the solidarity economy, and develop social technologies and knowledge to be socially and collectively owned by all those involved, fostering the development of self-managed organisations with autonomy and collective participation, linking creativity and challenging traditional values and practices. They also inspire dialogues between universities and society, between theory and practice, and between official programmes and projects based on solidarity economy principles. The practice is exercised in a dialogical way with the communities involved to produce income and to stimulate local development through popular education, the exchange of experiences, and the collective construction of self-managed spaces. Last and not least, let us not forget that the social incubator university programmes are also the place for students – young people taking undergraduate and graduate courses – to engage with all of the opportunities, enthusiasms and difficulties experienced by young people finding their way in the world.

Incubation methodology

The evaluation of the IADH project (IADH, 2011) identified a common framework methodology that has at its core an agreed set of socio-political and pedagogical principles. That being the case, in terms of processes and activities, the incubators vary widely. Consequently, this section is divided into two parts: principles and processes, where disciplinary issues are briefly discussed.

Principles

The participation of people as transformers, through self-management processses, of the reality in which they live is the basis of the incubation process. To achieve good results, participants recognise the importance of participation, and at the centre of this relationship is the tension between participatory processes (through which members develop their capacity for self-management, which takes time) and pedagogic issues around knowledge transmission (in which experts might want to pass on their knowledge more quickly). There are no strict rules, but the process should allow for the adjustment, readjustment and adaptation of those methods to ensure that members of the SEVs continue to own the process as they are inseparable components issues of teaching practices, research and extension.

The incubator team learns and teaches about self-management, engaging with technical and scientific concepts in a dialogical way, working between theory and practice, and research and outreach programmes, in ways that change how education is traditionally conducted by universities, joining 'scientific knowledge' to 'popular wisdom' in processes aimed at an attempted transformation of everyday practice.

Processes

The processes generally comprise three main phases: pre-incubation, incubation and post-incubation. The following discussion engages with the methodologies used by the incubators, highlighting some issues common to all SEIs.

The **pre-incubation** process consists of the identification, sensitisation, and preparation of groups. Once a proposal is received from a potential incubation group, a member of the SEI meets with a group that wants to explore the possibility of setting up an SEV to gather information about them and their issues, and to sensitise them to the incubation process. Through this process, members of both institutions (solidarity economy venture and incubator) get to know each other. They aim to understand the reality of the group's social situation and the behavior of the group's members, and to break the culture of silence that can mean that problems, oppressive power structures and solutions are not recognised and/or articulated. This 'discovery phase' takes into account the needs of the groups. Their voices are heard. At this point they begin to make the first steps towards mobilising to develop an SEV. Once a project has been worked up, it is approved by the SEI's evaluation committee.

In the phase of **incubation** proper, the SEI seeks to support the group's sustainability, which involves developing their managerial capacity and preparing a business plan. Central to this process is taking into account economic, social, local, environmental and cultural dimensions of the situation in which the group is operating. This necessitates a customised approach focused on the work process. Knowledge building is collective. Incubation includes contributions from a range of disciplines, and focuses both on the *specifics* of the project under consideration (examining the technical and economic feasibility of the project, developing productive capacity and technological improvements to processes and products leading to comercialisation, formalisation and legalisation of the project or process, and procuring the necessary documentation to produce and market the product) and, more widely, on *generic* issues such as enhancing management skills, the use of ICT in cooperative management processes, administration (legal and accounting aspects) and securing rights to subsidies and to social protection. There is a constant focus on creating a civic culture that strengthens community and civic values, such as cooperative/solidarity values, and understands the concepts of rights, incumbency, conflict mediation and consensus building. While the economic sustainability of the proposed SEV is vital, the cultural, social and political gains secured by participants in the incubation process stay with them throughout their lives.

After a period (not less than two years), the group is launched and enters the **post-incubation** phase, during which it receives periodic support to develop networks with other solidarity ventures. In this phase, the participants seek to consolidate the autonomy of the group, with regard to economic issues such as developing social and political relations, strengthening trust, and exchanging experiences. In some ways, the incubation process never ends. The pre-incubation and incubation processes are all steps towards dis-incubation, and as the SEV matures it gets closer to complete independence. Central to this is forming a self-managed, collective identity for the group and encouraging individuals to develop their own subjective experiences and capacity for self-actualisation. The methodology of the incubation process is centered on the production of a group with a collective identity and democratic procedures (Zornita, 2009, p 2).

Results and benefits

There are now over 100 SEIs in the 27 Brazilian states, involving some 700 professors and over 1,700 students, technicians, contributors and professionals. The IADH report (2011) indicates that there are over 20,000 solidarity economy ventures registered all over Brazil, with a total of over 1.5 million people participating in the solidarity economy.

More qualitatively, the social incubators have developed and disseminated solidarity economy practices by means of direct action, capacity building, advice provision, pedagogical approaches, formation lessons, joint construction lessons, continued follow-up and the incubation of teams, developing the capacity of a wide range of academics and students from a diverse range of disciplines to work with SEVs, and developing new lines of research. Most of the social incubators participate in solidarity economy forums, work with local authorities, and agitate for political change to the extent that we can now talk about a solidarity economy *movement* in Brazil, as shown in Figure 7.1.

The incubators have contributed to the development of economic forms that recognise cultural diversity (ethnicity, gender, 'race' and other forms of identity) and support the needs of diverse members

Figure 7.1: Mapping of the solidarity economy in Brazil

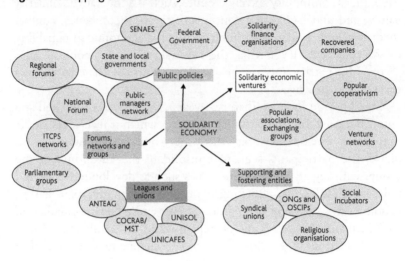

of society who need specific forms of support (for example, people with disabilities, drug users, ex-offenders and people with mental health needs), and people who are often invisible in society and in academia. Local Centres for Psychosocial Support are a good example of the type of organisation to have benefited from community-based income generation.

The IADH report (2011) attests to the production of university-based knowledge directly and indirectly attributable to social incubators. Apart from contributing to the academic output of its students and graduates (in terms of doctoral theses, Master's dissertations, articles published in journals and presented at conferences and other meetings), the social incubators offer other forms of knowledge production and dissemination through CDs, textbooks, videos, theatre plays, puppet shows, seminars and technical reports that (unfortunately) are not given the academic status they deserve.

The SEIs also contribute to other federal government programmes and actions, such as the Sustainable Rural Development Programme of the Banco do Brasil, and projects concerning food and nutritional safety, agrarian reform and family agriculture, fair trade, social technologies. New laws governing school meals, small and medium-sized enterprises and waste recycling also open new opportunities for incubators to support the commercialisation of new self-managed cooperatives.

Conclusion

Research highlights the following conclusions and recommendations with regard to incubation methodology. First, the capacity-building elements of the incubation process are extremely important for the long-term sustainability of SEVs. Capacity building of individual workers in SEVs needs to be long term, and here the importance of maintaining and developing networks to share knowledge and experiences is of note. In this context, the IADH report (2011) shows that the SEVs themselves rate the work of SEIs highly. The SEIs are seen as allies and partners for attaining established goals. The participants of popular cooperatives are very proud to have been able to participate in the incubation process.

There are, of course, still problems to be tackled, including continued difficulties in accessing financial services and credit. More capacity-building work needs to be done to enable SEI members to better understand market operation, support the commercialisation of new products and services, develop new technological processes, and help the SEVs to understand administration, finance and accounting. More could be done to enable the SEIs to monitor the progress of the SEVs, particularly those undergoing dis–incubation, as they may feel abandoned at this stage. Supportive networks are still underdeveloped. SEVs do not feel well informed or able to seek partnerships and access to other public policies and programmes. The incubators and their founders have developed knowledge in project management that could be more widely shared and owned, or socialised. Connections with public policy could be further developed, so that both universities and federal, state and municipal public policy departments are better able to finance incubators to ensure their stability.

The success of SEIs is intertwined with that of the solidarity economy in Brazil more widely, but it has to be recognised that there is still a deep gap between theory and practice between what is desirable and what is (currently) feasible (Melo, 2007). The experience of the SEVs reveals the continued existence of many difficulties that limit their potential for transformation and social reform, and the SEVs continue to face many barriers, including difficulties in creating more resilient organisations at scale. There can be a weakening of cooperative principles in the face of capitalist pressures at times of economic crisis, which can lead to intense conflicts and internal clashes within the cooperatives, triggered by the day-to-day pressures of self-management work, among other factors. Cooperators may give up working in a SEV when they are offered a job in the traditional market, and generally justify their decision with reference to the low income derived from cooperative work and feelings of instability arising from lack of a formal contract offering worker protection and rights. Some of these barriers could be overcome by creating more and better spaces of communication and integration among the incubator networks, exchanging knowledge and accomplishing political gains.

There are also workers, however, who opt for continuing to work in SEVs. They base their decisions on the social, political and cultural gains offered by such work, such as the constitution of new social relations and an increase in self-esteem, among others. Consequently, Melo (2007, p 14) argues that:

> ... it is important to highlight this harsh reality does not invalidate or weaken the importance of the sociopolitical gains emphasized in research on the Solidarity Economy, such as concepts such as 'citizenship', 'collective identities', 'new sociability', 'social capital', 'new work culture', 'autonomy', among others.... Therefore, the fact that a Solidarity venture can be a response to immediate needs – its purpose is economic as a work and income generation initiative – doesn't mean that it doesn't hold other potentialities.... Maybe exactly there – in these gains – lies one of the secrets of the permanence and development of the Solidarity Economy in the Brazilian scenario for over two decades.

In conclusion, self-management cannot be learned or taught theoretically; it is beyond the reproduction of principles expressed in any doctrine. Its apprenticeship occurs in the daily confrontation of conflicts generated between clasped social relations and the attempt to build viable possibilities to end the disconnection between people and their working relationships and practices, to build liberated forms of work and livelihood.

References

Cruz, A.C. (2006) 'Tese apresentada ao Programa de Pós-Graduação em Economia. M. A Diferença da Igualdade: A dinâmica da economia solidária em quatro cidades', Instituto de Economia, da Universidade Estadual de Campinas (Unicamp), Doutor em Economia Aplicada. Orientador: Prof. Dr. Marcio Pochmann. Campinas, SP.

Dagnino, R. (2016) 'Em direção a uma Estratégia para a redução da pobreza: a Economia Solidária e a Adequação Sócio-técnica.' Organização dos Estados Iberoamericanos para a Educação, a ciência e a cultura, Sala de Lectura CTS+I de la OEI. Available at www.oei. es/historico/salactsi/rdagnino5.htm (accessed 29 September 2016).

EM CONSTRUÇÃO (2006). Video Available at www.youtube.com/ watch?v=QuUYwn3GX1g (accessed 2 December 2016).

IADH (2011) *Relatório Final – Convênio Ministério Do Trabalho – Mte-Senaes/Iadh. Avaliação Do Programa Nacional De Incubadoras Tecnológicas De Cooperativas E Empreendimentos Solidários – Proninc Relatório Final (Versão Preliminar Para Discussão)*.

Laporte, A.L.A. (2013) 'Pedagogia da Autogestão', in *Universidade de São Paulo: Sistematização de Experiências de Incubadoras Universitárias Tecnológicas de Coooperativas Populares*, Brazil: São Paulo.

Melo, A.B.T. (2007) 'Novos movimentos sociais e economia solidária: uma breve cartografia da autogestão como processo de subjetivação. 151f', Dissertação (Mestrado) – Pontifícia Universidade Católica de Minas Gerais, Programa de Pós-Graduação em Psicologia, Belo Horizonte.

Parra, H.Z M. (1999) 'Uma experiência no fio da navalha', in F. B. and P. Ortellado (eds) *Humanitas publicações*. São Paulo: FFLCH/USP.

Pateo, F.V. (2008) 'Socializar o mercado ou desmercantilizar a sociedade: os caminhos dos empreendimentos solidários na busca pelo reconhecimento de seu trabalho. Trabalho de conclusão de curso', Faculdade de Economia, Administração e Contabilidade - FEA-USP.. Orientadores Profs. Eli Veiga e Reinaldo Pacheco da Costa.

Razeto, L. (1982) *Empresas de trabajadores y economía de mercado*.: Ediciones PET.

Singer, P.I. (2002) *Introdução à Economia Solidária*. São Paulo: Perseu Abramo.

Singer, P.I., Machado, J. (2000) *Economia Socialista*. São Paulo: Perseu Abramo.

USP (Universidade de São Paulo) (2013) *Incubadora Tecnológica de Cooperativas Populares. Articulando: Sistematização de Experiências de Incubadoras Universitárias Tecnológicas de Cooperativas Populares*. São Paulo: USP.

Zornita, K. G. S. (2009) 'O trabalho da fabricação do sentido.' SIICUSP – Seminário de Iniciação Científica da USP, seminar paper, São Paulo.

EIGHT

The role of universities in the sustainable evolution of solidarity economies

Luiz Roberto Alves, Marco Aurelio Bernardes, Victor Gil Neto and Waverli Maia Matarazzo-Neuberger

Introduction

Colleges and universities must be learning centres for new ideas and for change, offering guidance to other sectors that have the potential to serve as societal models. Contact with the everyday life of communities benefits students. This chapter analyses how the solidarity economy (SE) movement supports the development of citizenship awareness among students, discusses the socio-educational patterns presented by a community during the process of SE implementation, and shows how a university can accelerate the process whereby individuals and groups become involved in solidarity economy movements.

This chapter reports and reflects on a three-year initiative at the Methodist University of São Paulo that gathered students, professors and lecturers to support a local solidarity economy group from Montanhão in the São Bernardo do Campo district, a poor Brazilian community located in the ABC region, seven outskirt cities of São Paulo's Metropolitan area. Action research was the methodology applied, offering programmes and management tools, enhancing the community's social technologies repertoire and highlighting cultural and local knowledge in order to create the necessary conditions for sustainable local development, incorporating the principles of solidarity economy. The chapter discusses first how the university worked with community-based entrepreneurs to support them in the development of their businesses, before analysing the impact of a community bank and a social currency scheme on the entrepreneurs' experiences. In light of the results obtained, a paradigmatic shift is proposed, with a focus on mapping the social, environmental and economic relationships in the area, and bringing a sustainability perspective to the solidarity economy.

Poverty and the solidarity economy

An understanding of social inequality and poverty is essential to an analysis of the solidarity economy in Brazil. Inequality has been one of the consequences of the capitalist economy – especially in peripheral occidental capitalist countries – and this has become even more significant as a result of globalisation processes characterised by the destruction of economic regulations, the opening up of markets to external funding, and the reliance of local governments on international capital (Pochmann, 2005). During recent decades, the globalised economy has generated a multitude of economic crises, and the 1990s crisis changed productive processes and provoked unemployment, social inequality and the exclusion of entire classes from Brazil's formal economy. Job quality also changed as a result of company reorganisations and a continuing process of outsourcing.

Although Brazilian government policies have contributed to poverty reduction in the past two decades, there are still a significant number of people in the country living in extreme poverty. According to the Brazilian Institute of Geography and Statistics (IBGE, 2012), in August 2012, 10 million Brazilians had a monthly income of below US$25, which characterises extreme poverty. These people live in the outskirts and on the streets of Brazilian cities in conditions marked by violence, overpopulation, and a lack of basic services and infrastructure. The informal economy comprises 45% of the Brazilian workforce (PNAD, 2011). Without legal or institutional support, these informal workers are vulnerable to exploitation and poor and illegal working conditions. The costs of exclusion are borne by all Brazilians in the form of enhanced violence, weakened citizenship, and a society characterised by inequality. The lack of employment opportunities, combined with barriers related to gender and race, and lack of access to basic health and education services, results in the absence of autonomy (Marquez et al, 2009). Poverty is not just an absence of capital, and can be better characterised by the denial of fundamental rights. Poverty is complex and multidimensional, and includes inequality, informality and exclusion (Sen, 2000).

According to França Filho (2002), the idea of the solidarity economy emerges as a conception of another relationship between the economy and society, as another form of regulation from the market or the state. This regulation is oriented on a political society project articulated by a different logic and rationality, and with multiple sources of resources. The solidarity economy hybridises the economy, blending market, non-market and non-monetary economies. The enterprises it gives rise to sell products and services (market economy), receive public subsidies in recognition of their social role (non-market economy) and act in a voluntary way (non-monetary economy). The products and services offered by those enterprises are a response to the real demands of the local population, and so the logic of capitalist profitability is not the only driver of economic activity. As Polanyi (1983) said, 'economy' is one of a number of activities in any given society, and not the determining factor that controls how different groups relate to each other.

For Laville and colleagues (1994), what characterises the solidarity economy is a group of economic activities with a logic that is different from that of the market or state. It organises itself with an orientation on human factors, stimulating relationships, community ownership and reciprocity, and differing fundamentally from both capitalist forms of organisation – that value competition, individual interest and capital accumulation – and state economy, based on a central authority (the state) and institutional property. From a Marxist point of view, Gaiger (2007) considers three relevant characteristics of solidarity enterprises: the collective ownership of the means of production with no division between owners and employees; self-management, with no division between who 'plans and thinks', and who 'operates, commands and obeys' like in traditional enterprises, since all members participate in decision-making processes through an assembly; and, lastly, no profit for an owner of the enterprise, since the profits are shared by all members, and the way to distribute them is decided collectively.

Ogando (2012) argues that to evaluate solidarity economy enterprises a number of issues should be evaluated. These include economic indicators like infrastructure, the formal organisation of the solidarity economy venture, the way goods are marketed and sold, and the way the enterprise remunerates members. Social indicators should be considered, like how the enterprise emerged and was formalised; the educational, social and cultural background of its members; the nature of the participatory and democratic processes involved in running it; the level of participation in solidarity economic networks it undertakes; and the support it receives from external entities. Gaiger (2007) suggests another set of indicators related to the degree of solidarity and the entrepreneurship of the enterprises: collective activity, members' assemblies, participatory processes in setting the direction of the enterprise and coordinating its activities at a number of levels, participatory decision-making mechanisms, the status of members, participation in social and popular networks, and participation in and the development of social and community actions and initiatives related to improving the quality of members' lives. Indicators related to entrepreneurship are: raw materials and initial resources donated or acquired by members; business premises and/or equipment donated, borrowed or acquired by members; the final destination of production to members or to community commerce; the enterprise's ability to sell its products; sufficiency of income to pay for the enterprise's expenses; its capacity for rewarding members; formal linkages and payments for members and non-members; human resources investments; and vacation/weekend remuneration for members.

As a new field, the solidarity economy nests in a vast array of enterprises, from bankrupt companies recovered by their former employees to associations that organise recycling collectors and workers. No matter what reason or process has gathered people together in a solidarity enterprise, members must learn how to work together, sharing decisions and undergoing significant behavioural, cognitive, social and cultural changes. Universities can play an important role sharing this journey, which involves learning along the way.

The role of the university and the education process

There is a long learning journey ahead for those who choose the solidarity economy route. The potential for introducing change in economic models and in professional relationships highlights an awareness of how relationships should be built and how enterprises with social and environmental sources and consequences should be evaluated. One of the main aims of the education process of solidarity economy participants undergoing this journey should be to illuminate participants' self-image and their perceptions of their local reality, creating guidelines to promote change. Education is a vital process that can happen inside and outside universities, enhancing effective citizenship and political learning, not as a gift or a purchase, but as something won by the person and the group going through the process. The essence is pure solidarity.

Pedagogical principles can be based in Freirian concepts of 'generating themes': selecting everyday problems that are essentially rooted in the community's reality. This process can be a lens through which to explore the community's mindset in all its facets, understand its boundaries, and create new frameworks of meaningful knowledge that guide them down new paths. According to Freire (2005), 'generating themes' stimulates critical reflection about reality, facilitating analysis of all the dimensions that are part of it. 'Themes' that help generate solidarity economy responses could be related to hunger, employment difficulties, the community's relationship with its environment, its resources and needs, and relationships between the community and other institutional levels.

Dialogue is an essential resource in this process. As a way to 'pronounce the world', dialogue promotes reflection and action, using analysis as a way to transform reality, avoiding action for its own sake, without words, as just 'activism'. For Freire (2005), to be human is to be able to pronounce the world in order to change it. Dialogue does not happen when one wants to impose her/his world vision on others, and others want to pronounce that vision. Dialogue is an existential demand for pronouncing the world. It is not an exchange of ideas or a polemic discussion: it is a creative act that leads to change.

An example of a 'generating theme' that can be used with a committed solidarity economy community is to discuss how someone can make a living without a traditional, formal job. Participation in a dialogic educational process generated by this theme could empower individuals and make them realise the existence of other possibilities connected with cooperation, working together and creating new means and tools that enable them to manifest these new opportunities. This is a process of discovery and learning that can lead to new behaviours and open new possibilities in life. Being part of such a dialogic process can improve self-esteem and deepen a feeling of 'belonging' among the group, empowering its participants (Bourdieu, 2004). This feeling reflects itself in the group's collective actions, strengthens each individual and the group, and creates a collective intention to transform their reality (Santos, 1998). Individual participation in these dialogic situations transforms disorganised intuitions and feelings into a narrative that builds every time each group participant pronounces it, creating new ways to see the world. As Vygotsky (1998) said, a pronounced word is the human being's tool to transform reality. For Vygotsky, there are two ways to build concepts in the human realm: first, through the observation of quotidian reality followed by mental synthesis and decisions used to structure thinking and to analyse reality; and second, through scholarly education where individuals learn concepts by relating and combining them. The first process arises from quotidian concrete situations, and the second from analysis.

An education process focusing on facilitating freedom that allows individuals to change their perception about their selves and their realities, and empowers them to demand and exercise their rights, can create a culture of participation based on confidence, cooperation and a willingness to act collectively to transform their reality (Putnam, 2000; Kliksberg, 2002). Universities can bring a consciousness of what cultural dominant values are, questioning them, thus helping the group critically surpass its historical reality, while creating a new one. As empowerment does not happen in a spontaneous way, and when it happens it has a limited reach, universities and colleges can have a decisive role in supporting and embedding this process by mobilising groups around development projects they have created, developing the necessary technical and organizing skills, and facilitating access to financial resources (Cunha, 2002).

As critical loci, colleges and universities are learning centres for new ideas and for change. They guide other sectors and have the potential to serve as societal models. Although they are unique in many ways, their innovations are largely replicable by other institutions, and their mission and responsibilities for defining the scope of education give them a reason to update and re-evaluate their mission in a way that invites institutional learning and openness to sustainable thinking (Edelstein, 2004). Universities also transcend boundaries in space and time. With their senior professors and junior students, they also connect society's elders with its youth. With their interdisciplinary studies and many learned associations, they connect across intellectual and geographic boundaries and are thus participants across space (M'Gonigle and Starke, 2006). This was the task we undertook.

The ABC region and Montanhão

The ABC region

The ABC region is the south-eastern micro-region of the metropolitan region of São Paulo and covers an area of 841 km^2 occupied by 2,500,000 inhabitants distributed in seven cities. Located on a transit route, this well-known industrial region was designated to assist the development of São Paulo after the immigration process began in 1877 and a railway line was established by the British connecting São Paulo to Santos seaport. Thus the ABC region grew from 25,215 inhabitants in 1920 and today forms a significant part of the nearly 18.5 million inhabitants of São Paulo metropolis. Until the 1930s, immigrants, especially Italians, Spaniards, Slavs, and later Japanese, constituted a professional and cultural population. After World War II, the explosion of the industry-based capitalist project brought thousands of Brazilians from the poorest regions of the country to São Paulo, and especially to this region, attracted by the chemical, petrochemical, electro-mechanical and automobile industries that replaced the old-style furniture and textile companies established in the early 20th century, many of which were based on cooperative ways of working.

The socioeconomic development associated with the making of a new democratic experiment in the region would be unthinkable without the concurrence of the cultures of work, of renovation of public powers, and of learning about the economic and financial forces that since 1989 have organised themselves in forums, chambers and regional working groups. Today, the region has about 5,000 industries and more than 30,000 commercial outlets and service providers, with large industries accounting for 35% of available jobs. The capitalist restructuring that happened at the end of 1980s and in the 1990s meant that at least 20% of the workforce of about 1,200,000 citizens lost their jobs and became unemployed. This level of unemployment has been reduced by more than a half in the past ten years, with informal and precarious work replacing previously formal job positions. The dismissed workers had to look for other ways to survive. They used their severance payments to open small business, many to them in their homes. For those that could not fall back on even this small amount of money, the solidarity of poverty was the only possibility. The relationship networks that were established in the outskirts of the neighbourhoods were essential to helping those people to get together, talk about their situation, and together try to find a way to survive (Telles and Cabanes, 2006).

This is how solidarity economic groups appeared. In those groups people cooperated with each other in order to survive, with no other resource than each other's help. They did not have capital to hand, nor appropriate places or the necessary equipment to open small businesses. According to Sader (1988), the projects and practices of these 'organised people of the periphery' are a signal of victory over physical and symbolic disintegration; the acquisition of rights amid critical stress; the inter-communication of isolated groups to produce the condition of being a person within the associativity of workers; and the use of the wealth of the cities to promote fairer income distribution. It is a project of *humanity*, where the gap between 'knowing' and 'doing' diminishes. Thus, these cultures, organised around work and present since the beginning of the last century, are examples of social organisation: workers' parties, residents' and neighbourhood associations demanding better public service infrastructure, labour and credit cooperatives (such as the Società di Mutuo Soccorso, the old people's banks) and trade union movements. It seems that the region's culture, defined by work and its historically organised social basis, has guaranteed regional organism and cradled new managerial ventures.

Paradoxically, 56% of the region is still covered with Atlantic rainforest, and is therefore high on the list of Conservation International's 25 world priority areas for the preservation and conservation of biodiversity (Mittermeier et al, 1999). Most of this forested area is protected by federal, state and local laws and should be preserved in order to avoid dangerous climate change. Despite this, the area suffers from real estate speculation and the lack of proper urban planning. The region also hosts the greater part of the Billings reservoir. An artificial lake constructed in 1925 to generate hydro-electric power, Billings reservoir is now of strategic interest to the Metropolitan region of São Paulo, with water being an essential and scarce resource in the area. Most of the periphery of the ABC region is located within these domains and ecological interests are not considered when new districts and informal businesses are established.

Montanhão

Montanhão is a favela comprising 30 neighbourhoods, spread over Serra do Mar mountain range on the outskirts of São Bernardo do Campo and Billings Reservoir. It has 112,764 residents, 14.34% of the São Bernardo do Campo population. It occupies a mountainous area at risk of mudslides during the rainy season, and has no basic sanitation. Regulations making occupation in the protected Billings Reservoir area illegal have not prevented settlement. City hall data indicate that 20% of Montanhão families have no monthly income; 7% earn a minimum wage (approximately US$277)[1] and 18% earn up to the equivalent of two minimum wages. This means that over 44% of families have a monthly income lower than two minimum wages. Young people (from 15 to 29 years old) represent 26% of the total population (29,200 inhabitants) and most of them are under- or unemployed. In 2003, the Economic Department of São Bernardo do Campo registered 34 small industries, 377 trading companies and 1,880 services companies.

The community-based development projects in Montanhão that were the most successful were those that identified the potential to stimulate trade and services, keeping the profit inside community borders. Many of these projects were initiatives of the Associação de Promoção Humana e Resgate da Cidade Padre Léo Comissari (Leo Comissari Association to Promote Human Beings and Rescue Citizenship, or LCA), a local association linked with the Catholic Church that was established in Montanhão in the 1990s by Father Léo Comissari, who lived in Montanhão and ran the organisation for 10 years. LCA's aim is to support social entrepreneurship, based on solidarity, cooperation between members, and market-oriented skills developed by an educational process aimed at creating innovative survival solutions for its members. The association has registered 104 solidarity economy enterprises, and approximately 22 are regular participants of the meetings and programmes promoted by GAES, a group that support such enterprises.

Research conducted by the Fernand Braudel Institute (Guedes and Oliveria, 2006) in Montanhão showed that, despite the social and economic challenges they faced, people in social classes C and D improved their consumption patterns in ways that could be linked with changes provoked by the internal circulation of profits. Entrepreneurial skills can be seen as a distinctive feature of this community, and cooperative learning, responsible business practices, and education and technological development could continue to enhance this virtuous development cycle.

These solidarity economy societies build on past historical connections and experiences to create space for political action and social innovation. In the past, Italian and Spanish immigrants had been central to the formation of unions and forms of social support, organising work and capital in the new land. The experiences of the Società di Mutuo Soccorso, founded to provide help for Italian immigrants in the 1930s, and community and union movements developed during the 1950s, brought both immigrants from abroad and Brazilian migrant groups together, creating a common code for protest, work and social-economic development. Today's solidarity economy initiatives thus have a historical debt to these traditions and *societá*, inspiring their actions and helping to promote social initiatives to create common wellbeing, education, health, transport, environmental conservation and flood prevention actions. These historical movements have also led to mutual support actions such as community banks aimed at establishing a local currency at Montanhão, and the formation of new community associations. This symbolic construction has been taking place for more than a century. It is an ongoing project with significant fruits, a special ecology – troubled, but historically rich.

Building the solidarity economy in Montanhão

In 2010, the solidarity economy-focused LCA group, GAES, requested the support of the Methodist University of São Paulo to help 22 enterprises find solutions to the challenges facing them. A community project involving professors, lecturers and students, most of them from the business department, was created, aligned along three main axes: solidarity economy and culture; enterprise promotion and organisation;

and human and technological education. The university's role in the solidarity economy education groups was designed to be practical and reflexive. University educators participated in the groups' everyday activities, talking to them about the problems they faced, highlighting all facets, and stimulating the group to find solutions in innovative and cooperative ways. To be part of the entrepreneurship group coached by university members, the entrepreneurs had to agree to legalise their businesses and employment practices and to produce a business plan. As a result, only 12 entrepreneurs took part. This number was below the university's expectations and represents only about 10% of the total entrepreneurs enrolled at LCA, albeit more than 50% of the regular participants.

Table 8.1 lists the characteristics of the 12 enterprises that were part of the study.

Half of the participating establishments offered services, similar to the percentage of such enterprises found in the region as a whole, and included a bar and a restaurant, a glazier workshop, building services,

Table 8.1: Enterprises' characteristics

Enterprise name	Business nature	Foundation year	Leo Comissari network participation (in years)	Number of participants
Thie's Bar	Bar	1993	10	7
Cooperativa Arte da Costura	Clothes making	2009	1	6
Cooperativa Selecta	Soap production	2006	4	20
Auto Peças Rica	Motor repair services and compounds seller	1995	7	6
Flor e Arte	Flower shop			2
Cooprofis	Building services	2005	5	20
Grafica Nova Opção	Graphic services	2005	6	4
Mercado e Adega São Jorge	Food and drink small market	1990	10	2
Depósito de Material de Construção Matos	Building materials	2007	6	6
Mercado Gomes	Food and drink small market	1998	6	3
Helio Cristais	Glazier shop and services	2005	5	3
Minha Cozinha Restaurante	Restaurant	1993	10	2

a car and motorcycle repair garage and a graphics and printing office. Thirty-three percent of establishments represented the commercial sector, with two mini-markets, a flower shop and building structural materials shop. Only 17% or two businesses could be classified as industrial, both of them cooperatives, producing soap and clothes respectively. All of the entrepreneurs were part of the solidarity economy and alternative network of the ABC region (LCA), grounded in ethical and solidarity principles, with equal rights and obligations and committed to the following principles:

- share with equity;
- be guided by autonomy and self-management;
- help each other surpass everyday difficulties;
- respect the environment regarding raw material choices and production process;
- respect children's and teenagers' rights according to ECA (Children and Teenager Statute);
- practise fair trade;
- provide clear information about productive process, services and materials used;
- provide high-quality services and products;
- take part in LCA meetings, and respect and follow decisions made democratically and collectively;
- pay a monthly fee to support the network, related to a percentage previously defined by a general assembly of the LCA;
- give preference to services and products provided by other network components;
- be part of one of the committees of the LCA;
- supervise, evaluate and follow committee protocol;
- publicise the LCA and its members' activities, in order to improve the commercialisation of members' products;
- follow statutes and internal rules;
- check and control the committee actions according to LCA statutes;
- contribute to the LCA fund and present details of monthly cash flows to and from the fund;
- publicise LCA network products, membership and companies in all activities as an ethical guarantee of products and services provided.

The following paragraphs present three examples of the network's activities. These stories are typical of many of the participants and in providing them the intention is to allow the protagonists to speak in their own voices, to 'pronounce', about their background and reality and to show how they have overcome the obstacles created by a simple and poor life and the absence of local government support.

São Jorge mini market

Ever since he had been a teenager, the owner had used all the money he got to buy cakes and sweets to sell, with a small profit margin. He sold artificial juice to drivers in traffic jams, and to workers at the factory gate. At the age of 20, he began to work legally for building companies and then moved to a household appliance company and then to a car factory. Like many others, he was fired from the car industry in 1990 and set up the mini-market, which has been his only source of revenue. He has three employees and he was one of the first members of LCA in Montanhão, being enrolled since 2000.

Initial investment amount: US$4,400.

Gomes mini-market

The owner had a previous and unsuccessful experience in a city called Brasileira located in Piaui state. He immigrated to São Paulo and after losing his job at a building company he began this mini-market originally as a bar to sell sweets, beverages and alcoholic drinks. His target consumers were local workers who regularly went to the bar every day after work. Two years after establishing the bar he stopped selling alcoholic drinks and began to sell fruits, vegetables, beverages and sweets. After 2010 this mini-market began to grow and sell more items to a wider public.

Initial investment amount: US$1,375.

Cooperselecta Cooperative

The cooperative began with a group of six people, mainly women, whose objective was to develop environmental concern among the population regarding the improper disposal of used cooking oil. To achieve this objective, they decided to collect and to recycle cooking oil to produce soap in order to generate income for the families involved. LCA offered support and Parque Selecta Community Association a place for producing the soap. The Cooperselecta Cooperative was formally established in May 2010 in order to offer an alternative way to generate income for the local community. Qualifying programmes were developed specially aimed at young people who have extreme difficulty in finding a job in the formal market. The vision that inspired

Cooperselecta Cooperative members was to create new ways of working that valued workers and the planet, preserving the environment and generating a sustainable and social, environmental and economically fair income for local communities. Besides collecting cooking oil and producing and selling soap, members of the Cooperselecta Cooperative offered lectures to local schools, community associations and unions in order to promote environmental education.

Initial investment amount: US$1,100.

Results

During the first year, an analysis of the community and a diagnosis of its problems was conducted. An action plan was then developed based on the results obtained, with implementation beginning in August 2010. The action plan established four focus areas: business plan development; support for the development and launch of a community bank; social currency and micro-trust creation and development; and support for a municipal solidarity economy information exchange. To achieve the university's goals, monthly meetings with the 12 enterprises were conducted during which participants presented their businesses and their needs, and discussed their experiences to date, their hopes and fears, labour laws, human resource conflicts and management, negotiation skills, and how they could support and help each other. These meetings were used to attract more entrepreneurs to the network, and to discuss how they could work collectively and support their needs as a community. A social incubator was created in partnership with the city administration, together with a communication programme and an interdisciplinary group for developing skills. The following paragraphs describe the results obtained in each area.

Business plan development

The main goal of this area of work was to improve the performance of participating businesses to serve as an example for the community, attracting other participants and thereby increasing the number of businesses in Montanhão. Each participating business developed a business plan in order to understand and build on their experiences, enabling them to understand what factors had influenced the development of their business, and what factors were responsible for the resilience of their business. During this process, the university group helped to highlight weakness and strengths involved in their experiences, trying to build on strengths and diminish the weaknesses.

General assemblies were conducted with all participants at the beginning of the process to introduce them to procedures related to human resources management, marketing and logistics, and ways of working with public services and city hall. As the business and entrepreneur plans proceeded, individual guidance was available to support each entrepreneur's specific profile and needs. The business and entrepreneur plans were adjusted along this way, and the knowledge acquired influenced the development of managerial tools used to improve the efficiency of the business, such as tools to diagnose the needs and demands of local and neighbouring communities, methods of collective buying, and tools for determining the promotion of products and services, and pricing rules. University research groups and labs provided some technical advice in order to improve the quality of the process and final products and increase participants' competitive skills.

Participants received guidance in how to recognise the potential for expanding their business, and how to consider supply and value chains from the perspective of a producer, a distributor, a final consumer and a client. This process demonstrated the power that solidarity economy has to strength the productive chain, supporting and complementing all of the links within it. LCA agents followed the process in order to disseminate the lessons learned to other groups. The commitment to spread this knowledge was also assumed by each participant. All participants developed a business and entrepreneur plan at the end of the process that built on the history of the entrepreneur and their business and on a sectoral analysis of the enterprise. These were made available at the LCA library for the community to draw on, rather than being kept confidential. Other details relating to more sensitive information of a commercial nature, such as fixed and turnover investments, revenue projection and cash flow, and finance indicators like reporting results, profits acquired, investment return, equilibrium point and price compounds formation, remained private for each entrepreneur.

Establishing a community bank

University researchers attended discussions to define the operating model for the community bank. Regular banks cannot establish relationships with the informal economy sector, although the solidarity and popular economies are both recognised for their success in including social segments that are excluded from formal economy in valuable economic activity. The costs of borrowing are too high for many small operations. This is why Montanhão district, despite its formal and informal economy, lacks financial products like micro-credit, facilities to cash a bank cheque, facilities for the exchange of social currency to official currency, and even access to savings accounts.

The model approved established that the community bank would finance projects and entrepreneurs linked with the district solidarity economy network. Capital contributions for the bank would come from solidarity economy nucleus of the Getulio Vargas Foundation, from another university located in São Paulo, and from donations of other LCA partners linked with Italian unions from the Emilia Romagna Area.

Social currency and micro-trust creation and development

This is an essential area of work for expanding local economic activity, since credit for informal economic activities is only available at community banks. Micro-credit supports the development of new enterprises, and the development and formalisation of existing enterprises that could, with better equipment, improve their products and services.

The community bank offers micro-credit. It has a social currency named Comissari that is used by the entrepreneurs when they buy or sell products and services from other solidarity economy network establishments. Initial capital of US$1,100 was offered by LCA for an experimental period of time and currency circulation was restricted to establishments that were part of the network. Unfortunately, the currency is not used as often as it could be. Although the network entrepreneurs were encouraged to use the currency, it takes time to implement such an initiative and to overcome resistance to it. It is a huge cultural change and users must develop the confidence necessary to use the social currency in the same way they use the official one, and understand that it is based in a non-monetary economy, and supports values of reciprocity (França Filho, 2002).

Municipal solidarity economy information exchange

The municipal solidarity economy information exchange provides space for the Montanhão network and similar groups from other ABC region cities to exchange experiences and articulate their needs, which are formally discussed and organised in documents that can be used to generate proposals for public policies. The researchers offered training programmes, provided forum participants with auditorium facilities and support from the university communications and legal departments, and helped organise ideas and documents that emerged from the meetings.

The findings of the exchange forum can be summarised as follows:

- It is important to understand local cultural resources and create a basis for dialogue in order to cultivate shared ways of working where all the components have the same status. This leads to a recognition of the different approaches and visions shared by the community. This way of acting is essential for strengthening the community's identity and developing an awareness of its resources and characteristics, building a collective and empowered community in which residents feel they belong, and where they recognise their citizenship rights, and ways to change their social, economic and environmental reality.
- Skills in financial and human resources management and marketing should be tailored to community demands and are essential for obtaining micro-credit and consolidating business. The establishment of supply chains can be facilitated by local and chamber meetings, disseminating knowledge and sharing experiences, and helping enterprises to reduce their costs.
- Diagnosis, dialogue and information gathering permits the identification of new business opportunities that help solidarity enterprise networks to grow in specific directions, improving efficiency, building at scale, and solving supply chain gaps.
- Cooperative enterprises that gather more people together than family structures have more chances of been successful. Dialogue related to cooperative and solidarity skills must be enhanced to support the evolution of the community towards more innovative management models.
- Women play a significant role in the solidarity economy and represent 70% of all solidarity economy movements in Montanhão. They formed the majority in all planning meetings, assuming a leading role in all decisions and their enterprises were the most committed to solidarity economy principles. They were more patient than men, and more dedicated to the work of building partnerships, and to sharing their knowledge with the community. Men were more engaged with financial issues and focused more on results. This difference in behaviour may be related to different gender-based cultural expectancies. In Brazilian society, men are often assumed to be the ones to support their homes financially, while women are assumed to be more dedicated to social work, more committed spiritually, and more engaged with socially established goals. Women also face difficulties in the formal work arena: they historically earn lower wages than men, they may be discriminated against because

of their appearance, suffer the social costs of motherhood, illiteracy, and the prejudices of a macho Latin culture.

This chapter shows that Montanhão community members involved with solidarity economy enterprises were empowered through the actions developed by university representatives, although maintaining the cohesion of both groups was a challenge. This difficulty could be associated with lack of maturity of the group that was assisted by this programme, high expectations, cultural barriers and difficulties in overcoming fragmented points of view while acquiring a systemic vision where praxis and theory walk together. But that is the beauty of creating a collective knowledge that considers equally all sources, and can be accessed by every member involved, bringing a basis of hope that creating a more inclusive, sustainable and fair society is possible. Figures 8.1 and 8.2 present SWOT analyses considering the university and community points of view.

Figure 8.1: SWOT analysis from university point of view

Strengths	Weaknesses
Development of an entrepreneur plan methodology adapted to solidarity economy groups. Getting together the skills available in an academic environment to contribute to local development demands. Offering a real contribution to: empowering communities and improving quality of life at local level; spreading income around more fairly; increasing groups' self-esteem and motivation.	Unemployed workers are invited to be part of solidarity economy groups without understanding its principles and social and economic effects. Getting together professors, lecturers and students from different undergraduate programmes and departments that can and want to contribute with solidarity economy needs, overcoming interdisciplinary barriers and creating a board with autonomy to decide the next steps.
Opportunities	Threats
Developing students' technical and human skills through real and live experiences. The appearance of a new values platform based in collective development; association skills and environmental and local awareness.	Measure and consider all external interferences and their influence on the process. Solidarity economy should not be seen as a force for controlling the public, linked to one political party in clientelist ways. The programmes should be continued in the long term, not seen as one-off interventions.

Figure 8.2: SWOT analysis from community point of view

Strengths	Weaknesses
Collective development, association skills and environmental and local awareness create a value platform that empowers human-based relationship and facilitates better engagement with local characteristics. Acquiring management knowledge and tools.	Developing a structural dependence on the university and other partners. Political disputes interfering in the generation of shared common future goals. Treating the programmes as short term, rather than a continued and extended programme.
Opportunities	Threats
Acquiring knowledge and skills for developing entrepreneur plans and applying management tools adapted to their reality.	Lack of local leadership to continue the programmes and to continue to establish the community's needs and programmes from their point of view. Lack of confidence and reluctance to rely on associative linkages. Successful establishments being sold and the entrepreneurs having to start over.

Note

[1] Average exchange rate from 2012 of US$1 to R$1.95.

References

Bordieu, P. (2004) *O Poder Simbólico* (4 edn). Translated by Fernando Tomaz. São Paulo: Bertrand Brasil.

Cunha, G. (2002) 'Economia Solidária e Políticas Públicas: Reflexões a partir do caso do Programa Incubadora de Cooperativas da Prefeitura Municipal de Santo André, SP', Dissertação de Mestrado, Faculdade de Ciência Política, Universidade de São Paulo.

Edelstein, M.R. (2004) 'Sustaining Sustainability: Lessons from Ramapo College', in P.F. Barlett and G.W. Chase (eds) *Sustainability on Campus: Stories and Strategies for Change*. Cambridge: MIT Press, pp 271-92.

França Filho, G. (2002) 'A Perspectiva da Economia Solidária', in T Fischer *Gestão do Desenvolvimento e Poderes Locais*. Salvador: Casa da Qualidade.

Freire, P. (2005) *Pedagogia do Oprimido*. São Paulo: Paz e Terra.

Gaiger, L.I. (2007) 'A outra racionalidade da economia solidária. Conclusões do Primeiro Mapeamento Nacional no Brasil', *Revista Crítica de Ciências Sociais*, no 79, pp 57-77.

Guedes, P.M. and Oliveira, N.V. (2006) 'A democratização do consumo', *Braudel Papers*, no 39, pp 3-21.

IBGE (Instituto Brasileiro de Geografia e Estatistica) (2012) *Síntese de Indicadores Sociais. Uma análise das condições de vida da população brasileira*. Estudos e Pesquisas, no 29Kliksberg, B. (2002) *Capital Social Y Cultura: Claves Olvidadas Del Desarrollo. Banco Interamericano de Desarrollo*. Buenos Aires: INTAL.

Klink, J. (2002) 'O novo regionalismo à maneira do ABC: em busca de uma economia regional de aprendizagem', *Cadernos de Pesquisa*, no 8.

Laville, J.L., Belanger, P.R., Boucher, J.E. and Lévesque, B. (1994) *L'économie solidaire, une perspective international*. Paris, France: Lavoisier.

Marquez, P., Reficco, E. and Berger, G. (2009) 'Negócios Inclusivos em America Latina', *Harvard Business Review*, May.

M'Gonigle, M. and Starke, J. (2006) *Planet U: Sustaining the World, Reinventing the University*. Gabriola Island BC, Canada: New Society Publishers.

Mittermeier, R. A., Myers, N. and Mittermeier, (1999*) Hotspots: Earth's Biologically Richest and Most Endangered Terrestrial Ecoregions*. Mexico City: CEMEX.

Ogando, C.B. (2012) 'A economia solidária sob a ótica da Nova Sociologia Econômica', *Otra Economía*, vol 6, no 11, pp 117-124.

PNAD (2011) 'Série: PD248. Rendimento médio mensal domiciliar, por classes de Salário Mínimo, available at www.todospelaeducacao. org.br//arquivos/biblioteca/pnad_sintese_2009.pdf (accessed 15 March 2011).

Pochmann, M. (2005) *O emprego na globalização*. São Paulo: Boitempo.

Polanyi, K. (1983) *A grande transformação*. Rio de Janeiro: Campus.

Putnam, R.D. (2000) *Comunidade e Democracia: a experiência da Itália Moderna*. Rio de Janeiro: Editora FGV.

Santos, M. (1998) *Por uma outra globalização: do pensamento* único *à consciência universal*. São Paulo: Record.

Sen, A. (2000) *On ethics and economics*. Oxford: Blackwell.

Telles, V. S. and Cabanes, R. (2006) *Nas tramas da cidade: trajetórias urbanas e seus territórios*. São Paulo: Humanitas.

Vygotsky, L.S. (1998) *Formação Social da Mente*. São Paulo: Martins Fontes.

NINE

Fundos de Pasto: Community governance of common resources in north-east Brazil

Erica Imbirussú, Gilca Garcia de Oliveira
and Guiomar Inez Germani

Introduction

Discourses of natural resource sustainability have become mainstream since the Stockholm United Nations Conference on the Human Environment in 1972 and, as a consequence, the relationships between traditional communities and knowledge developed from their proximity to nature have been included in global debates. According to Castro (2000), this knowledge and its management are fundamental to biodiversity preservation. However, this is not uncontested. In mainstream economic theory, the self-regulating market is conceptualised as being capable of guaranteeing balance and efficiency in the use of natural resources, irrespective of traditional knowledge, and in this context Hardin's (1968) theory of the Tragedy of the Commons represents the orthodoxy in theories of common resources management. Without private property and a market in which to manage exchange, Hardin argued, rational self-interest will inevitably lead to resource depletion as it is in every individual actor's interests to maximise the benefit they accrue from common resources, while paying none of the costs.

As a counterpoint, Ostrom (1990) criticises not only Hardin's thesis, but also the conceptualisation on which it is constructed, namely game theory as formalised in the prisoners' dilemma and, Olson's theory of collective action, with its emphasis on rational self-interest. Against Hardin, Ostrom argued that the management of resources does not always become a 'tragedy' because communities are capable of creating institutions, formally or informally, which guarantee higher levels of sustainability in the use of natural resources through collective forms of ownership and/or management – and in fact Hardin argued that for him tragedy came from an *unregulated* commons, not from commons per se.

As a contribution to this book's focus on collective, solidarity economies, this chapter aims to investigate community management of resources, based on Ostrom's theory, in the *Fundo de Pasto* of Paredão do Lou, a community located in the city of Monte Santo, in the state of Bahia, Brazil, that has developed the use of common resources as its main strategy for social reproduction. These *Fundos e Fechos de Pasto* originated from the separation of two extensive landholdings in the context of the colonisation and occupation of the land (Garcez, 1987). In Bahia state, in 2015, these communities were represented by a total of 578 associations although, as we discuss in more detail below in the context of understanding how communities develop collective forms of resource management, many of the *Fundos e Fechos de Pasto* (FFP) communities have yet to be identified or are not yet organised into associations (Geografar, 2011).

The land, besides being a space for the production of livelihoods, also has the potential for conflict, especially when there are disagreements regarding property ownership. Communities fight for land rights to be regularised and stand up to those who want to illegally appropriate the communities' land, originally the *grileiros* (those who have occupied land illegally from the 1970s onwards) and, more recently, miners and wind-farms. In 2013, State Law 20.417/2013 was approved, which aimed to consolidate the formalisation of land ownership for some categories of traditional communities including the FFP; however, it has not become a more efficient way of guaranteeing community rights.

The history of this struggle for land rights is outlined in this chapter, which is divided into three parts. The first part introduces the FFP communities in Bahia, and describes their relationship with the natural world, as well as their fight for property rights. The following part analyses the management of common resources through orthodox theories and through Ostrom's alternative. The final part discusses the common resources management in the Paredão do Lou traditional community, which is a case based on the governance principles elaborated by Ostrom.

Understanding the lifestyle of the FFP in Bahia state

In Brazil, traditional communities are defined as:

> Culturally differentiated groups which have developed their own social organisation, occupy territories and use

natural resources as a condition of their cultural, social, religious, ancestral and economic reproduction, through the application of knowledge, innovation and traditionally transmitted practices. (Brazil, 2007)

Even though there is a wide range of spatial arrangements, usually both dwelling and working areas are close to each other, and constitute the territory from which the communities make their livelihood and maintain their culture. In this way, in FFPs, there is proximity between the inhabitants' lifestyle and their work, which consolidates their identity, their own way of living. In the FFP, this identity is represented by the farmer figure. Although complementary activities may also be developed (such as urban activities or waged employment), their identity as a 'dweller' is safeguarded and valued as it guarantees their collective identity and livelihoods through their connection to the soil.

Fundos de Pasto facilitate a unique lifestyle in which kinship relations unite members. According to Garcez (1987, p 21):

> Fundos de Pasto are collective properties, occupied by people who usually have common family backgrounds, where extensive communal grazing is the main activity, as well as precarious subsistence agriculture, mainly represented by the cultivation of corn, beans and cassava.

FFP communities use resources, especially grazing in common areas, in similar ways, but residents also have their own individual areas for cultivation. In the *caatinga* areas (a biome found mainly in north-east Brazil, including Bahia State, which has a very hot and dry climate) there is preference for goats in the *Fundos* and for cattle in the *Fechos de Pasto*, as they are well adapted to the environment. However, other animals, such as pigs and sheep, are also widely found.

According to the testimony of a resident of the Paredão do Lou *Fundo de Pasto*, *Fundos de Pasto* are:

> "… a share of land for nature preservation where people also let animals graze. Because we notice that wherever there is no *Fundo de Pasto*, there are fences everywhere, as well as no preserved nature, and when it is drought season, all we have is dry soil. So, it is basically an area for nature preservation." (Interview I, 2013)

To help the reader envisage this, the photograph in Figure 9.1 shows a *Fundo de Pasto* area in Lagoa da Ilha, in the city of Monte Santo, contrasted with an area of land not designated for such communal use.

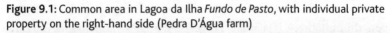

Figure 9.1: Common area in Lagoa da Ilha *Fundo de Pasto*, with individual private property on the right-hand side (Pedra D'Água farm)

Source: Marques (2013)

FFPs simultaneously provide opportunities for grazing and for a home, community life and work. They are a space in which a shared sense of identity is collectively built through working and living together. Nature preservation is integral to, and becomes meaningful as a condition for, social reproduction. These dimensions are central to how FFPs work, and are an obligation on their members.

FFPs are legally recognised by the Bahia State Constitution in article 178, which states that 'The State may give the use of concession rights for communal land to legitimate associations, especially in the Fundo de Pasto areas' (Bahia Legislative Assembly, 1989). This represents a legal advance since it recognises the FFP communities and hence guarantees their existence. On the other hand, it also restricts their rights and highlights the lack of understanding of state institutions about what these communities truly mean when it comes to their communal use of land.

The Bahia state land structure and its social and productive relations are rooted in Brazil's history of colonisation and consequently have characteristics inherited from the colonising country (Portugal): hereditary local elites, monocultures and slavery. The occupation of the national territory was facilitated through the grant of hereditary captaincies and *sesmarias* (abandoned lands offered by the Portugal Royal Court to new inhabitants, mostly from Portugal); in both cases, the concessions were overwhelmingly offered to those who belonged to the Portuguese elite. While in Portugal the *sesmarias* were restructured into smaller landholdings, in Brazil they had a different social function. Extensive landed estates were granted to members of the elite in order to secure the domination of the land and its inhabitants and in order to establish administrative political power. This form of domination often continues to this day.

The map reproduced in Figure 9.2 shows the distribution of *Fundos e Fechos de Pasto* associations in each city in Bahia state. There were 368 identified associations in 2010, with a wide range of ways of organising and struggling for land. In 2015, this number reached 578 (GeografAR, 2011). Each FFP identified and recognised by the state is legally represented by a local community association (which is mandatory according to article 178 in the Bahia State Constitution). These are currently organised in Bahia state into five regional associations that together form the State Association of the FFP Communities in Bahia, and include representatives from the communities and social movements, as well as advisers. Besides the fight for solutions to territorial and extraterritorial issues, the local and state associations play a fundamental role in the development of the communities' institutions.

The subsequent occupation of the countryside by the FFP communities happened through the breaking up of extensive landholdings that had previously dominated most of the state (Garcez, 1987). From then on, a communal lifestyle has been developed in the area, based on a close relationship with the natural world and the common use of natural resources.

Relations with nature: living among the caatinga biome

A better appreciation of the relationship between the FFPs and the natural world is necessary in order to properly understand how the communities work. Even though not all these communities actively work for environment protection, they do hold it in high regard, an issue that becomes even clearer during drought seasons.

Figure 9.2: *Fundos de Pasto* identified in each city, Bahia state (2010)

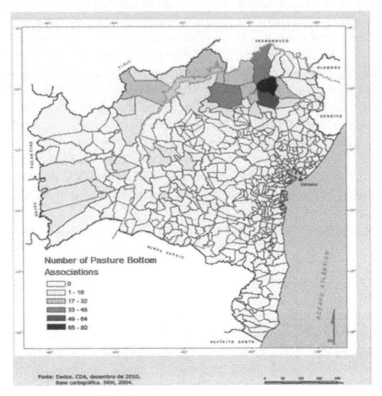

Source: GeografAR (2011)

Given the region's semi-arid climate, rainfall is irregularly distributed and concentrated in a two- to three-month period. Drought is a year-long event, and the temperature range is high. River flow is mostly periodical, and water volume is usually limited and insufficient for irrigation (Drumond et al, 2000). These factors preclude the development of forms of livelihood and culture that struggle to adapt to drought. Providing a livelihood and maintaining a community becomes more difficult during these drought seasons: the population, and especially the state, need to be prepared for these periods, even though it is not certain when a drought will begin or how long it will last. One of the best ways to mitigate the impact of drought is to preserve natural biomes, and local groups such as the Regional Institute of Small-Scale Agriculture (Instituto Regional da Pequena Agropecuária Apropriada, or IRPAA) from the Family Agricultural School of Monte Santo support positive approaches towards ways of coping with a semi-arid environment, as well as supporting environmental education that enriches these communities' experiences of developing strategies for coexistence with drought.

The Bahia semi-arid region shows great diversity of mineral resources in its subsoil and as a result mining is both an important economic activity in the state and one of the main reasons for socio-environmental conflict in the region. Mining operations have elicited complaints from communities about human rights violations and depletion of natural resources, in particular the pollution and destruction of water sources, the depletion of groundwater, and air and noise pollution. Mining has also intensified conflicts over land use, mainly because many traditional communities do not have any formal rights over the land they live on, which puts them in a weak position in the face of a business and development model that prioritises mining over the right to life of communities (IRPAA, 2016). The establishment of wind-energy parks in Bahia's semi-arid region has emerged as another source of environmental conflict.

The state and Fundos e Fechos de Pasto: traditional communities and land regularisation

FFPs are mainly located on land owned by the state, and communities usually have no property rights over the land. Land regularisation is the process by which communities seek to gain property rights over the land they live on, thereby gaining legal recognition and security of tenure. Only a few communities have been through formal processes of land regularisation, and even then some of them have failed to secure their rights. In this way, the land becomes fragmented between individual and common areas, without any consideration of the necessity of having common areas for these groups' livelihoods and culture, even though these characteristics were acknowledged as important in land regularisation processes established in the 1970s under the aegis of the Bahia Land Institute.

State Law 20.417/2013, which establishes guidelines for public and rural land regularisation, recognises the definitive property rights associated with territories occupied by some traditional communities; land rights for FFPs, however, can only be achieved through concession. This law is also responsible for conflicts between communities and major enterprises. Although communities were consulted when the regularisation guidelines were drawn up, some important issues were not addressed, while others that were contrary to the communities' interests were introduced, including the following:

- a distinction between traditional communities (who have traditionally occupied land that can become their own property) and *Fundo de Pasto* communities (who can only gain *usufruct* rights, rather than full ownership rights, over the land they occupy);
- a requirement for communities to identify themselves as FFPs before 31 December 2018;
- a distinction between 'land' and 'territory', given that communities seek the guarantee of their territories.

The first two issues constitute the *de facto* withdrawal of constitutional rights: the first because it transgresses the equality principle; the second because the concession of rights is limited to communities that go through a process of self-identification as a FFP before 31 December 2018, thus explicitly ignoring the political identity of communities that have not met the requirements of an artificial deadline. The discussion over this deadline for the acknowledgement of rights has become one of the main impasses for the legal process, and represents the main reason for FFP organisations to mobilise in order to fight for their rights.

For traditional communities, and in the case for the FFP closing, the distinction between 'land' and 'territory' is fundamental to understanding the specificity of each group and how their relationship with nature becomes a constituent of their very existence. 'Territory' for FFP communities is something broader than the physical basis or the 'land' alone. It is land where the social group has played out its life and developed a knowledge base that, over time, has ensured its existence and identity as a social group.

On the one hand, State Law 20.417/2013 could be a way to achieve legal land regularisation for FFPs. On the other hand, it represents new challenges and fears for communities and FFP organisations. For example, the process requires the engagement of communities that have not yet declared themselves as *Fundos de Pasto*, perhaps because they do not see themselves as being part of this category, or they do not know much about it, or even because they are afraid of further conflicts. FFP organisations have to support those communities that have already identified themselves, and actively identify new communities that would fit the criteria for becoming an FFP. This process has been criticised since it seems to disregard non-institutional ways of recognising communities, and as it also seems to imply that those communities that have not identified themselves before the stipulated deadline will no longer be seen as potential rights owners.

The first and the second items are consistent with the 169th International Labour Organization Convention on Indigenous and

Tribal Peoples (ILO, 2011) enacted in April 2004 by the Brazilian government. The third item is relevant because, once the community territory is regularised (rather than its land), the communities' culture and lifestyle ought also to be respected. This matters because the communities maintain their lifestyle and culture through a mix of individual plots and common areas. State Law 20.417/2013 partially guarantees that communities will keep their territories. Although the original proposals aimed to facilitate a participatory process, this has not happened as expected: in order to become recognised, it is mandatory for communities to sign up to a formal legal contract, the implications of which will be better understood in the run-up to the official deadline of December 2018. In this context, uncertainty has led to more intense conflicts over land ownership, and land has become the subject of disputes among miners, agribusiness, *grileiros* and developers of wind-farms and dams. And while the state should guarantee the security of traditional communities' occupation of their land, in reality it maintains the privileges of social elites, so that communities have no option but to fight in order to maintain their territory and their cultural values. To have common land represents the main strategy for communities to be able to live together within the *caatinga* biome. It means their identity and their social belonging, as well as their security, especially when they have not been able to produce a surplus.

Common resources management

Common resources are finite, shared resources, and their consumption by an individual group member results in fewer resources available for all. Typical examples of common resources are pastures, forests and fisheries (not exclusively natural resources). The study of collective action and common resources represents a social dilemma in which there are conflicts between private and collective interests (Ostrom et al, 2011). Orthodox theory argues that, in this context, individual private interests prevail. Possible solutions to avoid the destruction of such natural resources (the infamous 'tragedy') are only possible if an external individual interferes and enforces effective management (Ostrom, 1990). Another possibility would be for the common resources to be privately owned or privatised.

In contrast to Hardin's purely theoretical approach, Ostrom (1990) has focused her studies on existing small communities that have learned to cooperate for their own survival rather than competing for resources until they are exhausted. She argues that institutions, as well as formal and informal rules, can be created by communities themselves to determine actions in both general and particular circumstances. In this context, there is no need for external individuals or authorities to impose ways of managing common resources externally. Ostrom et al (2011) define 'robust' institutions as long-lasting organisations with operational rules that can be modified over time and sustained by collective choices.

Private properties are not exclusively economic phenomena, but also reflections of social patterns, competitive political dynamics and collective decision-making systems (Algrawal and Ostrom, 2011; Barry, 1992; Ostrom et al, 2011). Schlager and Ostrom (1992) argue that there are five categories of rights:

- *access*: the right to enter a property;
- *withdrawal*: the right to collect or extract resources and produce from the property;
- *management*: the right to manage how a resource is used, and how it might be improved;
- *exclusion*: the right to determine the right of access to resources by others and whether this right can be transferred;
- *alienation*: the right to sell or rent any of the previous rights.

These property rights can be subdivided into two categories: operational rights (access and withdrawal rights) and collective choice rights (management, exclusion and alienation rights). Operational rights can be defined and changed by collective choice rights. All the rules can be developed in a wide range of decision-making spaces, and it is from these spaces that they originate; this way, rules and rights are not similar concepts, and each right can result in a duty (Schlager and Ostrom, 1992). The authors also state that alienation is not the main right, as might be presumed to be the case with private property (Ostrom et al, 2011).

Examples of successful management of common property have been linked to collective action and the preservation of common resources. Ostrom (1990) argues that each resource's physical structure has an impact over group strategies and results. Accordingly, rules applied to one physical environment may result in completely different results if applied in a different environment. Physical and cultural group particularities limit the extent to which any one strategy can be generalised. Through comparing different communities, Ostrom argues that communities that have successfully managed their resources have developed a range of 'design' principles that address a range of common problems. The design principles presented in Ostrom (1990) and Ostrom et al (2011) are as follows:

- *Well-defined limits.* It is necessary to understand the resource's structure, size and border limits. The limits of a system of resources, as well as the group of individuals or family units that have rights over the resources, should be well defined. To have clarity over rules regarding social limits influences cooperation.
- *Equivalence between cost and benefit.* Rules must guarantee that the benefits associated with the use of common resources are allocated proportionally to contributions made. Proportional rules are believed to be more equitable. If inequalities are noticed, individuals may refuse to follow the rules that are considered to be unfair.
- *Collective choice agreements.* Most individuals affected by a regime of natural resource use should be able to participate in the processes whereby the rules are elaborated and modified. Ostrom argues that the existence of good rules does not imply that they will be fulfilled by all individuals if they did not have a part in saying what they should be, and are not able to change them when they do not work. This principle is the opposite of the assumptions of orthodox theory, which argues that there should be an external individual who would impose rules, and this would be the only way to establish communal organisation.
- *Monitoring.* Individuals who are in charge of monitoring the extent to which the rules governing the use of natural resources are transgressed have great responsibilities. They should be chosen by the community in order to be trusted by all.
- *Gradual penalties.* If rules are broken, there should be different degrees of penalty to discourage further violations and reinforce mutual confidence.
- *Conflict resolution mechanisms.* It is necessary to have local, effective and low-cost mechanisms for conflict resolution between internal and external individuals (such as government institutions, for example).
- *Rights acknowledgement.* The right of communities to create their own rules should be recognised by the government.
- *Connected enterprises.* When common resources are part of a bigger community, governance activities should be organised in a connected multiple-layer system. Small-scale units may act according to rules appropriate for local conditions, but large-scale institutions are also necessary to connect smaller-scale enterprises.

The lessons of these studies are that, even though there are many examples of these principles being of value, adherence to all of them is not necessary in order to achieve successful long-term management (Ostrom et al, 2011). Thus there is no unique way of developing an adequate resource management system, which also means that a model that is successful in one community will not necessarily be successful in other communities, even if they have similar resources.

Common resources management in the Paredão do Lou *Fundo de Pasto*

The Paredão do Lou *Fundo de Pasto* is located in the city of Monte Santo, in the state of Bahia, as illustrated in Figure 9.3.

Figure 9.3: Map of the research area location (*Fundo de Pasto* Paredão do Lou), 2013

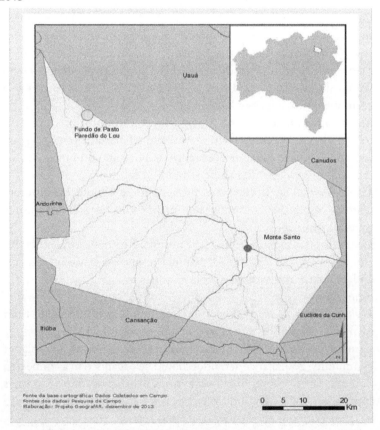

Source: Field research, 2012, elaborated by Marques (2013).

The Paredão do Lou community is represented by the Agricultural and Pastoral Paredão do Lou Farm Association, which is a non-profit civil society organisation, constituted by a board of directors and an audit committee, which takes decisions in assemblies. The association aims to represent 70 members and to be responsible for all the 181 residents of the 54 community family units. Initially, it was created in order to guarantee land regularisation processes when two *grileiros* inappropriately tried to take over the community land in the 1980s:

> "In the first attempt, the landowner was preparing to put up fence, but some lawyers argued that we should try to stop them, so we did and the landowner gave up. In the second attempt, a Monte Santo dweller, Agenor, bought some land and aimed to changes its designation from Monte Santo to Uauá, i.e. as his own land, including the Paredão do Lou area. There has also been resistance, but there has also been resistance from the land owner." (Interviewee I, 2012)

Following the second attempt to enclose the land, there was mutual resistance, which resulted in a judicial process initiated by a *grileiro* but which nonetheless eventually led to a favourable outcome for the community. In order to stop their land from being re-invaded, in 1985 the community initiated a land regularisation process. The ownership of the land was guaranteed by a document issued by the Bahia Land Institute in 1995, and since then there have not been any external conflicts.

There are many examples of solidaristic practices in the Paredão do Lou community. Productive land is distributed in smaller shares of between 5 ha. and 65 ha., the variation being proportional to how many children each family has. Each share can be subdivided if new family units are formed, or in the case of inheritance, but the individual shares of land, as well as the houses, are not usually sold. Having connections between the collective and individual areas is of fundamental importance, especially as a coping mechanism during the drought seasons. According to Brazilian environmental legislation, 40% of the *caatinga* biome should be preserved (which is its 'legal reserve'). However, what the community considers to be the preserved area is bigger than that stipulated by law because environmental preservation is so important to residents – so environmental preservation happens not through formal audit of legal requirements, but is a result of the local culture, as Ostrom suggested was possible.

Each farmer recognises the limitations of both the individual and the common areas in terms of the ability to provide livelihoods, so there are no internal conflicts over land. The *Fundo de Pasto* area is not fenced off from other communities, so it is effectively enlarged because of access to parts of the neighbours' land, which facilitates better animal husbandry. These adjacent areas are fundamentally important for the goats living in the *caatinga* biome as in the drought seasons the animals need to be able to graze widely to find new sources of food. Consequently, according to one resident, the relationship between different *Fundos de Pasto* communities:

> "… is peaceful because all the communities which have physical boundaries with *Fundos de Pasto* also have *Fundos de Pasto*, occasionally our animals walk towards other properties, and, the same way, we find animals from other properties in our land. In these cases, everyone is careful to look after the animal if it is ill or to return the animal to its owners." (Interviewee II, 25 years old, 2013)

Another example of solidaristic connections between communities is in their opposition to mining activities. Two mining companies are active in the local area and have attempted to explore the subsoil in the nearby São Gonçalo de Bento community, but with support from the Paredão do Lou association, the most destructive activities in the area were prevented.

Solidaristic animal husbandry

Goats are the most popular animals to be kept in unfenced conditions in the *caatinga*, because of their adaptation to the local biome. In Brazil, sheep are usually kept in pens as otherwise they might easily stray from the herd while searching for food or water, or whenever it rains. Pigs were once allowed to range freely, but because they used to eat the goats and lambs, the association decided to curtail this practice. There is currently one family (not an association member) that sometimes lets its pigs range freely, and this causes many complaints.

While the goats roam freely, the ownership of individual goats is identified through marks in their ears. A mark in the goat's right ear, called a *mourão*, identifies the family to which the animal belongs. A different mark in the left ear (a *diferença*) identifies which family member the animal belongs to. These signs can be observed in the photos in Figure 9.4. The identification process, which also accords respect towards animals, is defined through community consensus.

Figure 9.4. Identification signs in a goat's ears: *mourão* (A) and *diferença* (B)

Although it might seem that there is no system for distributing animals equitably, and, consequently, every individual might be interested in letting more and more animals graze in common areas for their own advantage (as per Hardin), this is in fact not the case. As few families have more goats than they need, cases of excessive grazing are the exception rather than the rule.

All produce that exceeds subsistence needs is sold in street markets in nearby cities and towns, but poor road conditions limit what is possible. Further, since there is hardly any surplus during drought seasons, the communities acquire what they need at markets with financial resources from the Bolsa Família programme.[1] Commercial transactions also take place through middlemen. During the drought seasons, there are few products on offer; even though the animals are more valuable during this time, their price is lower because they are usually underweight. Although often the intermediary sells at a higher price than the one paid to the peasants, the financial benefits are not passed on to the community. The lack of refrigeration infrastructure, high transportation costs, and difficulties in organising bigger sales may make the use of middlemen more attractive. Income in drought seasons comes mainly from government social programmes, such as the Bolsa Família.

This all shows that FFPs are not autarkic, subsistence communities. They have complex and solidarisitic relationships with other communities, with markets outside their territories and with the state, which provides them with resources they cannot provide themselves, especially during times of drought. Solidarity relations are thus intertwined with other markets and with the state.

Productive groups

Although the benefits of shared grazing areas are recognised by the community, there was little interest among residents in the association's two solidarity economy productive groups, despite persistent drought since 2011, which might be expected to encourage communities to seek other means of subsistence. Both groups, however – the caprine milk group, and the birds and garden group – were inactive at the time of writing. Residents preferred to focus on their individual areas. Usually, the same individuals are active the productive groups. There is also an underground dam group, which is in the process of development and is anticipating the end of the drought, and a group dedicated to the improvement of goat husbandry, which is awaiting funding to proceed with its activities. Moreover, there are collective resources such as the *aguadas* (well) and a flour mill, which, although it is privately owned, is available for community use because it is a productive resource. The details of these group activities are presented in Figure 9.5.

Figure 9.5 Map of productive areas in the Paredão do Lou *Fundo de Pasto* (2013)

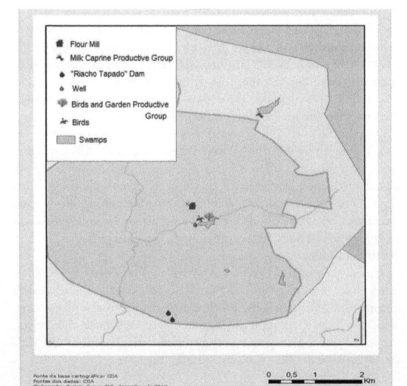

Anyone who participates in the productive groups is also expected to participate in all the collective activities it undertakes. As a rule, if anyone misses any taskforce activities, the work that is not undertaken needs be paid for, and this is organised through an attendance list. Payment can be fulfilled either through work or the monetary equivalent of the relevant number of working hours. Thus, it can be seen that the Paredão do Lou *Fundo de Pasto* has robust institutions of self-management.

Table 9.1 presents the rights related to common resources, regarding both the management of the *Fundo de Pasto* and the management of collective resources restricted to certain community groups. The table indicates that no one has the right of alienation of common resources under any circumstances. Neighbouring communities, such as well and dam users, are considered. The resources considered necessary by the community, especially water, cannot be denied. The Association has almost every right, except the right of alienation; the same way is true of the productive groups.

Table 9.1: Property rights over common resources in the Paredão do Lou community

	Property rights				
Common resources	Access	Withdrawal	Manangement	Exclusion	Alienation
Fundo de Pasto	Community	Community	Association	Association	No one
	Bordering *Fundo de Pasto* communities				
Productive groups: goats' milk, birds and garden	Community	Productive group members	Productive group members	Productive group members	No one
	Productive group members				
Water resources (well, dam)	Community	Community	Association	Association	No one
	Bordering *Fundos de Pasto* communities	Bordering *Fundo de Pasto* communities			

Source: Field research, 2013.

Table 9.2 systematises the relationship between the design principles for common resources defined by Ostrom, and links these to the nature of cooperation over common resources in Paredão do Lou.

Both the formal and informal community institutions have evolved over time in order to address the changing demands of common resources management. Ostrom et al (2011) argue that some communities accept that that there are non-cooperative users. In specific cases, the community forgoes payment from members who

Table 9.2: Design principles associated with the Paredão do Lou community

Design principles	
Well-defined limits	*Fundos de Pasto* formal area: 1.704 ha. Individual area, water resources (well, dam) and productive group resources: visually recognised limits. The use of resources is respected, both individual or collective.
Equivalence between cost and benefit	All the association members have proportional rights over the benefits. However, if a benefit is essential to non-members, they can also benefit. Community members have equal rights and should be mutually respectful even if their herds are of different sizes. Essential resources belong to everyone. Residents who cannot make financial contributions to the community are not penalised.
Collective choice agreements	Even though the rules have been put together during the process of living together, many of them have been formalised by the association. The association is also available as a space for discussion.
Monitoring	Formal monitoring is fulfilled by the association, through representatives for each area: Lajeado, Paredão, Sítio do Meio and Quixabeira. It is also undertaken informally by inhabitants.
Gradual penalties	Penalties depend on how serious are the infractions. Less serious infractions attract verbal warnings. More serious infractions may lead to exclusion from the association or even expulsion from the community, in extremely serious cases.
Conflict resolution mechanisms	Through the association.
Rights acknowledgement	The association legally represents the community vis-a-vis the state. Community land ownership through the association is recognised in Bahia State law.
Connected enterprises	Related enterprises include the collective resources beyond the *Fundo de Pasto* (a well, three dams), as well as the productive resources (goats' milk, birds, gardens and an underground dam).

Source: Field research, 2012-13.

cannot contribute financially, who are considered to be different from members who do not *want to* contribute. Both Ostrom's conceptions and community practices show that it is more important to have benefits guaranteed. As such, communities like Paredão do Lou are capable of maintaining its resources sustainably, through its system of livelihood and through both formal and informal institutions.

Conclusion

The *Fundo de Pasto* communities have their livelihood and culture guaranteed by the pasture system for small animals in areas of common grazing. Their way of life has been underpinned by relations of trust between members and connections between formal and informal institutions, internally and externally. In order to preserve their way of life, the communities have two main challenges: the management of common resources in an intensely hot and dry ecosystem, and disputes over land use and ownership.

State Law 20.417/2013 (which aims to regularise traditional communities) does not guarantee property rights for these communities. Three issues remain: discrimination between traditional communities, the deadline for FFP communities to identify themselves (31 December 2018), and discussions about the differences between land and territory, with territorial regularisation as the aim.

Generally speaking, the *Fundos de Pasto* in the *caatinga* biome facilitate the conservation of nature, and have the support of institutions such as IRPAA that develop methodologies for working in a semi-arid climate. The alternative theories of common resource management are important to explain how the management of natural resources works in these communities. The traditional theory presented by the concept of the Tragedy of the Commons assumes that communities are not capable of managing resources collectively, because rationality will always prioritise individual interests over collective ones. According to this theory, in *Fundos de Pasto* herders would act selfishly, and, consequently, the *caatinga* biome would be destroyed and there would be no social reproduction.

Ostrom's common resources approach provides an alternative that is critical of the traditional approach, holding that there is no unique path towards success in communities. Ostrom presented eight design principles that are helpful to better understand each community's dynamic and their own actions towards collective governance.

The Paredão do Lou *Fundo de Pasto* does not demonstrate all eight design principles. However, its way of life and the collective governance principles it adheres to ensures that the community remains closely knit and solidaristic, internally as well as externally. It has preserved the natural environment according to Ostrom's logic, both in terms of adapting to the *caatinga* biome, and in terms of the water use in a semi-arid climate. So even when considering the wide range of difficulties frequently faced by the community, its residents maintain their livelihoods and culture, in a sustainable and solidaristic way, and the community resists and exists.

Note

[1] Bolsa Família is an income transfer social programme that benefits poor families all over the country. Its main principle is that income support from the government to poor families promotes an immediate solution to poverty, while complementary actions aim to bring development to these families (MDA, 2003).

References

Bahia Legislative Assembly (1989) *Constituição do Estado da Bahia*. Salvador: Bahia Legislative Assembly.

Brazil (2007) Decreto n. 6.040 que institui a Política Nacional de Desenvolvimento Sustentável dos Povos e Comunidades Tradicionais. Available at: www.planalto.gov.br/ccivil_03/_ato2007-2010/2007/decreto/d6040.htm.

Castro, E. (2000) 'Território, biodiversidade e saberes de populações tradicionais', in A.C. Diegues (ed) *ETINOCONSERVAÇÃO: novos rumos para a proteção da natureza nos trópicos* (2nd edn). São Paulo: HUCITEC,/USP, pp 165-182.

Drummond et al (2000) 'Estratégias para o uso sustentável da biodiversidade da Caatinga', in Silva, J.M.C. and Tabarelli, M. (eds). *Workshop: Avaliação e identificação de ações prioritárias para conservação, utilização sustentável e repartição de benefícios da biodiversidade do bioma Caatinga*. Petrolina. Available at *www.biodiversitas.org.br/caatinga/relatorios/uso_sustentavel.pdf*.

Garcez, Angelina Nobre Rolim (1987) *Fundo de Pasto: um projeto de vida sertaneja*. Salvador: INTERBA-CAR.

GeografAR (2011) 'Mapa das associações das comunidades de fundo e Fecho de Pasto por município'. Available at www.geografar.ufba.br/site/arquivos/biblioteca/mapas/cbe3c99e41130accbc34e51b1dfb2903.pdf (accessed 2013).

Hardin. G. (1968) 'The Tragedy of the Commons', *Magazine Science*, vol 162, no 3859, pp 1243-1248.

ILO (2011) *Convenção nº169* sobre povos indígenas e tribais e resolução referente a OIT – Organização Internacional do Trabalho: Brasília.

IRPAA (Instituto Regional da Pequena Agropecuária Apropriada) (2016) *Carta do seminário das Comunidades atingidas pela mineração na região Centro norte Bahia*. Available at www.irpaa.org/noticias/1447/carta-do-seminario-das-comunidades-atingidas-pela-mineracao-na-regiao-centro-norte-bahia (accessed 22 Sept 2016).

Marques, L. (2013) 'Os fundos de pasto no município de Monte Santo (Ba) e a política de desenvolvimento territorial: comflitos e interesses territoriais no campo', Dissertação (Mestrado), Programa de Pós-Graduação em Geografia da Universidade de Sergipe, Aracajú, SE.

MDA (Ministério de Desenvolvimento Agrario) (2003) 'Programa Bolsa Família'. Available at www.mds.gov.br/bolsafamilia (accessed June 2015).

Ostrom, E. (1990) *Governing the Commons: The Evolution of Institutions for Collective Action* (5th edn). Cambridge: Cambridge University Press.

Ostrom, E., Poteete, A.R. and Janssen, M.A. (2011) *Trabalho em Parceria: ação coletiva, bens comuns e múltiplos métodos.* Translation: BETTONI. Rogério: Senac.

Schlager, E. and Ostrom, E. (1992) 'Property-Rights Regimes and Natural Resources: A Conceptual', *Land Economics*, vol 68, pp 249-262.

Part III
The social and solidarity economy and the state

TEN

The Danish low carbon transition and the prospects for the democratic economy

Andrew Cumbers

Introduction

In the last quarter of the 20th century, Denmark underwent a remarkable transformation in its energy system, moving from almost complete dependence on imported oil for most of its energy needs to becoming a beacon for climate change amelioration and a renewable energy role model. Lacking the vast hydro-electric resources of its Nordic neighbours, the country's success in building up a renewable energy capacity has been all the more remarkable. Key to this success has been the emergence of a wind power sector that has created 20,000 jobs and at one point in the early 2000s accounted for 50% of the world market for wind turbine manufacture (DEA, 2007).

Although it has rightly gained plaudits internationally for its leadership in tackling global warming (for example, IEA, 2006), rather less has been said about the social and political foundations of Denmark's low carbon transition. Perhaps this is because the latter has been founded on a very different set of social and political relations to the dominant global neoliberal model of energy governance and regulation. Rather than imposing the kinds of market discipline and private ownership on the sector apparent elsewhere, the Danish low carbon transition has been characterised by a more democratic and social model of economic development, combining high-level state support and institutional mechanisms on the one hand with bottom-up forms of mobilisation, collectivisation and ownership on the other. In short, it contains strong aspects of democratic engagement and social empowerment commensurate with Erik Olin Wright's call for actually existing alternatives to global neoliberalism (Wright, 2010). As such, it offers some interesting pointers towards more solidaristic forms of economic action and practice that are the focus of this book.

This chapter argues that the 'Danish model' evident here is associated with the high watermark of the Nordic variant of social democracy under capitalism with a high level of non-commodified social relations (Esping Anderson, 1990). While not an alternative to capitalism per se, it does offer elements of an alternative configuration of economic and social relations capable of moving away from a capitalist value ethos of individual profit maximisation towards one of social need, the common good and solidaristic values. But it also demonstrates some of the tensions and constraints in sustaining a socialised economic model in a broader landscape of continuing neoliberal encroachment.

Constructing the Danish model of energy democracy and low carbon transition

The oil crises of the 1970s exposed Denmark's increased vulnerability to imported oil as one of the most dependent countries in the Organisation for Economic Co-operation and Development, accounting for around 90% of the country's energy demand by 1973 (DEA, 2007). Rising oil prices, resulting from the geopolitical crises in the Middle East during 1973–74 and 1979–80, prompted a rethink of Danish energy policy. While the discovery of substantial oil and gas deposits in the North Sea ameliorated its short-term supply issues, long-term energy security remained a key public policy concern.

Like many other Western European countries at the time, Denmark experienced a deep and searching political debate over the country's future energy needs. Across the spectrum, most of the country's political parties and business establishment lined up in favour of the centralised model of nuclear power, a solution that both centre left and centre right politicians had been pushing since the 1950s. With the initial hike in oil prices in 1973–74, a National Energy Plan set out its stall to build five nuclear power stations that would meet a quarter of the country's primary energy needs (Hadjilambrinos, 2000). However, it was confronted by a diverse grassroots coalition championing a more decentralised alternative. This was also in keeping with the country's existing electricity system, which, unlike that in many other countries, had remained fragmented and under the control of local government (Cumbers, 2012).

The opposition coalition included both radical left and green elements but also included rural conservative groups suspicious of the centralising tendencies of the Danish political elite (Jensen, 2003; Andersen and Dreyer, 2008). The fusion of traditional localism and even mutualism with more radical energy agendas was important to the success of the anti-nuclear lobby. Additionally, a longstanding and enduring interest in wind power technology and the existence of scientific communities able to showcase and lobby for renewable energy in national policy forums and public arenas was also critical. The ability to link national political agency to broader 1970s environmental struggles and discourses was also key, particularly arguments about the limits to growth and the need for smaller economic units (Meadows et al, 1972). Campaigners were effective in public demonstration events, notably the Tvind school's giant windmill (Kruse and Maegard, 2008), helping to develop an alternative public narrative around clean and pure energy.

By the late 1970s, public opinion had shifted decisively against nuclear energy, with formal recognition evident in the social democratic government's 1981 Energy Package with a strategy to reduce reliance on imported energy including a strong component of supporting renewables. The energy strategy was also supported by a 1979 Heat Supply Law, which had two important effects from our perspective here; first, to encourage more efficient use of thermal energy and heating in combined heat and power and district (DH) heating systems; and second, to require such systems to run on a not-for-profit basis,[1] effectively giving an incentive towards cooperative ownership (IEA, 2006). This basic policy agenda remained in place until the late 1990s when broader neoliberal influences began to shift policy in a new direction (discussed later in the chapter). Its success can be measured both by the increased use of renewable energy - from virtually nothing to around 26.7% of total energy consumption while renewable energy now accounts for 46.7% of domestic electricity supply (DEA, 2013) – and by the growth of DH, which accounts for over 60% of heat supplied to Danish homes (DEA, 2007).

Three elements were critical in the emergence of Denmark as a renewables champion; these, I argue, were related to particular collective governance arrangements linking grassroots mobilisation around strategic state interventions. The first element was government funding for 30% of all investment in new wind turbines during the 1980s, reducing to 10% in the 1990s (Cumbers, 2012). What effectively amounted to a developmentalist state 'infant industry' strategy was critical for allowing Danish producers to develop a strong lead that was able to outlast competitors, notably in the US during fluctuating world market conditions for renewables in the 1980s (Mazzucato, 2011). A second element, emerging from the 1981 Energy Package or *Energipakken*, was forcing the large but publicly owned and regional electricity distribution networks to purchase a minimum quota of their energy from renewables on the path to rising national targets over time (Meyer and Koefoed, 2003). This commitment was strengthened even further in the 1990s with the setting up of 'feed-in' tariffs that guaranteed renewable wind farm producers a fixed price for their output, a step that encouraged the local public electricity utilities to invest in their own renewable capacity. The effect was to provide a stable, long-term investment environment for wind turbine that was the spur to development and rapid growth of the sector (see Figure 10.1).

Figure 10.1: Growth in number of turbines and capacity, Denmark 1977–2012

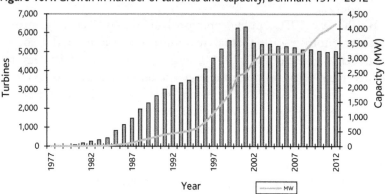

A third element of the Danish renewables revolution has been the creation of new forms of local collective ownership of wind turbines. Once again, an enabling state regulatory framework combined with grassroots action has underpinned this development. In particular, alongside tax concessions for those investing in renewables, the government introduced new laws – 'residency criteria' – that constricted turbine ownership to those living in the area of operation. 'Consumption criteria' laws were also introduced, limiting individual shareholding according to personal electricity consumption (Tranaes, undated). Although both sets of laws have been relaxed over time so that by the early 2000s it was possible to buy up land for larger wind developments, they have meant that wind turbine ownership remains dominated by either small-scale forms of private ownership (typically partnerships between local neighbours) or cooperative forms. The first Danish onshore 'wind farms', in the sense of large-scale activities that supplied more than a local neighbourhood, were cooperatively owned, although in the mid-1990s, individual ownership – especially by farmers in rural areas – took on an increasingly larger share. In more recent years, larger private and corporate investors have grown in importance. Nevertheless, as late as 2009 it was estimated that 15% of wind turbine ownership remained in cooperative hands.[2] Alongside this has been the creation of a number of collective bodies to represent renewable interests, notably the Danish Wind Turbine Owners Association, which has 4,000 members, representing 4/5 of turbine owners,[3] the Danish Wind Industry Association (with over 250 member firms) and the Nordic Folkecenter for Renewable Energy, a not-for-profit body for national and international advocacy. Within broader Danish civil society, such associations and a growing plethora of environmental and green think tanks and academics play an important role in countering corporate and state interests wedded to carbon-based technologies in lobbying for robust low carbon policies.

The overall effect of these developments has been to create an interesting experiment in community empowerment and public engagement around climate change politics, in effect a form of energy democracy. One obvious benefit has been the high level of public support for building wind turbines in residents' neighbourhoods compared with other countries. As Moller puts it:

> Wind energy in Denmark generally enjoys a high public acceptance. One of the cornerstones for maintaining public acceptance on a national scale as well as in local areas with dense wind turbine development was ownership. Public regulation granted a proportion of the wind capacity to be erected by publicly owned utilities and more importantly, legislation stimulated the formation of local wind energy cooperatives with limited ownership of shares in wind turbine projects within residents' municipalities. (2010, p 234)

Local economic benefits stemming from job creation and income-earning opportunities have clearly been important to community acceptance of renewables, but arguably as important has been the resulting public engagement and knowledge formation processes around energy issues.

At this point, it is also worth emphasising the continuing decentralised and democratic nature of the broader energy system compared with elsewhere. Although there have been a number of mergers of local electricity cooperatives and municipally owned forms since the end of the second world war, in particular to build more centralised thermal power stations, the national state has largely remained excluded from this system (Hadjilambrinos, 2000). As such, the system remains decentralised, although attempts to realise economies of scale have led to the creation of 10 regional transmission networks (which are amalgamations of 100 local cooperatives) (DEA, 2007). These regional and local public bodies still own the eight major electricity generating plants, accounting for 75% of total production (Hadjilambrinos, 2000, p 1119).[4] Although there has been a growing amalgamation of decision making in the electricity sector through the setting up of regional associations – ELKRAFT for the main island Zealand (which includes the capital Copenhagen) and ELSAM (for Jutland and the island of Funen) (Hadjilambrinos, 2000, p 1119) – that have wielded considerable power in national energy policy debates, it is important to emphasise the continuing democratic constitution of these organisations. All local and regional public energy bodies are subject to elections, while rural energy cooperatives are also democratically run by members. Of course, this does not mitigate against the capture of larger organisations by vested interests, but it has resulted in adding important deliberative layers and checks to the energy policy arena, particularly in contrast to countries such as the United Kingdom and France where the post-1945 centralisation of energy policy has created opaque and obscure institutional structures that allow corporate and political elites to exercise almost untrammelled power.[5]

As we have already seen, Danish energy politics are not without conflict, most notably between 'consumer interest' often aligned in the short term with established corporate high interests committed to centralised carbon-based forms of energy production and an alternative vision predicated on stimulating alternative energy technologies, subsiding infant industry and smaller-scale development. However, the decentred nature of this political economy has permitted experimentation and pluralism in the politics of energy supply to the extent that the local distribution companies hold differing views on wind power, with rural cooperatives often more supportive of the nascent technology than the more municipally based utilities (Heymann, 1999).

Relatedly, the depth of cooperative relations and associationalist culture in Danish civil society has also been important, to the extent that most citizens will be involved in a range of different associations thereby constructing complex and overlapping relations of identity formation. In these conditions, there is less of a danger that vested interests or 'principal agents' can fully capture economic agendas because economic communities and groups remain less bounded or framed by a 'silo mentality' and are more open and fluid in their constitution.

While it is important not to overemphasise the progressive aspects of this approach, it does allow a more open and agonistic public arena to emerge (Mouffe, 2005) that can promote alternative values to the economic mainstream. The thick civic and participatory culture within which Danish energy politics is embedded works against what Otto Neurath refers to as the 'tendency for one, and one loyalty to "devour" all' (Neurath, 1945, p 429). It also means that a diverse range of perspectives is represented in policy formation. Although wind power producers and cooperatives have been very scornful of the position taken by the electricity utilities in the 1980s in their opposition to the new technology, concerns about the cost of supporting new technologies through subsidies must be seen as a legitimate interest, particularly for poorer urban energy use groups in cases where the benefits of cooperative ownership can in effect be accruing to more affluent middle-class rural groups. The strength of the Danish model of energy democracy evident here means that different interests are represented, though of course this may not always lead to the policy outcomes favoured by left and progressive opinion.

The Single European Market and the neoliberal incursion on the Danish energy model

During the 1990s, what was effectively a national model of low carbon transition, framed by specific territorially based historical conditions and social forces, became increasingly entangled within the broader EU regulatory regime for energy and, in particular, the emergence of a neoliberal-inspired single market project. Although a broad consensus in Denmark had been firmly established by the 1990s to expand renewables and wind production, the means of achieving this became increasingly contested. At a general level, there remained a conflict between large utility distribution companies, particularly urban municipal organisations, much of the business lobby and centrist and right-wing politicians who favoured larger-scale developments (privately or state-owned) and reducing the cost of electricity to consumers, and the locally owned wind cooperatives, rural interests, turbine producers, and green and left groups who remained committed to more decentralised forms of organisation and continued widespread participation.

These tensions were played out in the planning process around renewables and wind power development, particularly between the spontaneous local development of small-scale turbines and the need for more effective high-level planning at national and regional scales. By the mid-1990s, the limits of the 'localised' model were becoming apparent, with the original phase of more anarchic and chaotic development giving way to a national strategic approach (Moller, 2010). The original spread of wind turbines lacked coordination and often occurred in environmentally sensitive areas (Moller, 2010). At the same time, the first generation of smaller and less efficient power stations was reaching the end of its operational life and requiring replacement, offering possibility for larger and more efficient turbines. A tension began to emerge between local community action and autonomy and national strategic objectives. The result was a new wave of legislation from the early 1990s onwards, requiring environmental impact assessments, greater planning restrictions and the creation of national and regional planning zones to regulate projects. The result was a steep decline in new onshore projects and a greater emphasis on offshore or larger, more concentrated, onshore projects in less environmentally sensitive areas (Moller, 2010).

Mixing into these national energy policy dilemmas, the EU single market agenda around energy began to take effect. In contrast to other Scandinavian countries, Denmark had a strong tradition of liberalism and decentralisation, even undergoing its own period of economic deregulation and proto-neoliberalism under a new right government in the 1970s. As a small open economy on the periphery of Europe, Denmark's political elites have historically tended to support lower trade barriers and greater European integration as a way of expanding markets for the country's manufacturers. Consequently, from the early 1990s onwards, governments of the centre left and centre right have been prepared to embrace large elements of the European Single Market agenda, although not membership of the Euro.[6] In particular, the European Commission's agenda to liberalise electricity markets, break up and 'unbundle' what were seen as inefficient and anti-competitive state monopolies and practices was fully integrated into Danish energy policy, particularly under the new conservative–liberal coalition that came to power after 2001. Even before this, however, a new Energy Act in 1999 effectively implemented EU rules and abolished the feed-in tariff (FIT), replacing it with the EU Commission's preferred alternative of tradable green certificates (TGC), which are based on electricity companies having to source a certain quota of total production from renewables.

From a distance, the battle between the FIT system and the TGC may seem an arcane and technical affair with little political interest, but it represented a critical fault-line for both Danish and European Union policy in the battle between neoliberal, market-driven reforms and a more state-directed and planned approach to low carbon transition. Critically, the support for the TGC system in Denmark came from the Confederation of Danish Industry, the main electricity utilities (and their desire to escape the cost implications of the FIT) and the increasingly powerful wind energy manufacturers who, as the global market leaders, clearly had an interest in a liberalised European energy market with a dedicated quota for renewables (Lauber and Schenner, 2011). However, the Act worked against the interests of turbine owners and those interested in investing in new technologies and products. Like many other 'open and fair market' solutions, it favours established companies, those that are able to take advantage of scale economies and tried and tested technologies against more innovative newcomers (see Meyer and Koefoed, 2003). This would be to the detriment of alternative forms of renewables such as solar energy, biomass or combined heat and power that would need greater investment and research and development. Additionally, allowing markets to operate in an unrestricted fashion means that green energy prices can fluctuate considerably with the demand for electricity, thereby providing little assurance for those seeking to invest in new technologies. This represents a classic example not just of market failure, but also of the inappropriate use of markets for public policy solutions (Meyer and Koefoed, 2003).

In Denmark the effect was to stymie further growth of onshore wind turbines, with the phasing out of the FIT seeing a massive tailing off in turbine construction (see Figure 10.1). Further marketisation has occurred through the integration of the Danish electricity sector into the common Nordic market, which has constrained the national government's ability to regulate prices by the introduction of a deregulated spot market for electricity that can greatly enhance market uncertainty, to the benefit of larger and established corporate concerns at the expense of smaller and more localised forms of ownership.

Between 2000 and 2010, the Danish wind power revolution effectively stalled, with no growth in wind power to the electricity grid (Figure 10.1; Ryland, 2010). Ten years of rule by a centre right coalition with an anti-environmentalist premier, Anders Fogh Rasmussen, have also clearly taken their toll. Rasmussen's government not only cancelled three new offshore projects on coming into office in 2001, but also cut government support for the previously successful policy of domestic energy conservation (Figure 10.1). Although the growing threat of increased foreign energy dependence (from Russian gas supplies) and Denmark's reputation abroad as a sustainable development champion caused the government to change tack in 2006, the cause of renewable energy and tackling climate change were set back considerably.

Low carbon aspirations and the future of energy democracy

Despite the blockages applied by the right-wing administration in the 2000s, public opinion in Denmark remains firmly committed to strong climate change amelioration objectives and renewable energy targets. One of the first acts of the new centre left government in 2011 was to raise the share of energy consumption by renewables to 50% by 2020. Although at the time of writing (October 2015) there was a new, but fragile, minority centre right administration, there is a strong consensus across all major political parties in favour of renewable expansion and the government has committed to Denmark raising all of its energy consumption from renewables by 2050. The main issues of contention, which the less environmentally prone right-wing parties and their supporters occasionally try to exploit, tend to be around costs[7] and compensation for properties affected by turbine development. Danish renewable policy has become a 'prestige project' now shared by political and economic elites for the country to be a global leader in the battle against climate change. Two think tanks have even come up with a Danish 'State of Green' brand identity as an aspiration for the country to compete in global markets on its green technology and environmental advantages (Realdania and Monday Morning, 2012).

The earlier aspects of bottom-up mutualism and energy democracy seem to be fading over time, and, as with the situation elsewhere, there is the prospect that energy resources and expertise will become increasingly financialised as assets that can yield rent-seeking opportunities for global and corporate elites (Hudson, 2012). One of the most serious political confrontations in recent years occurred when the ruling Social Democrats decided to sell 20% per cent of the state-owned energy company, DONG, to private investors including Goldman Sachs (Lockwood, 2015). This led to a split with the left-wing coalition partner, the Socialist People's Party. Meanwhile, cooperative membership of wind turbines has been in decline across the sector, particularly with the increased focus on offshore wind energy, which necessitates much greater capital investment levels. As such, there is an evident tension emerging in these developments between community ownership and involvement and private accumulation. To achieve its high renewables objectives, the Danish government needs high levels of capital investment, which can of course be achieved through public finance, but in an era of austerity, this is becoming more difficult. Attracting private capital then means providing highly attractive rates of return, which can only be achieved through rising consumer prices for energy, which in turn may serve to diminish public support.

Despite this uncertain outlook, a commitment to some form of collective ownership and involvement remains, some of which displays interesting characteristics in developing new forms of hybrid public and cooperative ownership. Perhaps the best example is the massive Mittlegrunden wind farm, which was constructed off the coast of Copenhagen in 2001 and provides 40 megawatts of electricity, equivalent to 3% of the capital's electricity needs. Ownership of the wind farm was originally divided 50/50 between the city's own municipal energy company and a specially created cooperative, although recently DONG bought the city council's stake. As a result, there are 8,700 residents with shares in the project, administered through the bespoke cooperative (State of Green, 2014). Significantly, around the same time, two other proposals were submitted for new offshore wind parks, one at Grenaa, a private proposal, which was the subject of considerable local resistance that stalled the planning process, and a second at Samsoe, which has been successful in also developing the public–public partnership model of cooperative–local utility ownership (Soerensen et al, 2003). Such examples suggest that the associational and collective ethos of Danish society runs deep and provide a cautionary tale for those of a neoliberal disposition.

Increased attention is now focused on developing a new generation of large offshore wind farms, which required massive levels of capital investment that are likely to be beyond small-scale forms of ownership. In the recent legislation around offshore bidding rounds, it was stipulated that developers must offer 20% of all new projects to local residents in the vicinity of wind farms, but cooperative ownership seems to be taking a more passive form through these kinds of initiatives than in the past. Overall, the Danish experience suggests developing tensions between neoliberal encroachment with deeply entrenched historical commitments to local participation, the decentralisation of economic power and more meaningful deliberative decision making. What is important from the perspective of the book is the way in which a continuing culture of mutualisation and localism takes expression over time in finding new forms to challenge the attempted appropriation of development processes by elite and vested interests.

Conclusion

The Danish experience with renewables holds some important positive lessons in articulating alternative solidarity economy initiatives. These relate to the potential for fusing decentralised and localised forms of mutualism and cooperative ownership with top-down state institutional mechanisms to forge social relations around need and the common good rather than private greed and surplus value. The experience points to the capacities that states have, to both engage in long-term planning and to construct and regulate markets to achieve key public policy objectives beyond neoliberalised commodification processes. It shows therefore how state levers and institutions can be used to foster non-market values for the common good, working for solidaristic over capitalist economic relations. Conversely, it shows how more participatory forms of collective ownership at the local level that are firmly rooted within existing civil society structures can combine to change the national policy discourse in a progressive manner.

Arguably there are limits to the extent to which the Danish approach is transferable elsewhere: Danish economy and society in the 1980s were very decentralised to start with, with a high level of existing associationalism in the forms of cooperative organisation, small firms and high levels of membership of collective associations such as trade unions and business sector organisations (Pedersen, 2006). How repeatable would this experience be today in more centralised states (such as the UK), political systems that have been captured by strong corporate interests (US), or even a country like Norway, with similar Nordic state–civil society traditions to Denmark, where energy policy has been captured by sectoral interests (Cumbers, 2012, ch 8)?

Perhaps the most important broader lesson from the Danish renewables experience relates to the renewal of public engagement and participation in the economy, evident not just through the proliferation of cooperative forms of ownership but also the formation of key industry and sectoral associations. Of course, these do not necessarily lead to progressive ends: the forms of cooperation evident here contain a large amount of economic self-interest in as much as they encourage public virtue. Thus it is a moot point as to how far the Danish experience here inculcates a more solidaristic set of economic practices and values. At the same time, they could lead to new forms of exclusions, particular of poorer electricity consumers who lack the income to buy a stake in new cooperative and community ventures. Additionally, as the DONG controversy illustrates, Denmark is prone to the same conflicts over resource appropriation occurring elsewhere between elite and increasingly financialised, rent-seeking interests on the one hand and a broader sense of the common good on the other. Danish society's continuing commitment to mutualism also sits uneasily with its recent history of growing anti-immigrant sentiment and the propensity since 2000 to elect more neoliberal and neo-conservative coalitions. Nevertheless, the creation and regeneration of 'knowledgeable publics' in the energy sphere, responding to the demands of earlier radical thinkers such as Dewey and Wright Mills (see Mattson, 2002), is surely critical in the battle to create economic and social alternatives to neoliberalism in the years ahead.

The Danish case also illuminates the growing conflict in the battle of ideas over economic development between an elite discourse that seeks to manage change from above in a way that is to the benefit of established interests, and which, in its latest neoliberal form, attempts to construct markets and maintain a sacrosanct commitment to private property rights and an idealised notion of competition (that at the same time masks the continued pursuit of powerful corporate vested interests) against an alternative vision of a deliberative and democratic policy formation. However, the argument here is that we need to go beyond a recent tendency in much critical left thinking (for example, Hardt and Negri, 2009; Holloway, 2010) that tends to juxtapose a 'top-down' and undemocratic model of economic decision making, whether of a statist or neoliberal kind, against a more virtuous bottom-up process of participatory economic democracy. Certainly, the Danish case demonstrates the possibilities for a more decentred form of public ownership that contains important elements of community-based and localised elements. It also shows the need to draw on non-state forms of collective organisation, particularly more traditional cooperative and mutualist forms that can play an important role in engaging a broader public in economic decision making. But the Danish experience also emphasises the importance of higher-level state coordination and planning mechanisms in achieving progressive policy goals in tackling climate change. In this respect, the recent influence of neoliberal policy formation and discourse in the Nordic states, the deep hostility to strategic planning and the use of market-based directives and procedures – driven in part by broader EU regulatory change – may pose a long-term threat to the persistence of the more cooperative tendencies and models developed to date.

Neoliberalism allied to a growing right populism throughout Europe and the world more generally are hardly conducive to the kinds of solidaristic economic practices and values articulated here. But, whatever the current difficulties from the broader political and economic landscape, the Danish case here points to the need for an economics of toleration and diversity in fostering different forms of collective ownership to achieve progressive policy goals where different traditions of the 'common good' are marshalled together in pursuit of common goals. In particular, Denmark's experience shows the possibilities of fusing social democratic inspired visions of state-led public ownership with both older traditions and newer experiments in grassroots mutualism. The diverse forms of collective ownership that seem to operate within Denmark also bring to mind Gibson-Graham's call for a left politics that 'work(s) towards a way of thinking that might place us alongside our political others, mutually reconizable as oriented in the same direction even if pursuing different paths' (Gibson-Graham, 2006, p 8).

Notes

[1] Denmark has long tradition of local electricity companies being run on a not-for-profit basis (Hadjilambrinos, 2000).

[2] Danish Wind Turbine Owners Association, http://energiayhistud.ee/wp-content/uploads/2015/01/Danish-wind-coops-2009.pdf.

[3] www.dkvind.dk/html/eng/eng.html (accessed October 2015).

[4] The actual oil and coal fired power stations are owned by the Danish state oil company DONG and Vattenfall, a subsidiary of the Swedish state-owned corporation. Gas distribution is also in the hands of either state-owned or municipal companies.

[5] British government decisions to embark on massive, high-risk and high-cost nuclear expansion both in the 1950s and today (with the recently announced deals with Chinese players to replace an older generation of power stations) involved almost no democratic accountability or critical public engagement (Cumbers, 2012).

[6] Economic liberalism has also run alongside an increasing nationalism and social conservatism, particularly in its immigration policy, which has become one of the most hardline in Europe since 2001.

[7] See the recent controversy generated by the right-wing think tank CEPOS's claims about the cost of wind turbines and the subsequent response by a number of esteemed Danish academics (CEPOS, 2009; Lund et al, 2010).

References

Andersen, P.H. and Dreyer, I. (2008) 'Systemic innovation in a distributed network: the case of Danish wind turbines, 1972-2007', *Strategic Organization*, 6(1): 13–46.

CEPOS (Centre for Political Studies) (2009) *Wind Energy: The case of Denmark*. Copenhagen: CEPOS.

Cumbers, A. (2012) *Reclaiming Public Ownership: Making Space for Economic Democracy*. London: Zed Books.

DEA (Danish Energy Agency) (2007) *Danish Electricity Supply: Statistical Survey*. Copenhagen: DEA.

DEA (2010) *Danish Energy Policy 1970–2010*. Copenhagen: DEA.

DEA (2013) *Energy Statistics 2013*. Copenhagen: DEA.EEA (European Environment Agency) (2004) *Energy subsidies in the European Union, a brief overview*. EEA Technical Report 1/2004. Copenhagen: EEA.

Esping-Anderson, G. (1990) *Three Worlds of Welfare Capitalism*. Cambridge, MA: Harvard University Press. Gibson-Graham, J.K. (2006) *A Post-Capitalist Politics*. Minneapolis, MN: University of Minnesota Press.

Hadjilambrinos, C. (2000) 'Understanding technology choice in electricity industries: a comparative study of France and Denmark', *Energy Policy*, 28: 1111-1126.

Hardt, M. and Negri, A. (2009) *Commonwealth*. Cambridge, MA: Harvard University Press.

Heymann (1999) 'A fight of systems? Wind power and electric power systems in Denmark, Germany, and the USA', *Centaurus*, 41: 112-36.

Holloway, J. (2010) *Crack Capitalism*. London: Pluto. Hudson, M. (2012) *The Bubble and Beyond: Fictitious Capital, Debt Deflation and the Global Crisis*. Dresden: Islet.

IEA (International Energy Agency) (2006) *Energy Policies of OECD Countries: Denmark 2006 Review*. Paris: IEA.

Jensen, I.K. (2003) *Mænd I Modvind (Men Facing Headwinds)*. Copenhagen: Børsen.

Kruse, J. and Maegard, P. (2008) 'An authentic story about how a local community became self-sufficient in pollution-free energy and created a source of income for the citizens', *The Commoner*, 13: 129-139.

Lauber, V. and E. Schenner (2011) 'The struggle over support schemes for renewable electricity in the European Union: a discursive-institutionalist analysis', *Environmental Politics*, 20, 508-27.

Lockwood, M. (2015) *The Danish System of Electricity Policy-making and Regulation*, EPG Working Paper 1504. Exeter: University of Exeter.

Lund, H., Hvelplund, F., Østergaard, P.A., Möller, B., Mathiesen, B.V., Andersen, A., Morthorst, P.E., Karlsson, K., Meibom, P., Münster, M., Munksgaard, J., Karnøe, P., Wenzel, H. and Lindboe, H.H. (2010) *Danish Wind Power: Export and Cost*. Aalborg: Aalborg University.

Mattson, K. (2002) *Intellectuals in Action: The Origins of the New Left and Radical Liberalism, 1945-1970*. University Park, PA: Penn State University Press.

Mazzucato, M. (2011) *The Entrepreneurial State: Debunking Public v Private Sector Myths*. London: Anthem.

Meadows, D.H., Meadows, D.L., Randers, J. and Behrens III, W.W. (1972) *The Limits to Growth*. New York, NY: Universe Books.

Meyer, N.I. and Koefoed, A.L. (2003) 'Danish energy reform: policy implications for renewables', *Energy Policy*, 31: 597–607.

Moller, B. (2010) 'Spatial analyses of emerging and fading wind energy landscapes in Denmark', *Land Use Policy*, 27: 233–41.

Mouffe, C. (2005) *On the Political*. London: Routledge.

Neurath, O. (1945) 'Physicalism, planning and the social sciences: bricks prepared for a discussion v. Hayek', *Otto Neurath Nachlass in Haarlem*, 202 K.56, 2 July.

Pedersen, O. (2006) 'Denmark's negotiated economy', in J L. Campbell, J. A. Hall and O.K. Pedersen (eds) *National Identity and a Variety of Capitalism: The Case of Denmark*. Montreal: McGill University Press.

Realdania and Monday Morning (2012) *2050 Something's Green in the State of Denmark: Scenarios for a Sustainable Economy*. Copenhagen: Realdania and Monday Morning.

Ryland, E. (2010) 'Danish wind power policy: domestic and international forces', *Environmental Politics*, 19(1): 80–85.

Soerensen, H.C., Hansen, L.K. Hammarlund, K. and Larsen, J.H. (2003) 'Experience with and strategies for public involvement in offshore wind projects', Paper presented at seminar on National Planning Procedures for Offshore Wind Energy in the EU, Institute for Infrastructure, Environment and Innovation, Brussels, June.

State of Green (2014) *Wind Energy Moving Ahead: Think Denmark White Papers for a Green Transition*. Copenhagen: State of Green.

Tranaes, F. (undated) 'Danish wind energy cooperatives', Part 4, http://ele.aut.ac.ir/~wind/en/articles/coop.htm, accessed June 2012.

Wright, E.O. (2010) *Envisioning Real Utopias*. London: Verso.

ELEVEN

Solidarity economy policy dialogue in Latin America: transferring Argentine experience of social currency to Brazil

Paul I. Singer and Heloisa H. Primavera

The solidarity economy

The solidarity economy (SE) is a mode of production originally conceived in Europe by workers as a defensive reaction against their proletarianisation by the first Industrial Revolution during the 19th century. Before they were forced to become wage labourers in the newly invented factories, these workers had been autonomous artisans, who used to sell their products directly to consumers or to merchants in the then widespread 'putting out' system. As wage workers they had to submit themselves to the orders of the employers, working very long hours to get a meagre wage (Singer 1975; 1977; 1980a). Poverty and insecurity became their lot: the business cycle periodically made many of them unemployed, and each advance of technical progress made the skills of many of them obsolete, turning them again into unskilled labourers and exposing them to the fate of long-term unemployment. In the defence of their status as autonomous producers, labourers unable to individually withstand the mortal competition of industrial capitalism invented the labour cooperative, which is the cornerstone of what is known now as social economy in Europe and elsewhere. Over a century later, this new mode of production evolved into very different forms and is currently most often referred to as social and solidarity economy (SSE) in intercontinental dialogues.

In our view, the historical origin of the SSE explains its main characteristics: the social and solidarity enterprise is the joint property of all persons who work in it. The cooperative was invented to escape oppression by capital, so equality is one of the main values of the SSE. The social capital of the cooperative is equally shared by all workers, who become members or associates of their enterprise. Each member has an equal share of the capital of the cooperative. From this fact derives equal rights of each of them to take part in decision making in their enterprise. Decisions are taken mostly in assemblies, in which all members take part with equal rights: one vote for each person (Singer, 1980b; 1983; 1987).

Cooperatives are *designed to be* democratic and egalitarian organisations and in order to remain so they *should not* have employees. Their principle is necessarily that anyone who is a member must work in the cooperative, and anyone who works in it must be a member. What distinguishes cooperatives from capitalist enterprises is that they are *associations of individuals who bring capital*, which means that, in some cases, each associate owns the firm to the extent that he or she invests money in it and decisions are taken by votes that are proportional to the amount of capital furnished by each associate. Capitalist enterprises are characterised by high levels of inequality in the distribution of decision-making power; usually a relatively small number of large investors or a manager make the decisions. The members of this group usually own the majority of the shares, and this enables them to take decisions without having to consider the opinions or desires of the other associates (Singer, 1980b; 1983; 1987).

While not all cooperatives in the global North are formed by associates who each contribute their capital to the collective, this issue has been a source of vivid debates in the space of the SE in Brazil, where most cooperatives are created by workers, the majority of whom are poor or very poor. In this the Brazilian experience is somehow different from the labour cooperatives in the global North. One of the most important challenges labour cooperatives face almost everywhere is the need for capital in order to develop their productive capacity, meet growing demands for their products and services, and to meet the needs of workers who would like to join the cooperative, but who are prohibited from joining it as they do not have the required amounts of money necessary in order to become a share-owning member who has made an investment in the cooperative. The need for more capital by labour cooperatives, that is those composed of associates who contribute their labour power, comes also from competition for market share with capitalist enterprises that are able to deploy scale advantages that increase labour productivity. Labour cooperatives are able to compete when more workers use the same equipment at different hours and thereby increase output without expanding fixed costs. In this case enlarged collective labour productivity, rather than increased individual productivity, enables the cooperative to sell its products at lower prices than its competitors.

Capitalist firms have more access to credit in order to finance investments than cooperatives for different reasons. Capitalist enterprises are usually owned either by wealthy families with existing business interests who are able to fund investments from their own resources, or are able to raise capital from banks, share issues, venture capital and/or investment funds. The fortunes of these families and the assets of these banks and funds function as collateral for new loans to enterprises that have valuable associates such as a strong track record and a positive balance sheet. This is not the case for labour cooperatives. Therefore there is the temptation for needy cooperatives to raise new capital by selling shares in the capital market. But if they do this they must give the new capitalist associates a proportional amount of decision-making power, thereby violating and diluting the essence of a labour cooperative, which is that all power to participate in decision making belongs to the workers, and only to them.

Since the interests of capitalists and of workers are completely different, enterprises that are owned by workers and capitalists cannot avoid engaging in these conflicts. For instance, capitalists always want to maximise return from their investments, which implies that the joint enterprise should always invest more, even if this implies taking out more loans, which leads to well-known capital accumulation dynamics and to ever-increasing indebtedness, and finally to the dominance of the coop by capital. The interests of the workers are that the cooperative fulfils its social programme, which has as its first priority the need to secure decent labour opportunities for its working associates, and as its second priority, the need to create opportunities for new worker associates. Workers as consumers may become indebted in order to satisfy the needs and wants of themselves and/or their families. But this is completely different from the permanent craving of capitalists for speculative investments in order to defeat rivals and to prove to everyone that he or she is a winner.

In order to fulfil their social programmes and/or merely to survive in the daily battle to sell their products at prices that at least cover their costs and preferably generate some surplus (which is completely different from the endless greed to earn ever more as an end in itself, which is the distinguishing mark of present-day capitalism), labour coops must provide their own sources of capital and credit, the accumulation of which is governed by their own principles of solidarity, equity and democracy (Singer 1993; 1997; 1999b; 2000; 2002).

The emergence of the solidarity economy in Brazil

These were the basic assumptions underpinning the launch of a new state secretariat in the Ministry of Labour and Employment in Brazil, created in 2003 as SENAES (National Secretariat for Solidarity Economy), which, at the time of writing (September 2016), was still in existence despite the removal from power of President Dilma Rousseff. It is absolutely necessary to emphasise that this secretariat was created as a result of a long-lasting engagement of activists in the Workers' Party with previously existing strong social movements such as the Landless Rural Workers' Movement (Movimento dos Trabalhadores Rurais Sem Terra, or MST) and the rising Brazilian Network of Solidarity Economy. This chapter discusses some of the achievements and obstacles encountered.

The SE may be viewed as a social movement that emerged in the 1970s, during the military dictatorships in Latin America. Leading cases include those from Chile, Peru, Colombia, Mexico and Brazil, all with very different strategies. Razeto (1990), Coraggio (1999) and Cattani (2005) have made significant contributions to the evolving SE.

We may consider a common characteristic of every SE model as being:

> … the fruit of the organisation of workers in the construction of a new economic model, their social practices being based on relations of solidarity partnership, and inspired by cultural values where men and women are protagonists and the purpose of the economic activity, and not the private accumulation of wealth in general and capital in particular. (Singer, 2002)

These new practices of production and consumption privilege collective work, self-management, social justice, care of the environment and responsibilities towards future generations. The SE movement has grown quickly not only in Brazil, but also in many other countries.

This development is due to a number of factors. First, it is a response to the resistance of male and female workers to increasing exclusion, urban unemployment and rural exodus as a result of the aggressive expansion of globalisation, rendering more and more people completely dispensable in terms of running the production and consumption machine. This opposition is expressed first as a struggle for survival, with the creation of an increasing informal market, where many popular economy initiatives pop up, including street vendors, parking watchers and many other activities generally focused on the reproduction of life, for individuals and families. Thanks to the initiative of several actors, such resistance is also expressed as associate, shared actions focused on the reproduction of life as well, but taking a further step by developing other structures for economic organisation based on values like life and solidarity, rather than profit and the indiscriminate amassment of money: this is the SE that is developing and growing at a quick pace.

Second, and particularly in Brazil, the growth of SE as a movement – going beyond isolated, independent actions, and organising itself into a more coherent movement connecting disparate networks and struggles – took a significant leap forward with the World Social Forums, a privileged space where different actors, organisations, initiatives and solidarity economy enterprises were able to develop an integrated strategy that resulted in the creation of SENAES. Alongside this secretariat, the Brazilian Forum of Solidarity Economy (FBES) was created in order to represent the SE movement in Brazil. It is necessary to acknowledge that these two organisations, plus the World Social Forum, led to significant levels of growth in the SE in Brazil, and in many ways structured this process.

The FBES is structured so as to build connections between the three segments of the SE movement: solidarity economy enterprises, advisory and fostering organisations, and public sector managers. The SE enterprises are, nevertheless, the leading performers and the target of the movement, making up most of the representation in all the FBES decision-making levels.

It is worth mentioning here some of the manifestations of the SE so we can understand the significance and heterogeneity of the SE enterprises segment: cooperatives (production, services, consumption, trading and solidarity credit); popular associations; production and service informal groups; recovered self-managed companies (former capitalist companies that went out of business and were recovered by the workers); solidarity and rotation credit funds (organised both informally or under several legal systems); solidarity exchange clubs and groups (sometimes using a social or community currency); networks and associations for trading and for supportive production chains; solidarity tourist agencies; and many others. For SENAES, the criteria for recognition of SE enterprises are the principles and values contained in the Charter of the Solidarity Economy, whose main points are the self-management of their internal organisation and the fact that they organise economic activity beyond the family network.

Another segment of the movement is formed by its advisory and fostering organisations, which are organised as non-profit organisations (NGOs) or universities (technological incubators and extension groups). These offer support and development services to the solidarity economy enterprises, either in the form of training actions (technical, financial, economical and political), or in the form of direct support (structure, consultancy, project development and/or credit offer) for the incubation and promotion of SE enterprises.

The third segment of the FBES is the public sector managers, formed of representatives of the local and regional governments, with programmes clearly focused on the SE. This segment is represented at national level by a network of public sector managers, holding a seat in the FBES National Coordination as one of the national public organisations/networks.

The FBES represents the SE movement at federal, regional and local level, through its National Coordination and state and local forums, and has links with domestic and international organisations, networks and associations.

A Charter and a Platform of the Solidarity Economy were initially created in 2003, and both initiatives are in continuous development. While the charter supplies the basic elements of the movement, the platform establishes the main targets to be attained and serves as a document to support the discussions within the SENAES and other public organisations. The Platform of the Solidarity Economy was fully approved by SENAES in its long-term plan of action, and details seven courses of action: social organisation of the SE movement; production, trading and consumption networks; solidarity finances; legal frameworks; education; communication; and the democratisation of knowledge and technology.

The main achievements of these 12 years of activity at SENAES, in which it is important to emphasise a constant exercise of participatory democracy, inside and outside the government, may be summarised as follows:

- *programmes and activities*, including support for associativism and social cooperativism; for the promotion of popular cooperatives; for regional, sustainable territorial development and the solidarity economy; for the treatment of solid waste; and for SE approaches to development;
- *a system of information on the SE*: a permanent system of information accessed by different users (unemployed people and small initiatives, as well as universities and organisations that provide support to cooperative, self-managed initiatives);[1]
- *an atlas of SE initiatives*: the publication of information resulting from a national mapping exercise, available in two different editions,

completed in 2007 and 2013, with the support of several universities and specialised NGOs. It reveals the existence of over 30,000 initiatives distributed in all regions of the country, involving three million people;[2]

- *national conferences*: in 2006, 2010 and 2014, national conferences on the SE gathered representatives workers, support institutions and different levels of government from all regions of the country.

In addition to these formal manifestations at national level, there is also a network of agencies in states of all regions and in many local governments, as well as inside the formal structure of public administration.

Given the impeachment and removal from power of Dilma Rouseff in 2016, the solidarity economy in Brazil will certainly face new challenges if it is to survive and prosper. At the time of writing, at least part of SENAES had survived the political changes. However, to understand the full potential of the SE, it is necessary to think more widely about what its possibilities could be. We will address this with an example of the development of social currencies in Brazil, as an exemplar of both innovative practice and as yet untapped potential.

A case study of social currency: from barter clubs to e-money as a tool for community development

Since the first government of the Workers' Party in 2003 (President Lula da Silva), a major issue in Brazil has been the formalisation of many informal, and consequently precarious, economic activities through the promotion of new self-managed economic activities with cooperative principles, through an active partnership with different levels of government and with contributions from support organisations. This innovation was initiated by the FBES, and the effectiveness of this policy and its evolution over more than 12 years bears witness to the bottom-up construction of a public policy.

One of the initiatives SENAES supported from the very beginning was the creation of social currency groups promoted by communities, especially those inspired by the Argentine model known as 'barter clubs'. Although barter networks using social currencies had declined in Argentina, in Brazil several initiatives developed and evolved into quite different models. The most significant one is certainly the Brazilian Network of Community Development Banks, which by 2015 had over 120 branches all over the country, supporting several hundred thousand small initiatives by new entrepreneurs and their families. In December 2015, during the 4th National Meeting of the Network of Community Banks, a new association named Banco Nacional das

Comunidades (National Bank of Communities) was created in order to legally represent all units in the country.[3]

It is important to understand the evolution of this particular model, due to its significance with regard to the persistence of political and financial crises, not only in Latin America, but worldwide. One of the major innovations of SENAES was its support to grassroots initiatives, which rarely get significant levels of support from national governments and/or central banks. A number of complementary currencies based on innovative economic theories, such as that of Silvio Gesell (1918), have emerged since the early 1930s and the Great Depression. The most famous and inspirational example occurred in the small village of Wörgl in Austria, where a negative-interest currency was used for two years and reduced unemployment significantly. Its multiplication was considered 'inconvenient' by the Austrian Central Bank, which prevented the spread of the phenomenon. The same issue would occur 60 years later in Brazil, in the small village of Campina do Monte Alegre in the state of São Paulo, where the 'Campino Real' community currency operated for two years, until the Brazilian Central Bank agreed to manage its closure so that a 'bad example' of a flawed local currency design would not spread (see Primavera, 2003). We must understand the rise of barter clubs in Argentina in this context: a group of underemployed professionals was inspired by an innovative multi-level marketing system that began to grow in Latin America in the 1990s, and whose main business was to form networks of distributors and consumers for a multinational company. They introduced the concept of the 'prosumer', coined by Alvin Toffler (1980) in *The Third Wave,* meaning that all participants should necessarily be *pro*ducers and con*sumers* in the network.

The first barter club (so called to avoid taxation of transactions) was then founded by 23 workers in a garage in Bernal, exchanging goods and services they themselves produced. Strictly speaking it was really an exchange group and not a barter club, insofar as some sort of currency was involved. Due to the ease of reproducing the system and the impossibility of controlling what occurred in the whole country by the founding group, without a professionalised system of registration and accounting, the concept was adopted by others who immediately began to dispute who could or could not issue a community currency, and thus destroying the very essence of the original product.

The Argentine model of barter club transmuted to Brazil

Perhaps the least visible, less studied and still most significant characteristic of Argentinian barter networks was their organisation of self-management at regular (sometimes weekly) assemblies of 'nodes' (units of exchange groups), at a regional level, and at monthly inter-zone assemblies at a national level, at which community currency activists periodically elected delegates charged with organising a set of rules from below, for the functioning of the network in all its aspects. That phenomenon was emphasised by North and Huber (2004) and North (2007) in a detailed field research project just after the 2001 political economic crisis.

Although Powell (2002), Hintze (2003), Coraggio (1995, 1999) and North (2007) have documented the emergence of barter networks, we nevertheless consider a more profound comprehension of the complexity of this phenomenon to be necessary. There is a need for a systemic analysis of barter networks that understands its economic, political, cultural and administrative aspects. Even though works by Gomez (2008, 2009) include a more complex, relatively detailed analysis of the phenomenon, we argue that a deeper, multidimensional analysis will enable us to clarify the difficulties of maintaining complementary currencies over time. Too often ideas have been imported from out of their context into a new environment, and the networks fail to grow. Too often, they disappear after some time or they stay small, despite the efforts of those few people who put much energy into developing something that in relation to its benefits should flow naturally.

In this context, the process of diffusion of the Argentine model of social currency to other countries in the region took place, and innovations were made elsewhere, mainly in cases where previous social capital existed. Thanks to the presence of different systems in other countries and the incessant interest of people keen to reproduce the Argentine phenomenon, the model spread to Brazil, Uruguay, Chile, Ecuador, Colombia, Peru, Bolivia, El Salvador, Honduras, Paraguay, Cuba and Venezuela. In some of these countries similar systems were already known, but the simplicity of the administration of the Argentine model meant that it could be easily installed and in many cases it replaced previous systems. Nevertheless, during the crisis of the system in Argentina, these early experiments, with the exception of some initiatives in Brazil, did not take off (Primavera, 2005, 2006).

In Brazil, the first barter club inspired by the Argentinian model was created in 1998 in São Paulo and is still in existence – an example of an autonomous, grassroots, self-management model operating without any support from the state. It was subsequently disseminated to other state capitals in the country such as Rio de Janeiro, Curitiba, Florianopolis and Porto Alegre among others, and in 2004 the First National Barter Groups Meeting took place, supported by the national government. While there are no recent official statistics, it is estimated that more than 200 local currencies exist in the country supporting barter systems that are self-managed and are supported by community organisations and/or universities.

In 2000, the Argentine model of barter clubs was officially introduced in Brazil at the first meeting of the Brazilian Solidarity Economy Network, in the village of Mendes, Rio de Janeiro state. This was the occasion at which the social currency model came into contact with the pioneering Banco Palmas, a particular micro-credit system that had been developed in 1998 in a favela on the outskirts of the city of Fortaleza, Ceará state, one of the poorest in the north-east. A few months later, the pioneering currency *palmares* was implemented with a lot of enthusiasm from local leaders. Two years later, at the end of 2002, with financing from the Dutch organisation STRO,[4] another project was implemented – Projeto Fomento (Promotion Project) – which launched the *palmas* social currency for the construction of a modest building which would offer SE training in the neighbourhood. Contracts were made with local businessmen and with providers of basic services such as gasoline, gas for cooking and public transportation. In 2006, this blend of micro-credit and social currency led to the initiative winning the Award for Social Innovation granted by the Bank of Brazil Foundation, the most important public bank in the country.

The support from the national government through SENAES would soon lead to the formation of a National Network of Community Development Banks to implement the *palmas* initiative in other regions in the country:[5] there are now over 120 such initiatives. In November 2009, during the Forum of Social Inclusion and Microfinances, the Central Bank of Brazil reversed a world trend and signed an agreement with the national government and the Instituto Banco Palmas to support the creation and networking of associative community banks. This represents a significant achievement: a recognition of the limits of the conventional money system and a recognition of the value of alternative proposals.[6]

It is also important to recognise that the current model of associative community banks with social currency in force in Brazil[7] creatively integrates the Argentine model of social currency with the strategy of micro-credit of the Banco Palmas and an important government aid initiative. This new approach obliged different social actors such as entrepreneurs, grassroots productive organisations and government entities to consider a different viewpoint before launching their new prototypes. We may assume that all the protoypes changed as a result of this process.

This is not, however, the only model in Brazil We can identify at least other types of social currency in the country:

- barter clubs inspired by the former Argentine model, most of which remain as small non-organised groups inside small communities, mainly in the states of São Paulo and Parana; some of them turn to the Community Development Bank model when they establish relations with local governments;
- short-term social currencies inspired by educational activities and used at events such as the World Social Forum (for example, the Txai currency used in Porto Alegre in 2005 and in Caracas in 2006), local SE fairs and the international Solidarity Economy Fair of Santa Maria, in the state of Rio Grande do Sul, with its Mate currency. Other frequent examples are found in universities among students with different goals, from exchanging used or new books to celebrating the experience of a non-monetary unit of trade such as the Grandino used at Universidade Federal de Rio Grande;[8]
- alternative currencies that have emerged since 2001 and are used by a growing community of youngsters promoting cultural activities, mainly in the music field. In recognition of the place where they started − the city of Cuiabá, in the state of Mato Grosso, inner Amazonian Brazil − these groups name themselves Fora do Eixo (Out of the Axis), meaning they are far away and isolated from the main axis of cities like São Paulo, Rio de Janeiro, Belo Horizonte and so on. These groups began by promoting cultural events involving new young rock bands, which soon started using a currency named Cubo Card. From these small beginnings, hundreds of different currencies evolved all over the country. They are mainly used to share resources to improve conditions for cultural production and performances, and address issues around intellectual property for CD and audiovisual materials. FDE is now a well-known, polemical brand among youngsters and 'altermondalist' activists (see Savazoni, 2014).

Reflections on processes of monetary innovation North and South

Social currencies in Latin America are extremely innovative examples of the SSE model of development, thanks both to their specific formats and the alliances through which they are promoted. Bearing in mind the fact that that developments in Brazil were inspired by the Argentine model, which had its problems, it seems useful to draw parallels with perhaps more effective initiatives in Europe, as they can provide inspiration for the project of expanding the scope of social currencies as a necessary innovation tool in both the global North and South. These include Sol in France,[9] the Regio system, launched in 2003 in Germany, and in particular the Chiemgauer model[10] and the WIR Bank, in Switzerland, created in 1934[11] and still in existence. Of particular note are more than 70 examples of local social currency in Spain that have emerged since the 2010 Eurozone crisis.[12] These range from very small localised groups such as Boniato (in Madrid) to local currencies based on waste recycling, the expanding Faircoin of the Integral Cooperative of Catalunya, the cultural Puma (in Sevilla) and the Ekhi (in Bilbao), which keeps demurrage (negative interest))[13] at the core of its model (Hughes, 2015).

The concept of a 'social' currency as an innovative concept characterised by the sovereignty of money issued by a *community*[14] over other parallel, complementary currencies issued by individuals (in the case of Local Exchange Trading Schemes or Green Dollars), enterprises or local governments was first proposed by Primavera (1999, 2000, 2001a, 2001b). A decade later, three different international meetings gathering academics and activists have taken place with 'social currencies' at their core – 2011 in Lille (France), 2013 in The Hague (Netherlands) and 2015 in Salvador (Brazil) – at which both academics and social currency activists, working together, have progressed the evolution of new, and necessary, theories to explain and analyse real-world developments in the field. A simple distinction such as 'social currency', to name a new social practice, can be left outside the field of theory, or can be taken as a starting point to renew theory as nature itself does through processes of evolution: 'differentiate, select and amplify' (Beinhocker, 2006). Guided by Beinhocker, we can track the transformation of a simple barter club in a Buenos Aires neighbourhood into a community development bank with an electronic social currency installed in the heart of a fertile public policy in Brazil. There are not enough comparative studies of this wide diversity of monetary innovation, but what is certain is that they all have ambitions to become much more significant such that they create *another market*, not just a special-purpose, complementary currency alongside state-issued money, but are generally fail to achieve this. That is why we believe new theory is necessary: we do not know enough about why some models grow significantly and others do not.

Such a diversity and proliferation of the financial mechanisms discussed here do not engage with the entirety of the field of *possible* models and proposals (rather than projects and theories), but are reflections of *realities* that already exist and could certainly be articulated more effectively in a synergistic way to face a crisis that is far from being overcome. In our view, the current global crisis is not just a temporary financial or economic crisis, but should rather be seen as a *paradigmatic* crisis, given the frequency with which financial 'crises' occur. These are an intrinsic part of the system, and it is hard to conceive of any kind of significant change without recourse to and the development of innovations that clearly disrupt the system (Primavera, 2006, 2013).

If we want to approach the current 'crisis which is not such' – since it is part of capitalism itself and not an unexpected, abnormal event – that is, if we want to change this state of affairs, it should be done in a systemic way rather than in the localised, partial and fragmented way that has been the case thus far. The innovations mentioned here are part of the SE as a new model of development, not just a component of antipoverty policy. Social currencies, in which the community is the sovereign money-issuing entity, and in which the creation and management of money by communities is a political practice, are more than a mere complementary currency within the traditional model of development. Hence we would stress the importance of cooperation by the distinct social actors in the development of social currencies, as in the case of the Brazilian Network of Associative Community Banks, the Sol project in France and the National Barter System of Venezuela. On the other hand, different financial institutions may create useful complementary currencies without the participation of their 'clients' such as the WIR Bank in Switzerland, cooperative banks and conglomerates of various-sized enterprises. Through new forms of cooperation, it should be possible to develop more robust incarnations of social currencies that facilitate solidaristic models for communities without relying exclusively on private bank and state-issued money.

The contribution of the SE to a new global economy

While much has been done, the challenge remains to coordinate different social actors, ongoing projects and initiatives to facilitate the emergence of new forms of living and exchanging within and without the SE. On the one hand, we are witnessing a wide range of 'monetary' innovations within the formal, capitalist economy (for example, bank cheques, sales coupons, company coupons, loyalty cards, airline miles systems, luncheon tickets and so on). On the other hand, we have the growth of a range of community currencies, forms of social money that have grown up outside the formal economy and, in some cases, overtly reject its values and systems.

With the exception of SENAES in Brazil, social currencies have not been taken seriously, either by governments and academics, as a tool to support the growth of a new, emancipatory economy based on concepts of sufficiency and solidarity. In this context, they have tremendous potential. The most political expression of subversion of the economy is the creation of money: the act of issuing one's own currency as a means of exchange is a way to return power to producers and consumers, the protagonists of the real economy who have been displaced by the privatised and speculative financial system.

It is no less true that for some pioneers of complementary currencies, the first approach was instrumental: a strategy to fight against unemployment and achieve social inclusion, trying to put those excluded by 'structural adjustment' on the map. However, the experience of the barter clubs' social currencies in practice led to a realisation of the extent of previously unrecognised possibilities for production and consumption, of the possibility of abundance in the context of apparent scarcity. Everything seemed possible: as value and price could be separated, cooperation and solidarity could be manifested.

There are two key features of social currencies that are central in understanding how they came to be crucial in underpinning an economy of solidarity. First, the social currency units used were never 'scarce', but always 'sufficient'. Members of the schemes could 'buy and sell' with social currencies or get financing because *trust* was the raw material for the groups that met regularly. There was then abundance without waste, 'sufficient abundance'. Second, when someone accumulated social currencies and they did not need, they were lent to someone who needed them and then returned without interest. This behaviour, which flies in the face of the capitalist economic paradigm, was possible because the 'sufficiency' of currency had eliminated the need for interest. It never occurred to anyone to ask why there was no interest: those who practised this new economy understood it better than finance ministers and bankers. They understood that a social currency is not a commodity, of value in its own right, to be traded for profit. This understanding of money as simply a medium of exchange undermined both the scarcity paradigm and the impulse towards competition that characterise capitalism (Kennedy, 1998; Lietaer, 2001).

We are living in a time of deep transition when it is necessary to make some assumptions about what might be possible. We share a fundamental belief that democracy represents not only an ideal, but also the most likely route to achieving sustainability. We say this in the context of Brazil, which, as the recent coup shows, has stretched the boundaries of possibilities of challenging inequality within the conventional economic paradigm to the limit, and, as a result, is facing considerable political obstacles.

In spite of this it is possible to be optimistic about trends towards a more participatory and democratic approach towards economic life, mainly represented by the diffusion of the SE paradigm in Latin America and the European Union. France has recently adopted laws for the promotion of the SSE, as a fundamental democratic model. In Brazil, as well as SENAES, a significant movement has evolved that has revitalised small rural properties, supported by a new Ministry of Family Agriculture, and this additional food production is enough to feed the whole country. Large landed properties are still able to sell their production into the world market. Alongside this, the social movement of landless workers (MST) now represents more than 1.5 million people and has been slowly expanding since the early 1980s. It follows the principles of organic agriculture, as do other similar initiatives that are less well organised but have a nationwide following. Ecological agriculture has proved to be efficient both in terms of quality of crops produced and in terms of protecting the environment. The quality of rice produced with this model is recognised as excellent and consumed nationwide.

When we consider the SE in Brazil, we must recognise that it represents currently 3% of GDP, involves 3 million people, and includes over 30,000 production initiatives. Among these, special reference must be made to the Brazilian Network of Community Development Banks, which issues its own social, local currencies, a truly life-saving venture in poor communities. Women are strongly involved in these initiatives, which are expanding worldwide. The full flavour of the diversity of the Brazilian SE can be gathered from the work of Bénédicte Manier (2012), who gathers together thousands of different ongoing global initiatives, in which women, young people, black people, indigenous communities and all kinds of minorities resist the exclusion that the system insists on pushing them towards.

Rethinking the economy is at the core of these transformations, which intersect with every social activity: livelihoods, energy production, healthy food production, protection of the environment and, of course, education. New forms of education in which students are challenged to create knowledge by having fun, instead of being bored, show how far these 'silent revolutions' may reach, solving problems with new global approaches, looking to the future as well as transforming the present. While the global capitalist economy now reaches into all corners of the world, alongside it a new economy is coming to life, an economy that is driven by indignation about the oppression of people and planet, and whose central principles are justice and sustainability. Another world is rising and we are happy, indeed, to be living in such a world.

Notes

[1] http://portal.mte.gov.br/ecosolidaria/sistema-nacional-de-informacoes-em-economia-solidaria/

[2] http://sies.ecosol.org.br/atlas

[3] www.institutobancopalmas.org/banco-nacional-das-comunidades

[4] www.stro.org

[5] www.bancopalmas.org.br

[6] www.bcb.gob.br/\pre\acordos_e_convenios\acordo_de_cooperacao_tecnica_BACEN_MTE_SENAES.pdf

[7] www.bancopalmas.org.br/oktiva.net/1235.nota/12311

[8] www.nudese.furg.br/index.php?option=com_content&view=article&id=84&Itemid=100

[9] www.dsi-experts.fr/sol/ and www.sol-reseau-coop

[10] www.chiemgauer.info and www.monneta.org

[11] www.wir.ch

[12] www.economiasolidaria.org/category/temas/moneda_social

[13] This is an innovation by Gesell that operates like a charge on those holding money, whose value decreases steadily over time. This encourages those holding the currency to spend it, thereby increasing the velocity of circulation.

[14] In other words, the community is the issuer of money and is thus sovereign in this respect, much as the state is sovereign in the case of state-issued money.

References

Beinhocker, E. (2006) *The Origin of Wealth. The Radical Remaking of Economics and What it means for Business and Society*. Boston, MA: Harvard Business School Press.

Cattani, A. (ed) (2005) *Dicionário Internacional da Outra Economia*. Porto Alegre: Almedina.

Coraggio, J.L. (1995) *Desarrollo Humano, Economía Popular y Educación*, Buenos Aires, AIQUE-IDEAS.

Coraggio, J.L. (1999) *Política social y economía del trabajo. Alternativas a la política neoliberal para la ciudad*. Madrid: Miño y Dávila.

Gesell, S. (1918) *Die natürlich Wirtschafordnung durch Freiland und Freigeld*. Hamburg: Gauke.

Gomez, G.M. (2008) 'Making Markets. The institutional rise and decline of the Argentine Red de Trueque', PhD thesis, Institute of Social Studies, The Hague.

Gomez, G.M. (2009) *Argentina's Parallel Currency: The economy of the poor*. London: Pickering & Chatto.

Hintze, S. (2003) *Trueque y Economía Solidaria.* Buenos Aires: PNUD/ UNGS Prometeo.

Hughes, N. (2015) 'The Community Currency Scene in Spain', *International Journal of Community Currency Research*, 19, A, 1-11.

Kennedy, M. (1998) *Dinero sin inflación ni tasas de interés.* Buenos Aires: Nuevo Extremo.

Lietaer, B. (2001) *The future of money. Creating new wealth, work and a wiser world.* London: Century.

Manier, B. (2012) *Un million de révolutions tranquilles. Travail, argent, habitat, santé, environnement. Comment les citoyens changent le monde.* Paris: Les Liens qui Libèrent.

North, P. (2007) *Money and Liberation. The Micropolitics of Alternative Currency Movements.* Minneapolis, MN: University of Minnesota Press.

North, P. and Huber, U. (2004) 'Surviving financial meltdown: Barter networks in Argentina', in P. North and U. Huber (eds) *Alternatives spaces of the 'Argentinazo'.* London: Antipode, pp 963-84.

Powell, J. (2002) *Petty capitalism, perfecting capitalism or post-capitalism? Lessons from the argentinian barter network,* Working Papers Series No 357. The Hague: Institute of Social Studies.

Primavera, H. (1999) 'La moneda social de la Red Global de Trueque en Argentina: ¿barajar y dar de nuevo en el juego social?', Paper presented at the International Seminar on the Globalization of Financial Markets and its effects on emergent countries organized by the International Institute Jacques Maritain, CEPAL (Comisión Económica para América Latina) and the Chilean Government, Santiago, 29-31 March 1999.

Primavera, H. (2000) 'Política social, imaginación y coraje: reflexiones sobre la moneda social', *Revista del CLAD Reforma y Democracia*, 17: 161-188.

Primavera, H. (2001a) 'Moneda Social: ¿gattopardismo o ruptura de paradigma?', texto de lanzamiento del Foro Electrónico sobre Moneda Social, http://money.socioeco.org.

Primavera, H. (2001b) 'La moneda social como palanca del nuevo paradigma económico', Cuadernos de Propuestas de la Alianza para un Mundo Responsable, Plural y Solidario, Polo de Socioeconomía Solidaria, Grupo de Trabajo sobre Moneda Social, París, F.P.H., http://money.socioeco.org.

Primavera, H. (2003) 'Dernier tango à Buenos Aires', *Revue du MAUSS*, 21: 113-118.

Primavera, H. (2005) 'Monnaie Sociale', in J.-L. Laville and A.D. Cattani (eds) *Dictionnaire de l'autre économie.* Paris: Desclée de Brouwer, pp 385-393.

Primavera, H. (2006) 'Projet Colibri: un rayonnement de l'économie solidaire?', in J. Blanc (ed) *Exclusions et Liens financiers: Monnaies Sociales, Rapport 2005-6*. Paris: Ecomonica.

Primavera, H. (2013) 'An Economy for the Common Good with Social Currencies', in J. Shantz and J. Macdonald (ed) *Beyond Capitalism. Building Democratic Alternatives for Today and the Future*. New York, NY/London: Bloomsbury.

Razeto, L. (1990) *Economía popular de solidaridad: Identidad y proyecto en una visión integradora*. Santiago: PET.

Savazoni, R. (2014) *Os Novos Bárbaros. A Aventura Política do Fora do Eixo*. Rio de Janeiro: Aeroplano.

Singer, P. (1975) *Curso de Introdução à Economia Política*. Rio de Janeiro: Forense.

Singer, P. (1977) *Economia Política do Trabalho*. São Paulo: Hucitec.

Singer, P. (1980a) *O que é socialismo hoje*. Petrópolis: Vozes.

Singer, P. (1980b) *Guia da inflação para o povo*. Petrópolis: Vozes.

Singer, P. (1983) *Aprender Economia*. São Paulo: Brasiliense.

Singer, P. (1985) *A formação da classe operária*. São Paulo: Atual.

Singer, P. (1987) *O Capitalismo: sua evolução, sua lógica e sua dinâmica*. São Paulo: Moderna.

Singer, P. (1993) *São Paulo's Master Plan, 1989–1992: the politics of urban space*. Washington, DC: Woodrow Wilson International Center for Scholars.

Singer, P. (1997) *Social exclusion in Brazil*. Geneva: International Institute for Labour Studies.

Singer, P. (1998) *Uma Utopia Militante. Repensando o socialismo*. Petrópolis: Vozes.

Singer, P. (1999a) 'Clubes de trueque y Economía Solidaria', *Revista Trueque*, no 2, p 39.

Singer, P. (1999b) *O Brasil na crise: perigos e oportunidades*. São Paulo: Contexto.

Singer, P. (2000) *Para entender o mundo financeiro*. São Paulo: Contexto.

Singer, P. (2002) *Introdução à Economia Solidária*. São Paulo: Editora Fundação Perseu Abramo.

Toffler, A. (1980) *The Third Wave*. London: Harper Collins.

TWELVE

Twenty-first century socialism? Venezuela's solidarity, social, popular and communal economy

Dario Azzellini

Introduction

Perhaps the country whose experiences have inspired solidarity economy practices more than any other is the Venezuela of President Hugo Chávez. The 1999 Constitution defined Venezuela as a 'participatory and protagonistic' democracy, advocating more direct participation and aimed at creating a 'humanist and solidaristic economy'. In 2006, the idea of participation was officially defined in terms of popular power, revolutionary democracy and socialism, which is defined as '21st century socialism,' because it does not follow pre-established guidelines or any one ideology but is under constant development, and includes a wide range of groups and organisations with structural, social and political differences (Azzellini, 2009b). The process of seeking and building 21st century socialism is guided above all by values such as collectivity, equality, solidarity, freedom and sovereignty (MinCI, 2007, p 30) and aims to build a solidarity economy that includes all with dignity.

The Bolivarian process[1] of social transformation is characterised by a 'two-track' approach (Zibechi, 2006): on one side, the state, the institutions and traditional left organisations, and on the other side, movements and organised society. It is a construction process 'from above' and 'from below'. Unlike previous social transformation processes that defined the state as the central actor and motor of change, and considered self-organisation necessary only until the revolutionary party had seized the state, in Venezuela the central agents of change are now the movements, the organised people. The state's role is to support them by being facilitator of the bottom-up processes that will enable the movements and the people to implement the steps needed to transform society. The state has to guarantee the material content necessary for the realisation of the common wealth. This idea had been retiterated on various occasions by Chávez, and it is shared by part of the administration and by the majority of organised movements (Azzellini, 2013, 2017). In an interview with the author, Carlos Luis Rivero, then Vice Minister of the Ministry for Popular Economy, explained:

> "We, as the state, do not see ourselves as representatives of the people. This is a society that must be constructed and led by its citizens in which the state must only be a promoter of that process of participation. But the state is not the transformative element. Entities must be constructed among the people that allow the effective transformation of the reality that we have – the political reality, the economic reality, the cultural reality, the social reality ... that's where the issue of participation comes from. There can't be any transformation without the participation of the people."

Since 2005, the declared strategy of social transformation ha been based on the development of local socio-political and economic organisations, following the idea of communal socialism, which connects not only with Marxist theory, but also with council communism, libertarian socialism and anarcho-syndicalism as well as with historical popular, indigenous and Afro-American experiences throughout Latin American history and traditional forms of indigenous collectivism and communitarianism (Azzellini, 2013). The creation of communal production and consumption cycles, combined with council structures of all kinds and on different levels as a strategy for the transition to socialism, is also based on István Mészáros' book *Beyond Capital* (1995). Local self-administration is meant to recognise socio-cultural economic space as a space to be shaped by communities (in contrast to the political-administrative space that orients official institutions' actions) (Harvey, 2006). The reorganisation of Venezuela's territorial geopolitics through a network of local self-administration aims also at overcoming unequal and antidemocratic geometries of power in the country (Massey, 2009).

Nevertheless, this process has proved contradictory and conflictive. While the new order is supposed to be created from below, the fact that the state controls resources and finally decides how to use them creates an asymmetry of power between self-organisation and state. Moreover, the inherent logic of institutions is to reproduce themselves and retain control over social processes, which contradicts the declared need for an autonomous and free constituent power in order to create the new order and not reproduce the old one. Consequently, this chapter outlines the main features of the envisioned social transformation, the experiences regarding the democratisation of the ownership and management of the means of production, communal self-administration, and the obstacles and contradictions inherent in the process.

Regardless of the very different contexts in which existing Venezuelan movements act, compared with most other movements in the Americas their forms of organisation and struggle as well as their goals are very similar to those of the new movements. Zibechi (2012) describes various self-organised structures in marginalised Venezuelan neighbourhoods along with experiences from other Latin America countries. The Venezuelan movements, communal councils, communes and so on are aimed at building autonomy, with, against and beyond the state. As Andrés Antillano from the Urban Land Committees put it in an interview with the author: "The relation with the state is not defined by us but by the willingness of the state to subordinate itself to the interests of the people".

The two-track approach, the primacy of constituent power and the council system

A key normative idea in the Bolivarian process is the priority of constituent power, understood not as a temporary moment of delegating power and/or sovereignty, but rather as a permanent creative force of the people, which imposes itself, in turn, on the constituted (that is, state) power. Constituent power is the legitimate creative capacity that resides collectively in human beings – the capacity to create something new, without having to derive it from what currently exists and without submitting to what came before. It has been, and is, the source of legitimacy for every revolution, democracy and republic. Historically, however, constituent power was limited in time and range to legitimate the constituted power. The question then becomes how constituent power can maintain its capacity to intervene and shape the present. This is what defines revolution: not the act of taking power, but rather a process of construction, an act of creation and invention (Negri, 1992, p 382). This is the global legacy of the Bolivarian process.

The idea of a constituent power not subordinate to the constituted power, as well as the concept of popular power, points us towards self-organisation, self-management and the institution of councils. With the beginning of Chávez's 2007 presidency, new mechanisms of participation and new councils, which would be built in different social sectors, were launched. And since the end of 2006, workers' councils, which can be considered the foundation of the Venezuelan socialist project, have become the official normative orientation for the organisation of workers and employees. As these councils facilitate cooperation and coordination on a greater level, they are intended to eventually replace the bourgeois state with a 'communal state'. Various 'popular power' councils (local councils and councils of workers, students, peasants and women, among others) are part of this structure and are being developed. At the heart of this process, as the most advanced element, are the communal councils and communes (Azzellini, 2013, 2017).

From good intentions to everyday practices

Looking at how the political guidelines orienting the process of transformation are implemented, however, huge difficulties and obstacles are apparent. The everyday practices of many institutions differ significantly from the official rhetoric because of political disagreement, classist or elitist thinking (not believing that ordinary people, workers, communities and so on have the knowledge or capacities to govern themselves), private interests (control, corruption) or incompetence.

Venezuela has to overcome the historical condition of producing and exporting primary resources according to the needs of the global North and of transnational companies (a situation that is socially, economically and ecologically unsustainable), and the productive forces have to be transformed in order to serve the social and economic needs of the majority of Venezuelan people. Venezuela produces only a very small part of what it consumes; it imports goods from unprocessed food to technology, textiles, toothpaste and bicycles – almost everything. At the same time the transformation of property relations and the management of the means of production are more conflictive than in any other field of the transformation process, since they directly affect the fundamental essence of the capitalist rentier model and the economic interests of powerful sectors. The workers and the organised communities are the only ones with an objective interest in transforming the economy and the relationships governing production.

Clearly, the asymmetry between the power of the state and the power from below means that bottom-up initiatives are easily influenced by state institutions and not the other way around, with the inherent risk of co-optation (Schönwälder, 1997; Goldfrank, 2001). In this case, initiatives from below are no longer the seedbed of the coming new society but rather an appendage of constituted power. The danger of reproducing the logic of constituted power and traditional approaches (such as hierarchies, representative mechanisms, division between those who govern and those who are governed, leaders and those they lead, and bureaucratisation) is compounded by the fact that, in order to respond to social rights, the Venezuelan state itself must be reinforced. This results in a growing bureaucratisation, which in turn impedes the opening up and subsequent transformation of society/institutions. The broadening of direct grassroots participation brings an increase in the conflict between the state and its popular base, especially in the sphere of production (where the interests at stake are high) as well as within the state, which itself becomes a site of class conflict. Since the Venezuelan state is a rentier state, class struggle is also mediated through the state: who has access to the oil revenues and where and how they are invested (Azzellini, 2014).

The democratisation of ownership and management of the means of production

From 1999 on, a series of initiatives were implemented to effect structural changes to the economy and to democratise relationships of property, work and production (Azzellini and Ressler, 2006; Azzellini, 2009a, 2010b). Between 2001 and 2006, the Venezuelan government – in addition to the nationalisation of the core of the oil industry – focused on promoting cooperatives. Venezuela was previously one of the Latin American countries with the fewest cooperatives. At the beginning of the Chávez government in 1998, there were only about 800 officially registered cooperatives with about 20,000 members all in all (Azzellini, 2012). The 1999 Constitution assigned the cooperatives special significance. They were thought to create a balance between social and economic interests, and received massive state assistance. The favourable conditions led to a boom in the number of cooperatives founded. In mid-2010, according to the national cooperative supervisory institute Sunacoop, 73,968 cooperatives were certified as operative, bringing the national cooperative membership to an estimated total of 2 million, although some people participate in more than one cooperative or have an additional job (Baute, 2009).

The problem is that the rapid growth of the number of cooperatives made it difficult to create effective mechanisms to control the use of governmental aid (Ellner, 2008). The initial idea that cooperatives would automatically 'produce for the satisfaction of social needs' and that their internal solidarity based on collective property 'would extend to their local communities, spontaneously' proved not to be the case. Most cooperatives still followed the logic of capital; concentrating on the maximisation of net revenue without supporting the surrounding communities, many put maximising revenues above the integration of new members. Many suffered from internal conflicts, which were mainly caused by inexperience with regard to managing social relations and undertaking management tasks. These problems were heightened by a lack of collective supervision mechanisms (Piñeiro Harnecker, 2007, 2010). Given these experiences, Sunacoop started to cooperate closely with the communal councils while promoting cooperatives. However, many supporters of the Bolivarian process assume that in the mid-term a solid cooperative sector will consolidate itself. The creation of a huge number of small companies, even if they are not in line with the cooperative philosophy, already represents a certain 'democratisation of capital' within the extremely monopolistic and oligopolistic market in Venezuela (Ellner, 2008).

In 2005-06, the state promoted the participation of employees in the management of their companies, mainly in state-owned enterprises and enterprises with mixed forms of ownership (state/cooperative). This drew on a model of co-management developed in the state-owned electricity supply industry during the entrepreneurs' strike of 2002-03, which was adopted by the enterprises' rank and file to ensure continuity of both the energy supply and maintenance services. As no legal basis for co-management was created, different models were introduced.[2] The model introduced in 2005 for expropriated factories, based on a model of co-ownership of the enterprise by both the workers organised in a cooperative and the state, proved not to be the emancipatory transformation project that was envisaged. Consequently, it was eventually rejected by the workers of the factories in which had first been introduced: they rejected the idea that it is ownership of the means of production through the cooperative that generates the right to take decisions regarding the cooperative.

This stand should not be confused with the critique of co-management by some traditional trade unionists, or even by some Marxists, who reject worker participation as neoliberal. The danger of co-management as a neoliberal strategy for the integration of workers in order to generate higher profits by tempering workers' demands to raise productivity always exists. As happens with nearly any cultural, social or political innovation, co-management has also been absorbed by capital and has contributed to the modernisation of the capitalist system. Nevertheless, in a serious project of social transformation workers cannot remain as wageworkers but have to assume responsibility over production and the workplace, otherwise no social transformation will be achieved.

In 2005, a new enterprise model was created to encourage companies to take a different path. The *empresas de producción social* (social production enterprises, EPSs) received aid from the state and had priority in state contracts. In exchange they had to invest part of their profits in their communities, introduce some kind of co-management in accordance with the preferences of the workers, and support the creation of cooperatives further down their production chains. The form of property, state, private or collectively owned, was not of importance. No generally valid criteria were established, so institutions created their own. Private companies favoured models of minority worker participation in ownership, with little or no participation in decision making. Many companies that did not fulfil all of the EPS criteria also registered as EPSs to take advantage of the government aid (Díaz, 2006, pp 157-8). Some state-owned companies created chains of suppliers and developed relationships for further processing with cooperatives, but in general reorientation could be forced on companies. Since the second half of 2007, no more EPSs have been founded. The name EPS has been used since then, still without any overall definition, as a designator for socialist production enterprises (Álvarez and Rodríguez, 2007) or enterprises of social property.

During and after the entrepreneurs' strike of 2002/03, workers took over several small and medium-sized factories as a protest against unpaid wages and redundancy payments. At first the government relegated the cases to the labour courts, until it began a process of expropriation in January 2005 (Ellner, 2006, p 85). Nevertheless, a systematic policy for expropriation in the production sector did not exist at least until 2007. Until then, expropriation had been mainly the result of the pressure placed on state institutions by worker occupations and mobilisation. After the government started a more systematic process of expropriation, increasing numbers of workers engaged in labour conflicts in private industries demanded nationalisation, believing that it would solve the problems faced by industry and workers. Nationalisation was mainly seen as a way to preserve jobs, without any consideration given to productivity or collective management. Meanwhile the property model preferred by workers and officially supported by government was the 'direct social property' model. This represents social property managed directly by the people, by factory councils, communal councils and communes.

In the context of industrialisation, in 2007, the government initiated a plan to build 200 new 'socialist factories'. The workers in the socialist factories were to be selected by the local communal councils and the required professionals sourced from state and government institutions.

These factories were considered to be direct social property, and the management of them was supposed to be gradually transferred into the hands of organised workers and communities. However, most institutions do little to organise this process and prepare employees for their new responsibilities, which generates growing conflict between workers and institutions. The same is happening more and more in expropriated enterprises as workers began to realise that while the fact of being a state employee might have saved their job and made it more likely that they would keep it, it did not fundamentally change working conditions, and nor has co-management or workers control been achieved.

With regard to workers' control, no common approach shared by the entire government exists. Different approaches coexist, and the situation is subject to constant change. This is also due – apart from different political positions in the left – to the fact that government institutions themselves are filled with contradictions and class struggles. So on the one hand, the government encourages workers to take over factories mismanaged by private owners. Here, Chávez and others spoke openly about workers' control, while cases of expropriation and nationalisation showed the political will for structural change. But on the other hand, institutions leave very little space for workers' initiatives after nationalisation and tend to try to stay in control of management and production. Nevertheless, a movement for workers' control arose. It started in the recuperated factories with little coordination at the beginning, and gradually extended to other factories and companies. In June 2011, a national platform for workers' control was founded at a conference attended by more than 800 workers from recuperated enterprises, CST (Consejos Socialistas de Trabajadores y Trabajadoras, Socialist Workers' Councils), rank-and-file unionists and workers' control activists (Azzellini, 2017).

Since 2013, a wave of conflicts has engulfed Venezuela's state companies. In most cases, the issue is not wages or even strictly labour demands, but rather disputes with management and ministerial bureaucracy. Workers took over plants to reclaim the movement for workers' control, transformation to socialism and production oriented towards satisfying the needs of the popular masses. In most state companies, there are conflicts over questions of participation and working conditions. In the private sector there were half a dozen new takeovers (Azzellini, 2017).

Council-based local self-administration

The idea of the commune as a site for building participation, self-government and socialism goes back to the communitarian socialist tradition of the Paris Commune, and also to Simón Rodríguez, José Carlos Mariátegui and indigenous and Afro-American historical experiences. The communal councils (CCs) are based on direct democracy and spokespeople, contrary to the principles of representative democracy: they are the most advanced mechanism of self-organisation at the local level. The most active agents of change in Venezuela have been – and continue to be – the inhabitants of the urban *barrios* and the peasant communities. CCs began to form in 2005 in the absence of legal regulation and as a bottom-up initiative. In January 2006, Chávez adopted the initiative and it began to spread. In April 2006, the National Assembly approved the Law of Communal Councils, which was reformed in 2009 following a broad consultation process involving councils' spokespeople. The CCs in urban areas encompass some 150-400 families, in rural zones, a minimum of 20 families, and in indigenous regions, at least 10 families. The heart of the CC and its decision-making body is the Assembly of Neighbours. The councils build a non-representative structure of direct participation that exists parallel to the elected representative bodies of constituted power.

At a higher level there is the possibility of creating socialist communes, which can be formed from various CCs in a given territory and can develop medium- and long-term projects of greater impact, while decisions continue to be made in assemblies of the CCs. Another important element in creating a commune is the integration of other organisations and councils to guarantee the participation and rights of minorities, and/or vulnerable or special interest groups in the nascent institution. Beyond the communes, certain territories can be declared communal cities, if they are totally organised in CCs and communes with administration and planning from below. In August 2015, there were about 45,000 CCs and 1,220 communes in Venezuela.[3]

This council-based, non-representative local self-organisation aims to create a 'new power-geometry'. The concept of power in radical geography, as elaborated by Doreen Massey, has been put 'to positive political use' following a 'recognition of the existence and significance, within Venezuela, of highly unequal, and thus undemocratic, power-geometries' (Massey, 2009, p 20). In this frame, the councils show 'how both the very nature of power-relations and the geography of those relations might be changed' (Massey, 2009, p 21). The CCs are financed directly by the state and its institutions, thus avoiding major interference from the municipalities. However, while the law does not give any entity the authority to accept or reject proposals presented by CCs, the relationship between CCs and state institutions is often conflictive, mainly caused by the slowness of constituted power's response to CC demands and by institutional attempts to interfere in their work. The CCs constitute a parallel structure that gradually draws power and control away from the state in order to govern on its own, and therefore they tend to transcend the division between political and civil society (that is, between those who govern and those who are governed).

In the context of forming communes and communal cities, it is important to differentiate between (absolute) political-administrative space and (relational) socio-cultural economic space (Harvey, 2006). The communes reflect the latter; they do not correspond to existing political-administrative spaces, and they can cross municipal or even state frontiers, given that the population defines and models its own socio-cultural economic spaces. The different spaces always overlap and so do different relations of power and dominance. These do not stop existing, but through the institutionalisation of the communes and communal cities the socio-cultural economic space, and the influence of the people in shaping it according to their will, is strengthened. The mechanism for building socialist communes and communal cities is flexible, and they themselves define which tasks will be taken on. This flexibility makes it possible to find one's own way towards self-government, which can begin with what the population itself considers most important, necessary or opportune.

The communal cities that have begun to form so far, for example, are rural and are structured around agriculture (Azzellini, 2010a, 2013, 2017). During a workshop in a poor neighbourhood of the south-eastern city of Barinas, Carmelo González, from the Autonomous Municipal Institute of the communes of Barinas, explained:

> Water, electricity, telephone and the establishment of the EPS. These are problems which are supposed to be managed by the communal assembly. This is your power and not ours as administrative officials. You have the possibility to hold the power in your own hands. This is something unseen. This is the creation of a new kind of socialism, which doesn't exist anywhere so far. If the commune becomes a reality in the whole country, in Barinas, in Venezuela we can attempt to construct a communal government here, doing the transition to socialism, toward the new geometry

of power. All of these forums and talks are also meant to bring the information into your community…. Because discussions create participation. And this participation will enable you to create government. And the government is not who is holding the power. The power is in your hands, in the possibility that you have to create this model of socialism…. We intend to learn collectively what you know because that is even more than we do. It's the knowledge of the people which is expressed right now. (Azzellini and Ressler, 2010)

It has to be stressed here that the approach of González is not shared among all state employees. Often they try to impose certain mechanisms, projects and procedures and it is rather rare that they put themselves at the service of the communities and popular organisations. Nevertheless, since 2010, the growing self-confidence, experience and determination of communities has strengthened the position of the entities of local self-administration. In December 2010, the National Assembly passed the Popular Power Law, the Social Auditing Law, the Public and Popular Planning Law, and the Law of Communes. Although there is no law that specifically regulates communal cities, several such organisations have emerged – so far, rural ones structured around agriculture. Despite the lack of regulation, the construction of communes and communal cities began several years ago; grassroots organisations have begun to establish communes, which are supposed to be supported by the Ministry of Communes, created in 2009. Instead the ministry has turned out to be biggest hurdle in the construction of communes. In 2011, it declared that it was supporting approximately 230 communes under construction, but it has never officially recognised any commune as 'established' and all communes complain about conflicts with the ministry relating to projects, planning and decision making. This is not much of a surprise, but rather a logical consequence of the inherent tendency of institutions to reproduce and perpetuate their power and stay in control of social processes. Since every commune declared as 'functioning' means a loss of power and political weight for the ministry, it will always tend to claim that the communes need the ministry. This tendency is even strengthened in times of profound structural changes when every institution is questioned.

The relationship between the Ministry of Communes and many communes under construction continued to be characterised by conflict for several years. Certainly, the ministry has provided important support, including workshops and funding for many communities, but it did not respect the autonomy of the communes and tried to impose itself on issues from territorial limits to specific projects. Although the number of popular initiatives to create communes increased massively from 2010, the ministry did not register any communes until the end of 2011 when, through a national mobilisation effort, the National Network of Communards (RNC) forced the ministry to officially recognise the existence of 20 communes. Almost all of the 1,200-plus registered communes in August 2015 were officially recognised after President Nicolás Maduro appointed Reinaldo Iturriza as Minister of Communes in April 2013. The RNC, the most important autonomous movement in pressing for the construction of communes, is a self-organised network that was born in 2008 and brings together communes and communes under construction from across the entire national territory. The intention of the self-organised network is to build in a democratic manner from below a communal state based on councils, and to continue to develop a constitutent popular process and to deepen the constitutent character of the people. The RNC was created as an institutional initiative after Chávez had called for the formation of a team to analyse the existing experience of the communes that had been formed autonomously from below. But when the Ministry of Communes was established and excluded the main commune activists who had been participating in the process up to that point, the existing 16 communes decided to split from the ministry and organise their own autonomous network.

The resulting RNC continued growing, with about 500 communes participating in 2015. There are regular gatherings of regional spokespeople, in regions ratified by the network, and national meetings are organised at least twice a year. There are also work commissions – in communications, for example – and thematic meetings, like those on 'socialist communal productive economy.' The RNC is totally autonomous. As it stated in the closing document to the 2011 annual meeting, the communes of the RNC work to:

> Assume the planning of the productive cycle (production, transformation, and distribution, thus promoting the cultural change of the models of consumption and consumerism)....
> Accumulate the technical and organic force for the means of production to pass progressively to workers' control (councils of workers) and of the communes in their various levels of aggregation, to develop the communal economy, in transition to Bolivarian socialism. (RNC, 2011)

The communal economy

Throughout the years, a focus of the government has always been to try to strengthen an alternative economy, often using different names for it: solidarity, social, popular or communal economy. A clear definition or distinction does not really exist. The strategy for the construction of an economy pointing beyond capitalist logics and the democratisation of economic cycles is based on the expansion and consolidation of a popular, social and communal economy, consisting of self-managed, state-promoted units. The orientation for this derives from a strategy of radical endogenous development: sustainable development based on locally-owned resources and potentials (not external ones), connected with the collective management of the means of production and a more active role of the state in the economy. The origins of endogenous development go back to the first proposals from CEPAL in the 1950s, which were further developed in later decades (Sunkel, 1993). The Venezuelan approach, however, goes beyond the original objectives of endogenous development: it is not only an endogenous production, but also has endogenous distribution as a goal:

> Endogenous development integrates the excluded population, and develops new forms of social and productive organisation in a self- managed way. Its core and substance are the men and women of every age and situation, which inhabit this country. It is based on education and training, on the knowledge and practice spread in the population, with a strong cultural component, and promotes the transformation of the natural resources through the development of productive chains whose links are represented by the phases of production, distribution and consumption, with a great respect for the environment and an increased sense for his protection. (Valles Caraballo, 2004, pp 23-4)

The idea of communal production and consumption cycles refers to the work of Mészáros, who proposes a 'communal system':

> Accordingly, in striking contrast to commodity production and its fetishistic exchange relation, the historically novel character of the communal system defines itself through its practical orientation towards the *exchange of activities*, and not simply of *products*. The allocation of products, to

be sure, arises from the communally organised productive activity itself, and it is expected to match the directly social character of the latter. However, the point in the present context is that in the communal type exchange relation the primacy goes to the self-determination and corresponding organisation of the *activities* themselves in which the individuals engage, in accordance with their need as active human beings. The products constitute the subordinate moment in this type of exchange relation, making it therefore possible also to allocate a radically different way the total disposable time of society, rather than being predetermined and utterly constrained in this respect by the primacy of the material productive targets, be they commodities or non-commodified products. (Mészáros, 1995, pp 759-60, emphasis in original)

After a certain amount of success for the first communal cooperatives founded by communal councils themselves to constitute enterprises following community decisions and maintain community control over them, several institutions started promoting communal cooperatives. In these new communal enterprises, the workers come from the communities. Through the CCs and communes, communities decide what kind of enterprises they need, what their organisational form should be, and who should work in them. Generally, the communities are supported by state institutions, especially by the Ministry of Communes, which helps organise workshops so they can discuss and better articulate what they want, and their preferred form of organisation for the communal enterprise. Therefore it is the same communities who decide what the structure and intention of their enterprise should be through a long process of training and debate (Azzellini and Ressler, 2010).

By the end of 2009, 271 enterprises of communal social property (EPSC) were founded by communities all over Venezuela. Furthermore, these EPSCs and the state were sharing responsibilities in 1,084 community-based social production units (ABN [Agencia Bolivariana de Noticias], 30 December 2009). The number of companies has grown since then, now that the EPSC has been demonstrated to be the most successful and promising model for a collective local company so far. With the introduction of the Organic Law of the Communal Economic System on 14 December 2010, a legal framework was created for the EPSC, and today there are thousands of these companies at the communal level.

While the communal cooperatives built with the help of Sunacoop were mainly productive enterprises, such as textile companies, bakeries, shoemakers and some agricultural production companies, the character of the companies changed when various institutions and even some state-owned companies started to support the model of the communal companies. Communities started to build EPSCs in various areas, from food production and construction materials to communal companies for local services. Some communities or communes even built or took over small factories, such as Polimeros Ocaña, a factory for plastic bags and packages near San Felipe, Yaracuy. The principal sectors where EPSCs are located correspond with the most strongly felt areas of need of the *barrios* and rural communities: the production or processing of food and production and distribution of construction materials. The nationalised cement factory, Cemento Andino, was the first cement company to set up community distributors for construction material and *bloqueras*, or block-making companies, producing big cement blocks used in the construction of houses, in the communities. As Zoraida Benítez from the Community and Vicinity department of Cemento Andino explained in an interview with the author, this initiative helped to reduce speculation and lower prices by eliminating intermediaries. This example was then followed by other state-owned cement factories.

There is a great deal of concern among communities about the environmental sustainability of the companies being set up. Communities engage with a number of environmental issues, from ecological agriculture to recycling, as well as initiatives to transcend capitalist relationships. In February 2012, the RNC began to hold regular meetings about the communal economy. Major topics for debate include the general orientation of a communal economy, the law on communal economy, ecological agriculture, the exchange of commodities without money, and the construction of sustainable production in the communes. A network of 13 local communal currencies used in communes is also an initiative of the RNC (Dittmer, 2011). The communes of the RNC have also developed cooperation initiatives with network members, and exchange experiences with each other. For example, a commune from La Guaira on the coast near Caracas regularly exchanges fish for goat meat from another commune from the mountain region of Lara, and the Siete Pilares Socialistas commune from Anaco in the state of Anzoátegui shared its experiences of constructing of a factory producing clay roof tiles. It visited another commune in Lara that had local clay resources and had already set up a factory for clay roof tile production. It learned how to produce tiles, set up its own project, and built six ovens for tile production. The tile factory is part of a decentralised factory for prefabricated houses. Once fully operative, it should be able to offer work to 1,340 people from the commune, which has 50,000 inhabitants.

Conclusion

To sum up, a great variety of different measures to promote structural changes in the economy, as well as the democratisation of property and the management of the means of production, have been put into effect in Venezuela. Some initiatives also aim to abolish the division between manual and intellectual work and eradicate capitalist relations. Other initiatives simply aim for a democratisation of capitalist relations. Despite errors and problems, a huge variety of cooperatives and other alternative company models have arisen over the years, a process that, at the time of writing (September 2016), had outlasted the transition from Chávez to Maduro. The search for an alternative economy is still on the agenda. However, the structural transformation of the economy has proved to be a titanic task, given the resistance of national and international capital markets and the bourgeoisie, and the difficulty of breaking with the reproduction and perpetuation of existing dynamics. The rentier economy has not been overcome so far.

Most traditional cooperatives, even EPSs and those founded through special state programmes, did not foster the development of alternative economies, but instead integrated themselves into the capitalist market. Nor is it surprising that it is extremely difficult to establish production processes that are not guided by capitalist rationality and are committed to social needs and the community. Concrete experience shows that even with regard to the simplest questions, the alternative enterprise models tend to fall back into practices governed more by competition than cooperation and to adopt hierarchical structures. Due to the lack of alternative distribution networks, the pressure to become part of capitalist commodity chains is high. To compete in a market for profit makes exchange value more important than use value. Direct management by communities has proven to be effective in facing some of these challenges, but matters like the division of labour and earnings have revealed themselves as very problematic because of the continued dominance of capitalist culture promoting inequality, competition and social hierarchies regarding work tasks.

Recognising the limitations of traditional cooperatives does not mean that cooperatives cannot play an important and totally compatible role in the construction of socialism, especially in the construction of a solidarity economy on a local level. Of all the alternative company models that have emerged since 2000, the enterprises of communal direct social property have been, up until now, the most successful model. In many cases these companies have managed to create a better balance between costs, efficiency and social dimension than state- or privately owned enterprises. Linked to local self-management processes and embedded in collective planning of the communities, the EPSCs respond to needs defined by communities themselves and are under their control. In networks such as the RNC, the communes exchange experiences around production and alternative economy practice, and build relationships of mutual aid and exchange of ideas and products. The range of products controlled and distributed by communities is constantly growing, and production is seen by communities as more reliable and appropriated than that controlled by the state or by privately owned companies.

Is also necessary to connect new companies and to create conditions for their independent functioning without economic support from the state if an economy that does not follow the rationality of capital is to be constructed. This is important for the question of whether processes of radical endogenous development will be successful, or whether there will be just a reload of import substitution policy under state bureaucratic administration, or even a continuation of the rentier model. One of the biggest contradictions the transformation process faces is that even most of the people in charge of the transformation of the economy have objectively little interest in doing so since they live off this rentier economy. The private appropriation of public finances and resources by clientelistic networks makes an endogenous industrial development strategy much more difficult. The most reliable instrument against corruption, and the only guarantee for a production oriented towards satisfying the popular needs, is worker and community control. This is also the reason for its many enemies, since it would mean the end of all privileges, one of the main roots of corruption.

The vast majority of enterprises of social property in Venezuela are not administered by workers and communities as they should be, but rather by employees of state institutions. At the same time, their internal organisational and working structures have not changed. The experiences of workers, in light of inefficiency or the incapacity (be it structural or specific) of the state to guarantee efficient production and a move towards a change in the social relationships of production, have contributed in a decisive manner to the strengthening of the movement for workers' control. This has resulted in fostering a class struggle where none previously existed. In nearly all companies nationalised by the state, we find conflicts about real participation or even workers' control.

Contradictions and conflicts (combined with class struggle) have also entered state institutions. On one hand, many state institutions are organising training for workers of nationalised or new state-owned enterprises in socialist politics, co-management and workers' control. On the other hand, the state representatives responsible for introducing a broader participation of the workers usually try to prevent the workers from being part of the transitional board of directors of intervened private enterprises, and almost always try to constrict the participation of workers in the enterprises. The question of workers' control and the change in the social relationships of production that this is automatically bringing up has provoked the deepest conflict inside the Bolivarian government since Chávez became President the first time in 1998. The conflict is an expression of class struggle: the struggle between those who want to overcome capitalist relationships, and those who do not want any profound and structural change in Venezuela's economic and productive model because they live well within it.

Nevertheless, those who dismiss the experiments in production and self-management made in Venezuela as doomed to failure because they are not guided by capitalist 'market' logics should bear in mind that the rules of capitalism are not laws of nature, even if the media and politicians want us to believe that capitalist economic categories have universal and transhistorical validity. Social structures are only valid for, and inside of, a set of human social relations. As such, capitalist categories simply represent the structure of rules in capitalist societies into which humans have historically entered (Agnoli, 1999). Since capitalist economic categories are the set of laws of a system built by humankind, they can also be overcome by humankind. In this context, the Venezuelan experiences are invaluable.

Notes

[1] A reference to anti-colonial fighter Simón Bolívar, 1783-1830.

[2] For a detailed analysis of co-management and workers' control in Alcasa and Inveval from 2005 to 2009, see Azzellini (2007, 2009a, 2011) and Azzellini and Ressler (2006).

[3] Ministerio del Poder Popular para las Comunas y los Movimientos Sociales, 9 August 2015, available at http://consulta.mpcomunas.gob.ve. For detailed analysis of the origins and development of communal councils, see Azzellini (2010b, pp 262-349).

References

Agnoli, J. (1999) *Subversive Theorie. Die Sache selbst und ihre Geschichte.* Freiburg: Cairá.

Álvarez R.V. and Rodríguez A.D. (2007) *Guía teórico-práctica para la creación de EPS. Empresas de Producción Socialista.* Barquisimeto: CVG Venalum.

Azzellini, D. (2012) 'From Cooperatives to Enterprises of Direct Social Property in the Venezuelan Process', in C. Piñeiro Harnecker (ed) *Cooperatives and Socialism. A View from Cuba.* Basingstoke: Palgrave Macmillan.

Azzellini, D. (2013) 'The Communal System as Venezuela's Transition to Socialism', in S.K. Brincat (ed) *Communism in the 21st Century. Vol. II: Whither Communism? The challenges facing communist states, parties and ideals.* Westport, CT: Praeger.

Azzellini, D. (2014) 'Venezuela's social transformation and growing class struggle', in S. Spronk and J.R. Webber (eds) *Crisis and Contradiction: Marxist Perspectives on Latin America in the Global Economy.* Leiden: Brill Press, pp 138-162.

Azzellini, D. (2017) *Communes and Workers' Control in Venezuela: Creating 21st-century Socialism from Below.* Leiden: Brill.

Azzellini, D. and Ressler O. (2010) 'Comuna Under Construction', Film (Caracas, Berlin and Vienna).

Azzellini, D. and Ressler, O. (2006) '5 Fábricas. Control Obrero en Venezuela', Film (Caracas/Berlin/Vienna).

Baute, J.C. (2009) 'Entrevista a Juan Carlos Baute/Presidente de Sunacoop', 16 January, available at www.sunacoop.gob.ve/noticias_detalle.php?id=1361.

Díaz, B. (2006) 'Políticas públicas para la promoción de cooperativas en Venezuela', *Cayapa*, 6(11): 149-183.

Dittmer, K. (2011) 'Communal Currencies in Venezuela', *International Journal of Community Currency Research*, 15, section A: 78-83.

Ellner, S. (2008) 'Las tensiones entre la base y la dirigencia en las filas del chavismo', *Revista Venezolana de Economía y Ciencias Sociales*, 14(1): 49-64.

Ellner, S. (2006) 'Las estrategias "desde arriba" y "desde abajo" del movimiento de Hugo Chávez', *Cuadernos del Cendes*, 23(62): 73-93.

Goldfrank, B. (2001) 'Deepening Democracy Through Citizen Participation? A Comparative Analysis of Three Cities', Paper presented at the 2001 meeting of the Latin American Studies Association, Washington DC, 6-8 September, available at http://lasa.international.pitt.edu/Lasa2001/GoldfrankBenjamin.pdf.

Harvey, D. (2006) 'Space as a keyword', in N. Castree and D. Gregory (eds) *David Harvey. A Critical Reader*. Malden: Blackwell.

Massey, D. (2009) 'Concepts of space and power in theory and in political practice', *Documents d'Anàlisi Geogràfica*, 55: 15-26.

Mészáros, I. (1995) *Beyond Capital. Towards a Theory of Transition*. London: Merlin Press.

MinCI (Ministerio del Poder Popular para la Comunicación y la Información) (2007) *Líneas generales del Plan de Desarrollo Económico y Social de la Nación 2007-2013*. Caracas: MinCI.

Negri, A. (1992) *Il Potere Costituente*. Carnago: SugarcoEdizioni.

Piñeiro Harnecker, C. (2007) 'Democracia Laboral y Conciencia Colectiva: un estudio de Cooperativas en Venezuela', *Temas*, 50-51.

Piñeiro Harnecker, C. (2010) 'Venezuelan Cooperatives: Practice and Challenges', Paper presented at the 28th ILPC, Rutgers University, New Brunswick, NJ, 15-17 March.

RNC (Red Nacional de Comuneros y Comuneras) 2011 'Culminó con Éxito IV Encuentro Nacional de Comuneros y Comuneras', 10 August, available at http://rednacionaldecomuneros.blogspot. com/2011/08/culmino-con-exito-iv.encuentro-nacional.html.

Schönwälder, G. (1997) 'New Democratic Spaces at the Grassroots? Popular Participation in Latin American Local Governments', *Development and Change*, 28(4): 753-770.

Sunkel, O. (1993) *Development from Within: Toward a Neostructuralist Approach for Latin America*. Boulder, CO/London: Lynne Rienner Publishers.

Valles Caraballo, C. (2004) *Para crecer desde dentro*. Caracas: Consejo Nacional de la Cultura.

Zibechi, R. (2006) 'Movimientos sociales: nuevos escenarios y desafíos inéditos', *OSAL (Observatorio Social de América Latina)*, 21: 221-230.

Zibechi, R. (2012) *Territories in Resistance: A Cartography of Latin American Social Movements*. Oakland, CA: AK Press.

Part IV
Policy translation between North and South

Being a Zapatista wherever you are: reflections on academic-activist practice from Latin America to the UK

Paul Chatterton

Introduction

Consider for a moment your day at work. What tasks do you do, what problems are you working on, what solutions are you generating? Are you supporting, and indeed, expanding, hierarchical, uneven relations that seek to control and dominate, or working towards a world a based on equality, openness and compassion? How would you even know if we were moving in the right direction? What do the thousands of micro-exchanges you engage in add up to? What about huge problems such as climate change, austerity politics, or even those overused behemoths 'capitalism' and 'neoliberalism'? Are you tackling these? Is it your responsibility to? Would you even know how to? Do you regard yourself to be a relatively fair, generous, giving, open person? Do you worry about being better, or don't you care? In sum, what's it all for?

These are some reflections on the thoughts that have passed through my mind during my academic career over the past 20 years, and are reflected both in my own experiences and in the debates in this collection: how do we build economies built on peace, justice and sustainability, and how do we embed this in our everyday practices? These considerations have led me to engage and experiment with a whole range of projects, people and places to try to find some answers and solutions to many of the problems we seem to face as a local and global society.

Early in my academic career just after the millennium, this soul searching took me to Latin America. The Blair government had just come to power in the UK and I felt dissatisfied with Third Way Blairism that had been ushered in (Giddens, 1998). Although it offered some social and economic concessions, it did not feel like a useful response to the problems we faced. We know the many shortcomings of this project and how it has merely extended privatisation and market forces into our lives. So I wanted to engage with social movements that seemed to be providing responses and solutions on the ground. I left academia and, with my partner Tash, went to Mexico to work and live with the communities affiliated with the Ejército Zapatista de Liberación Nacional (EZLN). The EZLN, or Zapatistas for short (named after the inspirational peasant leader Emiliano Zapata), has been one of the most prominent international popular movements against neoliberal capitalism since its uprising in 1994 (see Holloway and Pelaez, 1998; Ross, 2000; Subcomandante Marcos, 2001; Nash, 2002). I was intrigued by what they were achieving in terms of building autonomous infrastructure and popular democracy. At the university we were involved in a solidarity group called Kiptik (which translates as 'strength' in a Mayan language) and through a close friend an opportunity emerged to do volunteer work building potable water systems with rural communities. Immediately after our time in Mexico, we travelled to Argentina to spend a few months with various community projects in the wake of the 2001 political and economic crisis and tapped into a broader tide of popular self-management and uprisings against a bankrupt political and economic establishment across the continent. We wrote our experiences into a book to help leave a legacy of what we saw (see Chatterton and Gordon, 2004)

This chapter is a reflection on what we learned and what it means to bring these lessons home.[1] After an extended period in Latin America, we realised that our struggle was where we left off in the UK. The question at the forefront of my mind was what does it mean to be a Zapatista where I live? What would it mean to make the struggle against neoliberalism and the desire to build a solidarity economy part of everyday life, especially in terms of bringing a militant research agenda into a neoliberal university (see Colectivo Situaciones, 2003; Conti, 2005; Holdren and Touza, 2005; Malo de Molina, 2005; Cote et al, 2006; Shukaitis and Graeber, 2007)? Below, I provide some responses to this this question through six ideas that are based on the activities I have been lucky enough to develop with other fellow travellers since my return to the UK in 2003.

Antecedents and inspirations: the Latin American struggle for autonomy and self-management

Ejército Zapatista de Liberación Nacional and the struggle for autonomy

We had been working for about a month in the village of San Isidro, in the Zapatista autonomous municipality of Morelia. At the time I had been living for about a year in Chiapas, the most southerly state of Mexico, doing solidarity work with the Zapatistas through our solidarity group Kiptik. After raising enough money from donations and gigs back in Europe we'd meet with the Zapatista municipal water commission and get instructions about which village needed a water system next. We were laying out a gravity flow system fed from a spring a couple of miles away up the hill, and the head tank lay squarely in the middle of land reclaimed after the landowner fled in the land takes of 1996. The village overlooked Las Canadas, the deep canyons that lead down to the Lacandon jungle near the Mexico-Guatemala border.

It was winter in the Chiapas highlands and the freezing mornings gave way to clear blue afternoons. One Thursday, we were taking our usual lunchtime break, eating *pozol*, the ancient Mayan snack of ground maize hydrated with whatever river water was at hand. Packed with nutrients and carbohydrates, it was amazing how that stuff could get you through the day. We hunkered down under the tarpaulin we had erected to protect the drying cement of the newly plastered water tank from the heat of the sun.

"How many Zapatistas are there in your village back home?," Manuel, one of the representatives of the water commission, asked me out of the blue. "Not many" came my reply, resisting the temptation to say that I was from a city not a village. "Why not?" "Well I suppose no one cares enough, or they're too busy," I said, and then instantly regretted it.

In the silence that ensued I began to think about the inspiring struggles and people I had met back home in the UK over the past few years. People ripping up genetically modified crops, breaking into warehouses to hold free parties or military bases to dismantle jet fighters, blocking road developments or holding parties in the middle of motorways. The silent army of people organising free language classes for migrants or solidarity events against the poll tax, developing open source software, hacklabs and alternative news media. Under the bright inspiring lights of the Zapatista struggle, I had begun to forget just how many people continue to resist neoliberalism, the deadlock of consumer-led market fundamentalism and the patronising dead hand of representative democracy in a wealth of untold ways, often putting their own liberty on the line to struggle for a better, more equal society where everyone has a say in how it is built.

The silence was broken by Manuel, who seemed to be following my thoughts. "There are more Zapatistas than you think, Pablo. Having *guerros* [literally 'whitey' in Castellano] like you supporting us is great. But at some point you need to go home and connect with the Zapatistas where you live. You'll find them. And they'll find you. You just need to find a language to speak to each other."

My time in Chiapas ended soon after this, mainly as I got a job teaching international development at the University of Leeds in the UK. But it was also because Manuel's words had a potent effect on me. Living and working in Chiapas gave me my most remarkable and direct experience with autonomy as a struggle for survival, self-management and the common. Since January 1 1994 when the EZLN rose up against the North American Free Trade Agreement and 500 years of colonial oppression, and fought a short bloody war against the Mexican military, it has become a global inspiration for those fighting for dignity and against neoliberalism. Thousands of people continue to visit Zapatista communities to support and learn about their efforts to install a genuine process of autonomous development that fuses ancient Mayan customs, magical-realism, continental philosophy and Marxist-Leninism. In health, education, technology and democracy, EZLN has set up structures that genuinely try to meet local needs and allow all those affiliated to the Zapatistas to participate and flourish. The political process embedded in the Zapatistas is complex and often contradictory in terms of its relationship with the state. It is simultaneously against the neoliberal capitalist Mexican state that has privatised resources and land and further marginalised indigenous groups. At the same time, the Zapatistas have sought to create a political imaginary far beyond the nation state through novel structures such as the Caracoles and their Good Government Committees. There have also been infrequent moments when they have strategically supported certain elements of local and regional government and political groupings that would allow them to work towards their aims (see Holloway, 2010).

Taking back control: a journey with Argentina's popular movement

December 2001 in Argentina represented one of those exciting glimpses of radical fervour. Not of Marxist-Leninists, or trade unions, or party politicians. But a popular rebellion when many different groups joined together. People were more or less united in getting rid of political leaders and bosses who denied to the majority of Argentinians access to a decent quality of life. However briefly, the working-class *piqueteros* (the road blockers) were joined by the more middle-class *caceroleros* (part of the colourful and noisy Latin American tradition of taking to the streets to demonstrate by banging pots, creating what is known as the *cacerolazo*) and *ahorristas* (those who had lost their life savings) to create a dynamite combination that (briefly) brought down a government. The self-organising that multiplied after this created an insatiable appetite for popular power that still lingers today. 2001 was only a year in history. But what happened has links in the past and will go on into the future. It was a year that leapt around the world and inspired millions of people (see also North, 2007; Dinerstein, 2010).

What has happened in Argentina since 2001 is the story of possibilities for autonomy, community self-management and acting horizontally (Sitrin, 2006; see also Chapter Fourteen in this collection). There is so much to learn from and listen to. What we saw in Argentina were groups and individuals on the streets constantly talking about autonomy, taking back their lives from politicians and business leaders they long ago stopped believing in, not waiting for answers to come from someone else, but getting on with creating their own society. The 2001 crisis saw an upsurge of a range of autonomous groups – the *piquetero* movement, unemployed workers' movements, neighbourhood assemblies, Independent Media Centres, groups working for justice and human rights such as HIJ@S and the Madres de Plaza de Mayo, indigenous farmers' groups, squatted social centres, reclaimed factories, and experimental spaces and collectives.

What we learned from Argentina is that politics isn't something that is done far from where you live. It is about justice, self-organising, mutual aid and solidarity – in each community, family and workplace. It is about developing and living concrete alternatives to modern life under the capitalist economy, and it is also about making protest a part of everyday existence. It's about remaking the revolution everyday – or as the Zapatistas say, it's 'to walk thinking' (*caminar pensando*). This is the radical challenge we saw in Argentina – the story of which I have attempted to bring home to inspire myself and others into action.

In both Mexico and Argentina, I realised I went there to learn from them. As the infamous EZLN spokesperson Subcomandante Marcos has long pointed out in his eloquent communiques, 'We are all Zapatistas.' This message has been reinforced by the Occupy movement's slogan of 'We are the 99%.' The task of international solidarity, and developing projects that can tap into the potential for community self-management, now had to be translated into figuring out what it meant to be Zapatista wherever I was. I wanted to 'dig where I stand', and for me this was in the university sector as an activist-scholar. For me, an activist-scholar is someone who sees the value in radical education and the debate of ideas by public scholars which challenge the norm (Castree, 2006; Mitchell, 2008). I wanted to bring my activism into the university for a number of reasons. In spite of the way they are being re-engineered, universities are still amazing places of encounter, conflict, diversity, debate and resources, and it's crucial that we find ways to defend and expand these and open them up to others. Engaging with the activist world, while it raises the eyebrows of many senior colleagues, has the potential to excite and inspire. It is reflects education as a practice of freedom (Freire, 1979; Giroux, 1997; hooks, 2004). Defending education as a path to freedom and not as a route to debt, precarious jobs and conformity is one of the most important political tasks of our time. And it's also an essential antidote to the endless consumer parade that student life has become (Noterman and Pusey, 2012). It can also open up much-needed research agendas to provide new knowledge that can challenge, rather than reinforce, capitalism.

Six pointers for being an academic-activist Zapatista

Focus our education on challenging neoliberalism

As a university academic, we have significant power and influence over those we educate. But looking around university curricula, it's clear that there is very little content that actually faces up to and names the challenges of global capitalism and even less that begins an educational process to provide alternatives to it. So what would a Zapatista teach in a university? This was a key question on my return from Latin America into what I found to be an increasingly corporatised and instrumental institution.

In 2004, I co-developed a novel Master's programme called Activism and Social Change in the School of Geography at the University of Leeds with colleagues Stuart Hodkinson and Paul Waley and then later Sara Gonzalez. This programme was unlike many academic courses. It was infused with ideas about the possibilities of life after capitalism, and the abilities of people to manage their own affairs through mutual aid and solidarity. We tried to commit to workable alternatives to the daily grind of wage labour and monetary exchange, and a mistrust of those with blueprints or vanguardist leadership. We wanted to develop a programme that would introduce students to these concepts, not in a doctrinaire or theoretical way, but as living ideas that would catch their imagination and act as possible openings for how we might live more sustainable, just and equal lives. The really tough question we asked in the class was, what do we mean by 'activism', especially in the context of being in the academy (see Blomley, 1994; Russell, 2015)? Activism takes many forms, and visions of social change differ across time and space. Business activists, for example, have been the most successful activists of recent years. We did not want to fix ourselves to one particular ideological or political viewpoint – we certainly aren't all Marxists or anarchists. But we do see ourselves and our visions for social change as part of what has become known as the 'anti-capitalist', 'anti-globalisation' or 'global justice' movement, which has become visible at the summit sieges of Seattle, Prague and Cancun, and the World Social Forums (see Glassman, 2002; Mertes, 2004).

We wanted to forge new links between the university and broader social movements for change (Routledge, 1996). We developed modules in radical ideas, resistance movements, skills for researching and campaigning on social change, engagements with activists and campaigners and how to implement ideas, and a large action-research dissertation. In a situation where alternative ideas are marginalised and social movements are often repressed, there simply needs to be more of these kinds of radical education projects to help build and support campaigning and social movements. They also reclaim space within universities from depoliticised, or at least corporate-focused, education and career options. As universities become increasingly controlled by metrics, performance management, social surveillance and instrumental market-oriented learning, we need to create, expand and defend these forms of radical education (see Readings, 1996; Castree, 2000, 2006; Castree and Sparke, 2000; Bauder, 2006).

Develop resources and knowledge with and for social movements

Beyond teaching and learning, there needs to be a broader commitment to co-producing agendas for change with those outside the academy. This brings together very different positionalities, resources and assumptions, but ultimately academics need to align as equals with people in other sectors struggling for radical social change. Many civil society groups lack access to resources and here those in the university sector can be incredibly useful in terms of supporting work and co-developing resources. Moreover, social movements and civil society organisations can benefit hugely from the legitimacy provided by teaming up with university academics, who can assist with research analysis and access to resources (Chatterton et al, 2010).

To this end, I've spent a lot of time outside the walls of academia with a popular education collective called Trapese (Taking Radical Action through Popular Education and Sustainable Everything). In 2004, the collective started developing workshops in the build-up to the 2005 summit of the Group of Eight (G8) nations, which was being held in Gleneagles, Scotland. We toured the UK, Ireland and Europe giving workshops on the role of the G8, and the big issues on the agenda such as climate change and debt, with student unions, church groups, and peace and campaign groups. Our focus concerned understanding what the G8 meant, as an elite group of nations that sets the global agenda for the maintenance of the capitalist economy, and also discussing what workable alternatives existed to give people a sense that other worlds and ways of living are possible beyond that proposed by the G8. Here we introduced examples such as community gardens, workers cooperatives, and social movements such as the Zapatistas, union organisers and campaigns on climate change. We also focused on action planning and how people could empower themselves to take action both in terms of joining the protests against the G8 and also developing local campaigns afterwards.

Since then, we have developed a range of workshops and skill-sharing sessions. We found a huge demand for workshops that focused not just on the issues, but also on the skills and abilities people needed to engage with the issues. Working alongside these activist-oriented associations inspired us to create a handbook to teach people how to get involved in social change. In the end, the book was called *Do It Yourself, a Handbook for Changing our World*, which was edited by the Trapese Collective and published by Pluto Press in 2007 (Trapese Collective, 2007). The intention of the book was to blend ideas with a practical 'how-to' guide, covering sustainable living, decision making, education, health, food, cultural activism, media, direct action and free spaces. The crucial part of this project for us was that the reader could learn about the issues and then see practical advice on how they could translate ideas into action.

So what did we achieve by writing this book? Most importantly, we want education to inspire others to get involved in change. We have to address apathy, denial, powerlessness and often just a lack of time. This is easily done through templates for action, action planning, inspiring stories and crucial emotional support. My work with Trapese aims to take discussions on big issues such as privatisation, climate change, resource conflict, social inequalities and political apathy to the public, while at the same time talking about what kinds of workable alternatives are feasible. These issues are too important to lock up in academic seminars and journal articles.

Be committed to participatory organising and direct democracy

At its heart, Zapatismo is based on a very different political system from the one most of us in the global North experience. In the global North we are familiar with the everyday rhythms of representative democracy as currently practised – long electoral cycles, ballot boxes, letter writing to MPs, MP surgeries, TV debates. Yet is this all we can expect from democracy, and is it the best model for managing our lives? While not everyone has the inclination or indeed the ability to participate more in our democratic systems, there is much more that can be done. There is a huge difference between our present 'representative democracies', which are no more than liberal oligarchies where the state guarantees the reproduction of the existing social and economic order through its legal monopoly on violence, and 'direct democracies', based on self-government by everyone (Albert, 2004). Building the latter needs a commitment to full participation – which is a slow and difficult process. As the social and solidarity economy sector shows, a variety of tools exist to make democracy more connected and accessible – citizen's panels, neighbourhood assemblies, participatory budgeting and financial devolution to communities, consumer and producer councils, ordinances to limit the activities of corporations, media and news that is independent of corporate influence or advertising. It is about challenging the apathy and corruption of local authorities and exposing their desire to hold power and maintain the status quo rather than act as our representatives.

This is not just about giving the current system a makeover. It is a radically different, people-centred, direct form of democracy (Barber, 1984). Imagine communities being run very differently, where individuals felt their participation was needed, they could have their say, and things really changed. There is no central city council that decides everything. Instead there are dozens of community assemblies all talking to each other, broken down into different commissions for roads, food, health, education and so on. That is what this kind of direct democracy looks like. There may be more meetings, but local areas will start working for people, and many won't be tied up doing mindless, surplus or low-paid jobs – advertising, banking, making unnecessary consumer goods, generating mindless paperwork, transporting food long distances, guarding other people's wealth – that don't contribute much to what we really need.

A commitment to making decisions without hierarchies or leaders underpins much of this, where proposals are tabled and considered with the intention of understanding and incorporating many different needs. These can then be discussed by larger groups through delegates and spokescouncils. Nobody's views are ignored, and those who disagree are not simply shut out. Everyone gets a turn in this process, no-one is in power for more than a year, and there is a growing mistrust of those who offer ready-made blueprints or simple answers. There is no easy future roadmap, nor should there be. The future is worked out here and now, through a belief that everyone should have a say. To rediscover democracy, we need to create a civic culture that includes everyone, that holds those in power to account (or else throws them out), that stops corporations taking money out of localities, that invests in local food, education, housing and facilities, that creates a commonwealth.

Learning to manage our own lives is empowering. It is about not waiting for politicians, planners, local business elites or the media to tell us what will happen. A brief glance at localities around the world shows us the real outcome of an estranged system that we have left to political representatives: bleak outer estates, motorways that choke our cities, peanuts from planning gain, swathes of our cities handed over to modern-day corporate robber barons (pension companies, corporate banks, entertainment multinationals). Self-management is embedded in a belief that we can do-it-ourselves, that we have the necessary skills and ideas. It is about debunking the role of the expert – the architect, the planner, the teacher, the politician. Much legwork is needed so people gain the self-belief to manage their own lives. But it is possible and everyone can contribute more than they think. Examples abound – from self-managed communities and eco-villages, community-owned agriculture, self-build housing, workplace organising and strikes (Harvey, 2012). I have attempted to embed these practices in the various activities I have developed with others, ranging from housing co-operatives to self-managed social centres, and I touch on some of these in the next section.

Build infrastructure that embeds autonomy, self-management and mutual aid

Politics happens in place, and what I learned from my time in Latin America is that laying down infrastructure to support this is a vital task that can bring people together, sharing resources and relearning important repertoires of resistance and creativity that are rapidly being lost. The Zapatistas and *piqueteros* taught me that what we need is infrastructure that can support strong bonds of solidarity and mutual aid. Mutual aid involves the real effects that can result when people begin to work together towards common goals (Kropotkin, 1972, 1987; Marshall, 1992). These are the bases of creating greater understanding, compassion and care. It is an antidote to the rightward drift in thinking represented by the easy stereotyping and lazy misunderstandings that we commonly hear. These grow when we don't often meet or talk to people who are different from us.

There has always been a push towards creating free or communal spaces; reclaiming these enables much of what is discussed here. Without the control of physical space, it is difficult to build commonality and connection between disparate groups (Hodkinson and Chatterton, 2006; Pusey, 2010). The enclosure of space is a reality of urban life through gentrification, displacement and speculation. All of this means that land and property have become commodified, out of the reach of most people on average incomes, and spaces held in common have been reducing rapidly. Finding and extending places for encounter in environments unmediated by consumer relations or profit is one of the most significant challenges of our neoliberal times. Common places seek opportunities for transformative dialogue and mutual learning, as well as conflict, where anyone is free to enter and contribute. Participatory research practices and spaces are needed for building understanding, encounter and action that are inclusive, that nurture creative interaction with others outside electoral politics, and can lead to critical reflection (Pain, 2003; Kindon et al, 2007; Pain and Kindon, 2007).

Relearning social interactions based on these ethics is important if we are to respond to multiple problems collectively rather than individually. By showing solidarity and mutual aid we can balance our individual desires for consumer goods and money with those of more collective goods such as peace, environmental sustainability and equality. How we put this into practice is more difficult, but it involves at first recognising the ways in which consumer society, the wage economy and hierarchical working practices affect us. Daily we are surrounded by examples of voluntary interactions that are not connected to the state or the money economy. We just don't value them, but they have always been the bedrock of healthy human relationships. It's not difficult to find examples. For instance, what we might call the 'solidarity economy' is growing all around us through time banks, local exchange trading schemes and other alternative currencies, cooperatives, credit unions and participatory budgeting (North, 2010).

One of the ways I have helped to lay down infrastructure to support radical place politics has been through my involvement in social centres. Social centres have always been a vital part of the infrastructure of radical social movements, and recently in the UK and Ireland struggles in our cities and communities have given energy to a whole network of places. The demand to mark out a place – giving us space to breathe, take action and experiment with managing our own lives collectively – is an almost universal desire among radical groups today. These autonomous spaces come in many different guises – small info shops and resource centres, radical arts centres, music and cinema spaces, and large social centres with meeting spaces and bars, often with housing cooperatives attached, providing low-cost accommodation. Social centres also have deep roots in struggles for collective, common space throughout history and connections around the world. The most immediate examples are the occupied *centri sociali* of Italy and an impressive array of well-established autonomous political spaces in European cities like Berlin, Barcelona, Milan and Amsterdam, with their strong tradition of squats (see Ruggiero, 2000; Mudu, 2004; Montagna, 2006).

Locally, I helped to set up a social centre called the Common Place in Leeds in 2004. The specific aim of the Common Place social centre was to build a local network of resistance in the lead-up to the G8 summit in Gleneagles, Scotland. But beyond that, the Common Place became a cornerstone of local political organising and self-managed politics for over half a decade. A dense network of people committed to social change and the practices of self-management formed around the Common Place. It became a vibrant hub for alternative ideas and over its five-year period featured a vegan café, DIY magazine, radical film festivals, regular gigs and a licensed bar. Towards the end of its life, the Common Place changed emphasis and was taken on by a workers' cooperative that now runs it as a music venue.

My desire to lay down infrastructure that could help promote self-managed solidarity economy expanded into housing. In 2004 I set up a housing cooperative named Xanadu with five friends. This was part of a network of small radical housing cooperatives in the UK called Radical Routes.[2] It was an inspiring experience in self-managed housing, which led to a wider experiment in self-managed cooperative housing through the Low Impact Living Affordable Community (Lilac) project.[3] I was a co-founder of Lilac, the first low-impact, affordable cohousing cooperative in the UK, and was involved in its development for six years (Chatterton, 2015). As well as building houses, the Lilac project has built a community of people who have been prepared to pioneer radically different ways of living, and is registered as a bone fide cooperative society for the benefit of its members. The framework adopted by Lilac embeds common ownership and the social relations that underpin it. Like all cooperatives, it has to subscribe to the seven principles of the International Co-operative Alliance (ICA) that stress voluntary membership, member control and economic equality. This protects against asset stripping or the accumulation of private wealth or resources. Lilac also attempts to promote closer interpersonal relations through a co-housing model that literally designs in more social interaction. The use of a mutual home ownership model creates a novel relationship to housing tenure, and attempts to foster identities as collective rather than private home owners. It links housing value to national earnings rather than average house prices, which shifts housing away from being a speculative commodity that can be bought and sold according to the vagaries of market conditions. I am now involved in a national alliance to expand community-led housing through city-based pilots across the UK. What we urgently need are radically different meso-level, middle-out, institutions that can both embed common ownership and economic equality and also re-equip participants with skills for decision making and communication based on openness and compassion (see Parag and Janda, 2014; Roelvink et al, 2015). In this journey we need to guard against co-optation by the kinds of localism embedded in the Big Society agenda that emerged under the Conservative-led coalition government in the UK of 2010 and have been stripped of the kinds of values outlined in this chapter. This kind of localism divests the state of the responsibilities of basic welfare functions and devolves them to a resource-limited and fragmented civil society (see Featherstone et al, 2012). We need the continuation of centrally coordinated state level support and resources – not as instruments of control but of facilitation, in order to enable and harness the growth of a diverse, strong and self-directed civil society.

Being strategic

Taking a strategic approach to the issues we are working on is crucial to success. This might mean slowing down and deliberating on both ends and means. How often do we stop to consider what we are actually trying to achieve, what we think the problem is, where we are heading, and how we are doing along the way (see Wright, 2010)? What I saw in Latin America was people who got organised, knew their context and what they were up against, and spent time building up an understanding of each other and what they needed to do. There are a number of key elements to this strategic approach I want to highlight.

The first is our overall approach – what does it feel like? Those who align to the radical left face a number of key challenges in terms of how to pitch their arguments and the alternatives they propose. How do we make our view of the future seductive, feasible and substantial? Duncombe (2007) explored how progressives often fail to capture the popular imagination and are often perceived to be dogmatic and moralist. Language that falls into models of telling others what is right and wrong or what people ought or ought not to be doing risks alienating people, as well as overlooking the huge amount of latent creativity that resides in all of us. Accessibility is an important byword. Without becoming trivial or superficial, we need to find ways to be relevant and use humour and satire in ways that will focus attention on injustices.

We need approaches, tactics and places for political becoming that can be made and remade by participants and embrace socialising as a part of everyday politics. We need to invite others to engage more experimentally and creatively in social change with us. When Holloway and Pelaez (1998) talked about 'reinventing the revolution' they were referring to a more participatory process – a revolution as the Zapatistas say, 'that is made by walking'. Participants aim to self-critique their own practice and impacts, and seem to be genuinely open to dialogue rather than seeking self-congratulation. Conversations about social change need to be open-ended. We need to embrace the messy politics of the possible. This is unsettling terra incognita for most of us. It requires relinquishing control and acknowledging that we don't have all the answers and that the solutions need to be co-produced.

Getting messages out in ways that connect and inform is also a real challenge. What I saw through the Zapatistas was attempts to blend different styles – populist, intellectual, traditional – to create novel forms of communication that can't easily be stereotyped or marginalised. Regular communiqués reflected on local and national issues but were presented in wider global contexts in ways that inspired and enlivened.

Finally, making time for evaluation and reflection is crucial. Tools like consensus decision making, facilitation training and a commitment to non-violent communication (NVC) are crucial here. Consensus is can be used for decision making to agree proposals in a dialogue between equals where outcomes can be owned by everyone. What consensus tries to do is unleash the creative genius of decision making across the whole community (Starhawk, 2011). Further, NVC, an approach developed by Marshall Rosenberg in the 1960s, can improve communication practices by focusing on self-empathy (tuning into one's own experience), empathy (listening to others with compassion) and self-expression (allowing individuals to express themselves authentically to inspire compassion in others) (Rosenberg, 2003). Among the Zapatistas and autonomous groups in Argentina, participation is central and enacted through roundtables, participatory assemblies, affinity groups, neighbourhood assemblies, and in the former case, enshrined through revolutionary law aimed at women.

Oh, and take the odd risk ...

It would be great to think that our efforts could lead to success and social change that rolls out unproblematically. But of course, the history of efforts for social change is also one of struggle, conflict and repression. Being a Zapatista unfortunately also means facing up to powerful and organised forces aimed at thwarting our efforts. Groups in Latin America are no strangers to direct and often brutal repression. The Zapatistas face regular incursions into their communities through direct military intervention as well as proxy conflicts fought through paramilitary groups. In Argentina, autonomous groups faced severe repression during and after the military dictatorship of the 1970s and 1980s. Many are still organising for recognition and justice in face of the mass disappearances and tortures during that period.

At several points during my efforts with others to bring home the spirit of the Zapatistas, this more repressive reality became apparent. Here I want to dwell on one event – an attempt to close down Drax, the largest coal-fired power station in the UK. This was the most reasonable thing I ever did.

On 13 June 2008, 29 of us stopped a train carrying 6,000 tonnes of coal to Drax power station. We did it peacefully, safely and with respect to all those we encountered. Why Drax and why coal? At the time, Drax was the single biggest source of CO_2 emissions in the UK. It produces 22 million tonnes of CO_2 a year, and uses 60,000 tonnes of coal per day. It emits the same amount of CO_2 as Croatia. Inevitably we were arrested. The West Yorkshire police mobilised 600 police, a boat and a helicopter. It took them 12 hours to remove us from the top of the coal hoppers, as we had locked ourselves to whatever fixed structures we could find. We were detained for 24 hours in Leeds and our houses were searched. We were released on bail and charged under the 1861 Malicious Damages Act, a charge reserved in the past for highwaymen and train robbers.

So why did we do it? The scientific case was clear. I was closely watching scientific arguments unfold in 2007 and 2008. In November

2007 the Intergovernmental Panel on Climate Change stated that climate change was happening more rapidly and more severely than previously thought. Around the same time, James Hansen, then the chief scientist to the US government, wrote a letter to former Prime Minister Gordon Brown urging him to stop the expansion of coal power. In it he stated: 'If we continue to build coal-fired power plants without carbon capture, we will lock in future climate disasters associated with passing climate tipping points.'[4] Hansen had given a testimony in the US stating that future generations would perish if unabated coal burning was not stopped. A new wave of coal power stations was announced in the UK with no plans to deal with old and existing coal power like Drax. The elixir of carbon capture and storage was a long way off. We knew that coal was the key to whether we would tackle climate change or not and we knew every tonne counted. There needs to be a global moratorium on two thirds of fossil fuel reserves to avoid a 2°C global temperature rise. Worse of all, we knew our region emitted more tonnes than any other: in what is locally called megawatt valley, five carbon-spewing monster power stations dominate the Yorkshire plain and the Humber estuary. Every year, Drax adds 22 million tonnes of CO_2 to the global budget. We knew there were workable alternatives to coal, but these were not being pursued. Our argument was simple – make an urgent transition to a low carbon economy and decarbonise electricity production by 2030, and have a moratorium on fossil fuels. There was also a strong political case. We looked into parliamentary action on stopping coal – letters to MPs, lobbying, parliamentary questions, select committees and commissions judicial reviews, university reports and injunctions; all had been critical and stressed the need for action. But none had actually stopped emissions. That is why we turned to civil disobedience and citizen action.

After one of the most demanding and stressful years of my life, we stood trial in front of a jury in July 2009. During the trial, we stated that we believed what we did was not unlawful as it was a reasonable and proportionate response. We put forward a defence of necessity (to avoid death or injury) and prevention of crime (unlawful damage/ public nuisance). The defence case was disallowed by the judge at a pre-trial hearing and our esteemed global witnesses, including James Hansen, were not able to attend. We defended ourselves without lawyers or barristers and acted as our own witnesses. While the judge allowed us to proceed, he was only interested in facts, not motives. He didn't want to establish why we did it, only whether we did it.

I was first up in the witness box. The judge interrupted my defence and said: "The jury is only deciding in trial what happened and whether or not you were involved. They are not concerned with why you did it. Motive in a case like this is quite simply irrelevant. I also ruled that any evidence about global warming and consequences of burning fossil fuels at Drax are inadmissible, irrelevant to stopping a train." You can see what we were up against.

After a one week trial, it took the jury two hours to return a guilty verdict. This was not surprising given the pressure that the judge applied to them. I received a one-year conditional discharge and a £1,000 fine. During my probation I was subject to Multi-Agency Public Protection Arrangements (MAPPA) whose remit is to 'support the assessment and management of the most serious sexual and violent offenders'. MAPPA deals with domestic extremists in conjunction with the National Extremism Tactical Co-ordination Unit and includes 'environmental protesters'. As one newspaper put it after the verdict, were we heroes or terrorists? That is for the reader to decide, but coal burning continues unabated around the world and momentum gathers for a moratorium on fossil fuel burning. As an aside, our convictions have now been overturned after they were deemed unsafe when it was revealed that undercover police had infiltrated our group. The lengths that the state will go to undermine groups that challenge the status quo is considerable.

Conclusion

Trying to stay true to the spirit of Zapatismo is a rocky road. I have chosen to 'dig where I stand' in the university sector as an activist-academic (see also Fuller and Kitchen, 2004). Like other sectors, my own workplace is being increasingly privatised, regulated, monitored and managed; there is less and less scope for freedom, serendipity and non-instrumental thinking. Embodying the spirit of Zapatismo in this context has never been more urgent. As I have outlined here, it requires a commitment to education and learning about neoliberal capitalism, developing resources and knowledge that is of direct use to those struggling for change, committing to more direct forms of democracy, building infrastructure for self-management, being strategic, and taking risks. Much of the activity I have outlined is about staying strong in dark times, and keeping the momentum going for radical activity in a more hopeful future. But it's also about laying down openings and possibilities right now. It's about constantly seeking cracks, possibilities and connections, realising that we are resisting and creating, negating and producing. As John Holloway (2010) so eloquently suggests, being a Zapatista is about being in this world with all its problems and compromises, but also being against it, as well as building our hoped-for world beyond it. While many of these examples might seem like micro-examples, I want to stress the need to keep an eye on the bigger structural picture: the need to build meso-level institutions that support social activism, grow popular (even revolutionary) power, embed strong values to avoid co-optation, and find ways to avoid rebooting or re-embedding further capital accumulation and divisive social and spatial practices (Harvey, 1972; Anderson, 2004; Ruddick, 2004). None of this is easy or quick. Ultimately, being a Zapatista wherever you are requires patience, openness, strength and compassion. It is a long journey with no clear endpoint, but it is a journey I encourage you to embark on with others.

Notes

[1] See also Chatterton (2005, 2008a, 2008b, 2010); Chatterton et al (2010).

[2] www.radicalroutes.org.uk[3] www.lilac.coop[4] www.greenpeace.org.uk/media/press-releases/worlds-leading-climate-scientist-writes-to-brown-20071219

References

Albert, M (2004) *Parecon: Life After Capitalism*. Verso: London.

Anderson, J (2004) 'Spatial politics in practice: the style and substance of environmental direct action', *Antipode*, 106–125.

Barber, B (1984) *Strong democracy. Participatory politics for a new age*. San Francisco, CA: University of California Press.

Bauder, H (2006) 'The Segmentation of Academic Labour: A Canadian Example', *ACME*, 4(2): 228–239.

Blomley, N (1994) 'Activism and the academy', *Environment and Planning D: Society and Space*, 12: 383–5.

Castree, N (2000) 'Professionalism, activism and the university: whither "critical geography"', *Environment and Planning A*, 32(6): 955–70.

Castree, N (2006) 'Geography's New Public Intellectuals?', *Antipode*, 38(2): 396–412.

Castree, N and Sparke, M (2000) 'Professional geography and the corporatization of the university: Experiences, evaluations, and engagements', *Antipode*, 32: 222–229.

Chatterton, P (2005) 'Making Autonomous Geographies: Argentina's popular uprising and the "Movimiento de Trabajadores Desocupados" Unemployed Workers' Movement', *Geoforum*, 36: 545–561.

Chatterton, P (2008a) 'Becoming a public scholar academia and activism', *Antipode*, 40(3): 421–428.

Chatterton, P (2008b) 'Using Geography to Teach Freedom and Defiance Lessons in Social Change from "Autonomous Geographies"', *Journal of Geography in Higher Education*, 323: 419-440.

Chatterton, P (2010) 'Autonomy: The Struggle for Survival, Self-Management and the Common', *Antipode*, 42(4): 897-908.

Chatterton, P (2015) *Low Impact Living: a field guide to ecological affordable community building.* London: Routledge.Chatterton, P and Gordon, T (2004) *Taking Back Control: A journey through Argentina's popular uprising.* Leeds: University of Leeds.

Chatterton, P, Hodkinson, S and Pickerill, J (2010) 'Beyond scholar activism: making strategic interventions inside and outside the neoliberal university', *ACME*, 9: 245-275.

Colectivo Situaciones (2003) 'Sobre el militante investigador', available at http://transform.eipcp.net/transversal/0406/colectivosituaciones/es/print.

Conti, A (2005) 'Metropolitan proletarian research', available at www.ecn.org/valkohaalarit/english/conti.htm.

Cote, M, Day, R and de Peuter, G (2006) *Utopian Pedagogy: Radical Experiments Against Neo-liberal Globalization.* Toronto: University of Toronto Press.Dinerstein, A C (2010) 'Autonomy in Latin America: between resistance and integration. Echoes from the Piqueteros experience', *Community Development Journal*, 45(3): 356-366.

Duncombe, S (2007) *Dream: Re-imagining Progressive Politics in an Age of Fantasy.* New York, NY: The New Press.

Featherstone, D, Ince, A, Mackinnon, D, Strauss, K and Cumbers, A (2012) 'Progressive localism and the construction of political alternatives', *Transactions of the Institute of British Geographers*, 37: 177-182.

Freire, P (1979) *Pedagogy of the oppressed.* London: Penguin.

Fuller, D and Kitchen, R (eds) (2004) *Critical Theory/Radical Praxis: Making a Difference Beyond the Academy?.* Vernon and Victoria BC, Canada: Praxis (e)Press.

Giddens, A (1998) *The third way and the renewal of social democracy.* Cambridge: Polity.Giroux, H A (1997) *Pedagogy and the politics of hope: theory culture and schooling: a critical reader.* Boulder, CO: Westview Press.

Glassman, J (2002) 'From Seattle (and Ubon) to Bangkok: the scales of resistance to corporate globalization', *Environment and Planning D: Society and Space*, 20(5): 513-533.

Harvey, D (1972) 'Revolutionary and counter-revolutionary theory in geography and the problem of ghetto formation', *Antipode*, 4: 1-2.

Harvey, D (2012) *Rebel cities*. London: Verso. Hodkinson, S and Chatterton, P (2006) 'Autonomy in the city? Reflections on the social centres movement in the UK', *City*, 103: 305-315.

Holdren, N and Touza, S (2005) 'Introduction to Colectivo Situaciones', *Ephemera*, 5(4): 595-601.

Holloway, J (2010) *Crack Capitalism*. London: Pluto Press.

Holloway, J and Pelaez, E (1998) *Zapatista! Reinventing Revolution in Mexico*. London: Pluto Press.

Hooks, B (2004) *Teaching community: A pedagogy of hope*. London: Routledge.

Kindon, S, Pain, R and Kesby, M (2007) *Participatory action research approaches and methods: connecting people participation and place*. London: Routledge.

Kropotkin, P (1972) *Mutual aid: a factor of evolution*. London: Freedom Press.

Kropotkin, P (1987) *Fields factories and workshops tomorrow*. London: Freedom Press.

Malo de Molina, M (2005) 'Common Notions Part 1: workers inquiry, co-research, consciousness-raising', available at http://transformeipcpnet/transversal/0406/malo/en/print.

Marshall, P (1992) *Demanding the impossible: A history of anarchism*. London: Harper Collins.

Mertes, T (2004) *A movement of movements. A Reader*. London: Verso.

Mitchell, K (ed) (2008) *Being and Practicing Public Scholar*. Chichester: Wiley- Blackwell.

Montagna, N (2006) 'The de-commodification of urban space and the occupied social centres in Italy', *City*, 10(3): 295-304.

Mudu, P (2004) 'Resisting and challenging neoliberalism: the development of Italian Social Centres', *Antipode*, no 36, 917-941.

Nash, J (2002) *Mayan Visions The quest for autonomy*. London: Routledge.

North, P J (2007) 'Neoliberalizing Argentina?', in K England and K Ward (eds) *Neoliberalization: states, networks, peoples*. Oxford: Blackwell.

North, P J (2010) *Local Money*. Dartington: Green Books.

Noterman, E and Pusey, A (2012) 'Inside Outside and on the Edge of the Academy: Experiments in Radical Pedagogies', in R Haworth (ed) *Anarchist Pedagogies: Collective Actions Theories and Critical Reflections on Education*. Oakland, CA: PM Press.

Pain, R (2003) 'Social geography: On action-oriented research', *Progress in Human Geography*, 27(5): 649-657.

Pain, R and Kindon, S (2007) 'Participatory geographies', *Environment and Planning A*, 39(12): 2807-2812.

Parag, Y and Janda, K (2014) 'More than filler: Middle actors and socio-technical change in the energy system from the "middle-out"', *Energy Research and Social Science*, 3: 102-112.

Pusey, A (2010) 'Social Centres and the New Cooperativism of the Common', *Affinities: A Journal of Radical Theory Culture and Action*, 4(1): 176-198.

Readings, B (1996) *The University in Ruins*. Cambridge, MA: Harvard University Press.

Roelvink, G, St Martin, K and Gibson-Graham, J K eds (2015) *Making other worlds possible: performing diverse economies*. Minneapolis, MN: University of Minnesota Press.

Rosenberg, M. (2003) *Nonviolent communication: A language of life*, Encinitas: Puddledancer Press.

Ross, J (2000) *The war against oblivion: Zapatista chronicles 1994-2000*. Monroe, ME: Common Courage Press.

Routledge, P (1996) 'Third Space as Critical Engagement', *Antipode*, 28(4): 397-419.

Ruddick, S (2004) 'Activist geographies: building possible worlds', in P Cloke, P Crang and M Goodwin (eds) *Envisioning Human Geographies*. London: Edward Arnold.

Ruggiero, V (2000) 'New social movements and the "centri sociali" in Milan', *Sociological Review*, no 48, 167-186.

Russell, B (2015) 'Beyond activism/academia: militant research and the radical climate and climate justice movement(s)', *Area*, 47, 222-229.

Shukaitis, S and Graeber, D (eds) (2007) *Constituent Imagination: Militant Investigations, Collective Theorization*. New York, NY Oakland, CA: AK Press.

Sitrin, M (ed) (2006) *Horizontalism: Voices of Popular Power in Argentina*. Oakland, CA: AK Press, London.

Starhawk (2011) *The Empowerment Manual: A Guide for Collaborative Groups*. San Francisco, CA: New Society.

Subcomandante Marcos (2001) *Our word is our weapon*. San Francisco, CA: Seven Stories Press.

Trapese Collective (2007) *Do it yourself A handbook for Changing our world* Pluto, London,

Wright, E O (2010) *Envisioning Real Utopias*. London: Verso.

FOURTEEN

Living *sín patrón*: lessons from Argentina's societies in movement

Marina Sitrin

The workplaces recuperated by their workers in the last years have created more jobs with new forms of production grounded in relationships of *compañerismo*. They have demonstrated that the problem of the economy was not labour cost, but boss cost [*costo patronal*]. Zanon, Brukman, Gatic, Durax, are examples of these experiences that today have begun to inspire workers in other countries in crisis. Their stories, histories and dreams, while contagious, also carry a quantity of self-organised projects, and help others discover the possibility of living *sín patrón* [without a boss] deciding their own destinies. (Lavaca Collective)[1]

Introduction

This chapter explores some of the movements that arose in Argentina soon before and after the popular rebellion of 19 and 20 December 2001 – movements whose forms of organising, such as *horizontaldad*, prefigurative politics and *autogestión*, closely coincide with movements that have emerged over the past 20 years across vast geographic areas. It then explores what sorts of lessons communities and societies in movements such as Occupy, the 'movements of the squares' and the climate justice movement can learn from the Argentine experiences – using the framework of working and living *Sín patrón* to help guide the discussion.

In recent decades, people have been finding ways to resist various crises (economic, political, social and environmental) by organising together. Examples include: the Zapatistas declaring a resounding '*Ya basta!*' ('Enough is enough!') in 1994 in the face of institutional power and creating dozens of self-governing communities; the 2001 popular rebellion in Argentina, where people sang '*Que se vayan todos, que no quede ni uno solo!*' ('Everyone must go, not even one should remain!') in

257

the streets, and which led to the citizens creating alternative horizontal, non-hierarchical assemblies, recuperating workplaces, establishing popular media outlets and building autonomous communities on the periphery of cities; the hundreds of thousands of people around the globe organised in neighbourhoods and entire communities, often led by women, to defend land, water and air using forms of direct democracy and direct action; and the Occupy movement and the movements of the squares, mobilising millions around the world and looking to one another instead of the institutions that created the crisis.

This type of organising, without hierarchies and in the spirit of resistance, is creating something new, focusing on social relationships and prefiguring participants' desired ends. This way of relating is referred to by some in Argentina as 'living sín patrón' (without a boss). Borrowing from the recuperated workplace movement, which uses the slogan sín patrón to describe workplaces after they are recuperated from the owners, this idea is taken a step further to mean how people are trying to live from day to day and how they are changing individually and collectively with and within this aspiration. Many now describe an existence where their lives are their own – not dictated from above, without bosses or the market determining the value of their relationships – and use the shorthand living sín patrón to help reflect this way of living/being/doing.

What has been taking place around the world, from the Zapatistas to Occupy and the movements of the squares, is part of a new wave that is both revolutionary in the day-to-day sense of the word and without precedent with regard to consistency of form, politics, scope and scale. Separately many of these forms are not 'new', but taking them together makes them so. These new forms have been practised for over 15 years in Argentina and encompass a diversity of groupings, classes and geographic locations.

Societies in movement

The movements described in this chapter paint a small part of a much larger picture of societies and communities in movement. These are not traditional social movements, with participants mobilised around particular slogans or a single demand forethought and pre-organised by a coordinating committee. Nor do they use pre-formed tactics to meet a set strategy. The movements emerge from necessity, use the assembly form, and having found demands on governments to be fruitless, with governments either ignoring their needs or refusing to meet them, they turn to one another, creating horizontally and self-organising autonomously. The participants in these movements have generally not been politically active before, and most identify as neighbour, grandmother, daughter or sister. They do not organise with party or union structures and do not seek representative formations. They come together in assembly forms, at first not out of any ideology, but because being in a circle is the best way for people to see and hear one another. They strive for horizontalism because they do not want to replicate those structures where power is something wielded. They do not begin talking about power or empowerment, and end up creating new theories and practices of what it means to change the world.[2]

I use the term 'societies in movements' to help describe these movements, and to reflect a conscious break in the concept and framing of social movements. This is not done to create another theoretical framework, but to provide a loose description that allows for more creative engagement than those so far offered in the contentious politics field. First articulated by Raúl Zibechi in relation to Bolivia in the early 2000s, the phrase is used here both with the literal meaning (societies/communities that are moving), and also as a way to help go beyond the structures imposed by social movement theory. Zibechi argues:

> The old pattern of social action began with a strike in a workplace, backed by a general strike and demonstrations. In the new pattern of action, the mobilisation starts in the spaces of everyday life and survival (markets, neighbourhoods) putting ... societies in movement, self-articulated from within. And not laying siege, as transpired under colonialism two centuries ago, but rather boring from within until cracks emerge and, later, partially smashing the system. (2010, p 77)

I take this further and extend it to people creating their own communities, not just those organised in geographic locations. I find it a more appropriate way of speaking about these non-state centred movements that have emerged over the past two decades, thus broadening the understanding.

Occupy and the movements of the squares

Between 2011 and 2012, millions of people gathered in plazas and squares around the world, variously declaring: 'No nos representan!' ('They don't represent us!') in Spain; 'Ya basta!' (with reference to the Zapatistas) in Greece; 'вы нас даже не представляете!' ('Vy nas dazhe ne predstavlyayete!' or 'You can't represent us – and you cannot even imagine us!') in Russia; and 'Kefaya!' ('Enough!') in Egypt during the protest against President Hosni Mubarak's government that sparked it all.

People came together in the 'no', the refusal, and began to talk about alternatives. Turning their backs on the state and institutions that brought them to this moment, they turned to one another, forming assemblies and over time, networks and groups of self-organisation (Roos and Oikonomakis, 2013; Sitrin and Azzellini, 2014). The media were incredulous, constantly asking, 'What do they want?' The traditional left was equally disbelieving, as well as angry when the movements did not accept their leadership. And social scientists reacted with a combination of both, concluding that these were not movements but appearances, 'we are here' moments (Tarrow, 2011).

The comparisons made between Argentina in the years after the economic collapse and the current movements are astounding, even down to the critique they have both received from the traditional left and social scientists, most being described as 'flash in the pan' events rather than movements, and non-serious due to their focus on building social relationships and prefiguration rather than parties with an eye to state power.

A number of years have passed since the plaza occupations, yet the reverberations continue. As the Spanish 15-M movement participants reflect, the movement was *una clima*, a climate, sensation and way of being. This echoes societies in movement in Latin America over the past decade, where, for example, people in Argentina speak of being children (*hijos*) of the popular rebellion of 2001 when referring to their continued use of *horizontalidad* and autonomy (Falleti, 2012; Sitrin, 2012). Looking to Latin America, and Argentina in particular, not only helps us to understand what has been taking place with the movements of the squares, and to envision possible ways forward, but opens up an entirely new way of thinking about power, movement, society and ways of living *sín patrón*.

Argentina's 'Que se vayan todos': MTDs and recuperated workplaces

On 19 and 20 December 2001, an economic crisis, precipitated by years of unprecedented privatisation in Argentina, came to a head. When the Argentine government froze people's bank accounts, they were no longer silent. Hundreds of thousands went into the streets banging pots and pans (*cacerolando*). People were not organised in any formal grouping, they merely saw their neighbours in the streets, *cacerolando*.

There was no specific chant or demand, but a song: '*Que se vayan todos, que no quede ni uno solo.*' Their protest worked. They forced out four consecutive governments. The movement has since been referred to, by others involved in movements in Argentina, as the 19th and 20th.

Rather than organising political parties or looking to take over the state, people came together and formed assemblies in their neighbourhoods and took over workplaces. Those neighbourhoods which already had high numbers of unemployed residents and high levels of existing self-organisation exploded with more projects and participants. New movements, groups and networks emerged, from media and art collectives, to popular kitchens, after-school programmes, groups for reflection and a massive bartering network. Due to space limitations, this chapter addresses only a few such formations: the Movimientos de Trabajadores Desocupados (Unemployed Workers' Movements, or MTDs); and recuperated workplaces. This is a selection that represents a diversity of class and identity as well as geography. All of these movements functioned with assemblies, coining the now widespread term *horizontalidad*.[3] As this chapter show, *horizontalidad* is a social relationship that emerged in the space of rejecting hierarchical forms of organising, and over time has been described as both a tool and a goal for emancipatory relationships (Sitrin, 2006; Zibechi, 2012).

While some movements have diminished in number, and a few have even disappeared, the forms of organising inspired by the popular rebellion continue. As activist Emilio described in late 2014:

> 'All the energy that was released on the 19th and 20th ... did not slow down. There was an epoch change: it has been more than 10 years and we have a government with a long continuum of *Kirschenrismo* and the many changes in Latin America, but the important energy is citizen participation, to join an assembly to discuss problems, listen, create tools through direct action, and struggle with road blockades.... That is not stopping, not at all, the opposite.' (Cited in Sitrin, 2014)

Argentine recuperations

'Occupy, Resist, Produce'[4] – this slogan represents one of the most straightforward yet sophisticated movements in Latin America over the past two decades. With over 350 recuperated workplaces in Argentina, workers are creating new relationships to production, often challenging the capitalist mode of value production (DeAngelis, 2006; Santos,

2007; Zibechi, 2010; Holloway, 2010). Similarly, workers have been organising in Uruguay, Brazil and most recently Europe, recuperating their work through horizontal assemblies and a vision of an alternative form of value production.

The process of workplace recuperations in Argentina arose from economic necessity. As with so many other things related to the popular rebellion, workers took the situation into their own hands. Not organised by unions, parties or any other external force, they self-organised horizontally (Zibechi, 2006). Workers are not staging sit-ins, strikes or occupations, but recuperating, almost always insisting on the language of *recuperar* meaning to recover, reclaim or take back. Implied is that something was already theirs (Ruggeri, 2014). They organise looking to one another, and most all explain how they organise by describing *horizontalidad* (Vieta and Ruggeri, 2009).

During a recent visit to Argentina, in early 2015, I heard of a flurry of recuperated restaurants, along with many other new workplace recuperations. I was excited about checking them out, and taking what some joked was a gastronomical tour of the movements. Andres Ruggeri, a long-time organiser and scholar with the recuperated movements, suggested lunch at *Los Chanchitos*, a typical neighbourhood tavern restaurant, serving *asados* (barbecued dishes), homemade pasta and local wines, and whose survival is due to those who regularly eat there from the neighbourhood. Now that the workers have taken it over and recuperated it, it is even more popular, with the neighbourhood regulars showing up to help defend the process of recuperation, and making a point of eating there all the more. Adding in the people like myself, choosing to eat there in solidarity, the result was that the meetings I intended to have here were impossible, as the workers were too busy running the restaurant, with an ever-present line of people waiting outside.

Then, wandering around looking for Nac & Pop, one of the three recently recuperated fast-food chains, serving *choripán* (a type of sandwich with chorizo), I was happily surprised to find it on one of the busiest corners of Buenos Aires, where Congreso meets the Avenida de Mayo. Across the large intersection and park opposite the bookstore of the Madres of the Plaza de Mayo, there is a small storefront grill with a sign that reads 'Nac & Pop sín patrón' and 'Trabajador@s de Nac & Pop en lucha'. There were many other hand-written posters as well, addressing issues of the day, such as police violence and xenophobia.

I spoke with a few of the workers, with others on their shift occasionally coming over to chime in. The four workers I spoke to (as well as all the others, from what I gathered from the photos adorning the restaurant) were under 30 years old and pretty alternative-looking – one had dreadlocks, another brightly coloured died hair, many had piercings and black seemed the colour of choice for clothing. They explained they were generally from neighbourhoods with high levels of unemployment, known for work precarity and day-to-day violence related to poverty. Some of the young workers were migrants and none would ever have imagined getting involved in political organising before this. They described their situation thus:

> "Nac & Pop is now called Nac & Pop sín patrón (without a Boss) because we, the workers, are managing and running it ourselves."
>
> "Around a year ago we began to notice a real change with the owners and management of Nac & Pop. We were not getting paid, they were making more and more excuses why they were not paying us, we worked in black, meaning without a contract or any social support. We then noticed that many people were having their shifts changed and were being moved around from one restaurant to another and we realised they must be closing some of the locals."
>
> "We knew we had to do something but didn't know what. None of us had previous experience, not in unions or with organising groups – we had no relationship to the union. We are all young and most are immigrants and mothers, and many have families. We were in difficult situations but had to do something, we just did not know how or have the tools ... but then a few *compañeros* in one local suggested we could recuperate the workplaces ..." "But we did it. Though not without big challenges ..."
>
> "Most of what has changed is the climate at work. In the beginning it was very difficult because we had to decide everything, what steps to take, who had what responsibilities and how to share them, making the schedules, figuring out how to do assemblies since we did not have any tradition or experience with them and just winning space and respect for all was huge."

Having spent time with workers in many dozens of recuperated workplaces over the past decade and more in Argentina, it is remarkable how similar this brief description in 2015 is to what other workers have described in other recuperation processes – the feeling of a lack of alternatives and fear, yet coming together and deciding to recuperate.

Also consistent is the feelings people express, finding a new dignity through discovering that together they can take back their work and lives.

Centrality of community

The community and neighbourhood are involved in the vast majority, if not all, of the recuperation processes.[5] Many begin by showing support with food and financial donations, and in those cases involving direct confrontation with the police – 60-70% of recuperations (Vieta, 2008) – the workplaces are defended by members of the community, with the majority coming from the neighbourhood in which the workplace is located.

Historically, the close ties between neighbours and workers are important when looking at the plethora of workplaces that also now double as social community centres. Recuperation is not so much a case of workplaces suddenly opening themselves up to the community, but rather the extension of a relationship that always existed, with the formation of community centres being one of the logical outcomes of this relationship. When the people of the city of Neuquén, southern Argentina, where the tile factory FaSinPat is located, say '*FaSinPat es del pueblo*', they really mean it: FaSinPat is of the people, and the people are FaSinPat. Some of the workplaces, such as the metal shop IMPA, and the Hotel Bauen, in downtown Buenos Aires, opened as community spaces in the first weeks of their recuperation, even before they began production/service. Others, such as Chilavert, Globo and Nueva Esperanza, evolved into community spaces more slowly. Beginning with a few events each month, many now hold almost daily activities for the community, organised by the neighbours in collaboration with the workers. These community events range from music and dance performances, to political talks and films, and classes in everything from tango and salsa to basic computer literacy and writing. The activities and programmes are up to the desires and imaginations of the neighbours.

In 2004, people throughout Argentina began to organise *bachilleratos*, alternative high school programmes. In a country that used to have some of the best public education in Latin America, after the economic crisis both access to and the level of education plummeted. There are now tens of thousands of people participating in the *bachilleratos* process. Students, together with a teacher/facilitator, choose their course of study for their degree, and these choices are often things such as cooperativism (the study of how a cooperative works) or socialism. A large number of the *bachilleratos* are held in recuperated workplaces.

The recuperated workplaces' relationship to the state has changed over time. To begin with, it was characterised by police repression and eviction orders. As the years passed, and the state began to regain a degree of legitimacy, various mechanisms were created to encourage autonomous movements to engage with it (Sitrin, 2012). One such measure was a law on cooperation granting workplaces the option to become cooperatives. This enables workplaces to function legally for a period of time, allowing them to apply for government loans. At the same time, there are regular attempts to evict workers from recuperated workplaces, even those that have requested legal status.

Placido, a worker at the recuperated print shop Chilavert, explained that while the state offers loans to some workplaces, it is 'always putting obstacles in our way, like inspections, permits ... and right when you are going to get back to work, there is another bureaucratic obstacle that takes all your time and you end up doing nothing' (Sitrin, 2012, p 198).

Lessons learned

Considering all of the challenges faced by the various movements, internal and external, recuperated workplaces have in many ways most successfully withstood the test of time. One of the many reasons for this is the concrete nature of the project. In contrast with, say, neighbourhood assemblies, recuperations arose from necessity and continue to be based on that same necessity. When thinking about the current movements, from Occupy to those in defence of the land, the importance of identifying need and concretising the struggle based on that need is paramount. Another reason for the success of recuperations is the depth of their embeddedness in the community – a relationship of reciprocal need over time.

Unemployed Workers' Movements

The Argentine *piquetero* or Unemployed Workers' Movement (MTD) first arose in the 1990s, and took off after 2001. Generally led by women, unemployed workers in the northern and southern provinces took to the streets by the thousands, blocking major transportation arteries demanding subsidies from the government (Svampa and Pereyra, 2003). Instead of using party brokers or elected officials, as was the norm, people came together in assemblies, deciding horizontally what to do next. The *piquete* (picket) was developed to stop all transit, as there was no option to strike or take other forms of collective action. It was on the *piquete* that the assembly experience deepened and relationships among neighbours, who supported one another often for days at a time, created the solidarity and forms of self-organisation that were to form the basis of such movements in the future. Over time, people began to refer to the *piquete* not so much as the shutting down of something, but the opening of something else (Zibechi, 2012).

The organisation and consistency of the blockades forced the government to introduce unemployment subsidies in Latin America. Within a few years of the emergence of the *piquetes*, many groups evolved into movements, expanding their strategies and tactics. Some movements continued to make demands on the state, while others, those to which this chapter refers, decided no longer to look to the state, abandoning the *piquete* and focusing their energy on the new relationships and forms of *autogestión* learned on the blockades. As Neka, one of the organisers of the MTD Solano, explained: 'The most marvellous idea is not to think of the future and deposit your life in the hands of others who will then guarantee this future, but rather the recuperation of life and live it in a way that is different' (Sitrin, 2006, p 242).

In these areas, movements sometimes squatted land, built housing and gardens, raised livestock, and created alternative methods of education and healthcare along with many other creative and subsistence projects. Most had a group for reflection, meaning anything from weekly discussion on popular topics, to study groups discussing books related to movements and autonomy, and regional and national gatherings.

With the example of the MTD Solano, some of the initial projects, beyond the bakeries and kitchens, were things such as fish hatcheries, shoe production from old tyres and acupuncture classes. The MTD of La Matanza, outside Buenos Aires, created a school, run by the movement and neighbours, a small sewing shop and an elaborate bakery from which many in the neighbourhood bought products. In La Plata, the MTD took over land to build housing, and the MTD in Allen, Patagonia, developed a micro-enterprise called 'Discover'. As a *compañera* explained: 'They named it "discover" because through the MTD they discovered the value of *compañerismo*, the value of solidarity. Through the MTD, they discovered experiences that enable one to express oneself beyond words' (Sitrin, 2006, p 109). The micro-enterprises produced clothing, shoes, bread and other food products.

Lessons learned

Of the movements described in this chapter, the MTDs suffered the worst effects of the struggle with the new governments, with many of the movements splitting, becoming incorporated, co-opted or just dissolving over time. As of 2015, a number of movements continued, striving for autonomy and *autogestión*, though not without many challenges and internal divisions. Even while the Kirchner governments offered subsidies to the movements, it was with so many strings attached that many found the relationship impossible. As El Vasco from the Movement for Social Dignity in Chipolleti described it: 'The relationship with the state will always be contentious, it will always be a sordid war, always' (Sitrin, 2012, p 202). Now that there is a far right government, the movements will likely suffer even more direct repression. As for lessons learned, first, participants would say that the movement needs to maintain its own agenda – not function in response to whatever the government does or does not offer, but rather decide what it wants and organise towards that end, meaning in particular that the relationship to the state must be carefully handled and done in such a way that it is based first and foremost on the movement's desired goals. Another difficulty was infiltration and disruption – not a new issue for movements, but nonetheless destabilising. Participants recognise the need to have group and movement agreements on how to deal with disruptive behaviour early on in the group's formation. Groups also need to agree in advance how lack of participation in collective projects will be handled. Lastly, many reflect on the importance of being dynamic in terms of how participants relate to one another: not turning relationships into ideologies, and keeping horizontalidad and autonomy as processes and not end results – not theories to ascribe to, but forms that are ever changing and must be so. Of the many positive outcomes from the MTDs, the focus on concrete projects, as with the recuperated workplaces, was key in maintaining unity and consistency in organising. A focus on collective and individual reflection was also central to the individual and collective success of the movements.

Conclusion: overarching lessons for living *sín patrón*

> The state cannot be used to transform the world. The role that we attribute to it should be revised. (Zibechi, 2003, p 202)

There is no formula for living *sín patrón* and creating a new world. There are, however, some common characteristics from the societies in movement described in these pages that over the years have been effective in changing social relationships, deepening self-organisation and autonomy, and resisting co-optation and incorporation. So much more can and should be said for all areas, and this section is written to open a conversation.

Horizontalidad

Horizontalism is a rough and imprecise translation of *horizontalidad* since it is more of a relationship than an 'ism', and in fact eschews ideological frameworks implied by 'isms'. That being said, horizontality is not descriptive enough to capture the relational aspects of the word/practice. Variations on horizontalism have become a global way of speaking about social relationships that are both directly democratic and strive for different relationships –ways of relating that are about the process as a part of the end, and a process that is ever-changing, as the end is never reached, with each change in the process changing the concept and each change in the concept changing the practice. This way of relating, where all can be heard and various facilitation tools are used to help make it possible, is one of the foundations of living *sín patrón*.

It is important to learn from the Argentinian experience that this is a process and not a thing or something that exists because one wishes it so, but a process that is constant and has to be struggled with collectively. It is a tool as well as a goal, as movement participants learned and shared in the early years of the struggle. One of the challenges that almost always emerges is the question of leadership. Leadership and horizontal relationships are not antithetical – what is necessary is open and non-hierarchical discussions and relationships to address the issue of leadership and create a space that some call 'leaderful' – where all are encouraged to lead. It is also important to have accountability structures in place, that again, are horizontal and based in the consensus of the group, so as to be able to address tensions and issues of power as they arise.

Autogestión as power

> 'The difference is thinking about power as a noun, to arrive at power, to obtain power, as if it was a thing, and power is a verb.' (Sergio, cited in Sitrin, 2006, p 195)

Autogestión, self-organisation with *horizontalidad* in this case, is the means that most movements use to organise alternative ways of being, doing and relating. Rather than looking to others, people find ways to do it themselves – with the 'it' ranging from taking back their source of work to preventing mining in their region and creating alternative forms of adjudication and justice. While the site of the self-organisation is sometimes different, it is nonetheless the core of the organisational form. In the land defence movements or HIJOS, for example, the struggle is territorial, yet some participants have other jobs or responsibilities that bring them back and forth to the blockades, projects or assemblies.

Inextricably linked to concepts of power, projects *autogestionadas* are outside the decision-making spheres of the state or institutions of power, and instead are organised directly by those participating in projects and struggles. Part of the intention behind horizontal self-organisation is the relationships created in the process of the collective project, not just the outcome of that project. This concept of power with *autogestión* began in the early days after the popular rebellion in Argentina and has continued (with many ups and downs) over the past decade. As Paula, a neighbourhood assembly participant in Buenos Aires, reflected after two years of new movement construction: 'These movements are thinking of a distinct kind of power: the power of transforming daily relations. Besides, when one talks of dominance, it is the need to build different social relations in the present, then later think about a future society' (Sitrin, 2006, p 193).

Autonomy: 'what do we want?'

Both *autogestión* and power from below link to the concept of autonomy – not in the theoretical sense of autonomous Marxism, but as a logical expression of relationships that are not determined by institutions of power and instead are self-(auto)organised. The cooperative Lavaca describes it thus:

> 'The way we understand autonomy is: The autogestión of personal and collective projects. The free flow of new forms of thinking and doing. The exercise of freedom, understood as a form of social power. So as to develop these objectives we have created a series of tools.' (Sitrin, 2012, p 59)

Lavaca is an example of one of many groups that struggled with the question of autonomy as it relates to receiving subsidies from the state.

In particular, after the law on cooperation was passed and other groups in addition to recuperated workplaces could apply for government funds, Lavaca was one of many that decided to do so (after much debate). Soon afterwards, when it found it was not receiving enough to survive and was in engaged in constant battle with the government, which was taking up a great deal of its time (see Placido's earlier comments with respect to Chilavert), it decided to self-organise again without external funding. At the same time, it had a conversation about what it wanted. As Claudia from Lavaca said, "We had to begin again and ask ourselves – but what do we want?" This seems like a simple question, but, as she explained, once there is government engagement in a movement, the agenda often changes, and what the movement wants sometimes comes second or gets put on the back burner, as the government's proposals and offers are presented with such urgency they are generally discussed first.

Lavaca decided that what it wanted was to maintain its autonomy and self-organisation as a media producer – without the interference from the state and without paying the 18% tax that all media makers are required to pay. After organising with 60 other independent media outlets, in the streets and in the courts, it succeeded. Now, independent media do not have to pay any tax on their income. This means that many cooperatives can now survive on their self-organised work, where they could not before. Autonomy here came from the question, 'What do we want?'

The centrality of affect and new subjectivities

> 'It's about being able to create a new relational mode.... When this new form of politics emerges it establishes a new territory, or spatiality. And how is this sustained? It cannot be supported through ideology. In the beginning, the assembly consisted of people from all walks of life, ranging from the housewife who declared, "I am not political," to the typical party hack. But there was a certain sensibility, I don't know what to call it, something affective. And that generated a certain kind of interpersonal relationship between people. It generated a way of being and a certain sense of "we", or oneness, that is sustainable.' (Martín, cited in Sitrin, 2006, p 232).

Many movement participants have used the phrase '*política afectiva*' (affective politics) to explain part of the base from which their organising and motivating derives, affect meaning affection and love, a relational emotion, based on one's own feelings, but not separated from the group or the collective.

Concluding to begin

To begin living *sín patrón*, based on the experiences described in this chapter, people must organise together, in non-sectarian ways, grounded in horizontal forms while creating new affective relationships. From this base, it is key that concrete projects emerge that help meet people's needs. Challenges from the state, internal hierarchies related to accountability and leadership issues must all be addressed from the start, with guidelines and forms of mediation, among other things, so as to avoid divisions and disruption of the movement's agenda.

Developing specific concrete projects for survival and sustenance, together with the social relationships described allows for the flourishing of a new sort of value – one that while still under capitalism is also beyond capitalist value relationships, and instead creates new forms of relating based on and in relationships of solidarity. It is this, as is discussed in other chapters, that helps in the development of solidarity economies.

Notes

[1] http://www.lavaca.org/deci-mu/deci-mu-la-vida-sin-patron

[2] The descriptions in this article come from prior fieldwork in all of the locations cited; some variations on the descriptions and interviews have been published, while many others have not.

[3] Lavaca, comprising the cooperative and collectively run media site (Lavaca.org) and paper *MU*, came up with this concept. It came out of collective experiences, and thus it would not want to be credited with inventing the term, particularly now that it has become more widespread, but to the best of my knowledge, it was Lavaca's persona/political experiences together with learning from and sharing those of other autonomous movements in Argentina that resulted in this expression.

[4] This slogan has been borrowed from the Landless Workers' Movement (Movimento dos Trabalhadores Rurais Sem Terra) in Brazil, whose slogan is 'Ocupar, Resistir, Produzir'.

[5] In everything I have ever read, and every conversation I have had with participants in ERTs and those supporting them, I never once heard of a situation where a workplace was recuperated without support from the community.

References

DeAngelis, M (2006) *The Beginnings of History: Value Struggles and Global Capital*. London: Pluto Press.

Falleti, V (2012) *Movilización y protesta de las clases medias Argentinas: Cacerolazo y Asambleas Barriales*. Buenos Aires: CLACSO.

Holloway, J (2010) *Crack Capitalism*. London: Pluto Press.

Marcos, S. (2001) Interview by G Marquez and R Pombo, *New Left Review*, http://newleftreview.org/II/9/subcomandante-marcos-the-punch-card-and-the-hourglass, (accessed 17 September 2015).

Roos, J and Oikonomakis, L (2013) 'We are everywhere! The autonomous roots of the real democracy movement', *Comparative perspectives on the new politics of dissent*, pp 1-28.

Ruggeri, A (2014) *Que Son Las Empresas Recuperadas?*, Buenos Aires: Continente.

Santos, B de S (2007) *Another Production is Possible: Beyond the Capitalist Canon*. New York: Verso Books.

Sitrin, M (2006) *Horizontalism: Voices of Popular Power in Argentina*. Oakland, CA: AK Press.

Sitrin, M (2012) *Everyday Revolutions: Horizontalism and Autonomy in Argentina*. London: Zed Books.

Sitrin, M (2014) 'Defending the Earth in Argentina: From Direct Action to Autonomy', *Tidal Magazine*, available at http://tidalmag.org/blog/everyday-revolutions/defending-the-earth-in-argentina-from-direct-action-to-autonomy.

Sitrin, M and Azzellini, D (2014) *They Can't Represent US!: Reinventing Democracy from Greece to Occupy*, New York: Verso Books.

Svampa, M and Pereyra, S (2003) *Entre la Ruta y El Barrio: La Organizaciones Piqueteros*, Buenos Aires: Editorial Biblos.

Tarrow, S (2011) 'Why Occupy Wall Street is Not the Tea Party of the Left: The United States' Long History of Protest', *Foreign Affairs*. Available at www.foreignaffairs.com/articles/north-america/2011-10-10/why-occupy-wall-street-not-tea-party-left.

Vieta, M (2008) 'Autogestión and the worker-recuperated enterprises in Argentina: The potential for reconstituting work and recomposing life', Toronto: Programme in Social and Political Thought, York University. Retrieved May 2009 from http://lsj.sagepub.com/content/35/3/295.abstract

Vieta, M and Ruggeri, A (2009) 'The worker recovered enterprises as workers' co-operatives: The conjunctures, challenges, and innovations of self-management in Argentina and Latin America', in D Reed and JJ McMurtry (eds) *International Co-operation and the Global Economy*, Cambridge: Cambridge Scholars Press, pp 178–226.

Zibechi, R (2003) *Genealogía de la revuelta. Argentina: la sociedad en movimiento.* Montevideo: Nordan-Letra Libre.

Zibechi, R (2006) 'Worker run factories: From survival to economic solidarity', in T Ballve with V Prashad (eds) *Dispatches From Latin America: On the Frontlines against Neoliberalism.* Cambridge, MA: South End Press, pp 339-349.

Zibechi, R (2010) *Dispersing Power: Social Movements as Anti-State Forces*, Oakland, CA: AK Press.

Zibechi, R (2012) *Territories in Resistance: A Cartography of Latin American Social Movements*, Oakland, CA: AK Press.

Zibechi, R (2013) 'Is it Possible to Defeat Monsanto?', Chiapas Support Network. Available at http://compamanuel.com/2013/10/23/raul-zibechi-it-it-possible-to-defeat-monsanto.

FIFTEEN

The social and solidarity economy in Argentina and the UK: convergence from opposite directions

Molly Scott Cato and Paola Raffaelli

Introduction

This chapter explores the commonalities and differences in the history of the development of the social and solidarity economy (SSE) in the UK and Argentina, and in particular how the need for social security and welfare in the 19th century was resolved through mutual organisation in both societies. It discusses how this welfare provision was then absorbed into the state in the UK, while in Argentina it became part of an independent SSE with significant legislative underpinning and political support, particularly from the Peronist Party during the 20th century. In the final stage of comparison, we highlight the unpicking of the welfare state in the UK, which has led to an increased need for voluntary welfare provision, branded as the Big Society, and discuss attempts in Argentina to encourage cooperative entrepreneurism. As well as providing an account of the social function of the SSE, in keeping with a central theme of this collection, the chapter also explores how the need to make a rapid transition to sustainability works alongside the need for social justice to suggest a reciprocal relationship between the development of the SSE in these two societies, North and South.

Although historically the unmet need for social welfare was tackled through mutual organisation in both societies, in the UK social welfare came to be exercised primarily through the state, governed by national legislation on minimum standards and then implemented through local authorities. This led to the heyday of the welfare state for the three decades following the end of the Second World War. In Argentina universal state welfare was the provider of basic needs, such as health and education, complemented by civil society, unions and religious institutions. However, as discussed in more detail later, the politics of austerity – that is, the opportunistic actions of the opponents of state provision to exploit the 2008 financial crisis to achieve their long-held aim of reducing welfare provision – has reduced the differences between North and South, as the scope and depth of payments and services has been reduced, leading to a situation where voluntary and solidarity organisations have been forced to fill gaps that would once have been the responsibility of the state.

Solidarism in the UK and the rise and fall of the welfare state

When the history of Britain is taught in schools, the advent of the welfare state is usually dated to the publication in 1942 of a report by William Beveridge called *Social Insurance and Allied Services* (Beveridge, 1942). However, prior to this state-administered insurance system there was a network of mutual and membership organisations that ran a myriad of social and health services from hospitals to funeral parlours. This was the era of the 'friendly society', an insurance-based system established and managed by working people for their own interest and that of their fellows. It was a classic example of a solidaristic welfare system to fill the gap that had been created in large part by the movement of workers from rural areas to the industrial cities that gathered pace in the 19th century.

While few today would question the extent to which the welfare state has brought great benefits, there are some who regret the passing of the voluntaristic and solidaristic forms of welfare provision that predated it and was effectively eliminated by it (Yeo, 1976). And the welfare state is now coming under attack from a different and new direction: the politics of austerity operates like a self-fulfilling prophecy that raises fears about the cost of providing decency and security for all and by creating this fear thus undermines the sense of solidarity and universalism that the welfare state relies on for its success.

There is little question that this narrative is being successful in undermining the social attitudes that underpin the political economy of welfare in the UK. In parallel with a rhetorical attack on the solidarity underpinning the welfare state in the UK, we have witnessed an undermining of the principle of universalism. Examples of policies that target specific groups and move away from universal benefits include:

- the withdrawal of child benefit from higher earners;
- the introduction of high university fees, with an implication that students should look to their own family to fund their studies;

- the rolling out of a 'Universal Credit' that is anything but, as it is conditional on tightened eligibility criteria, signals the return of the 'deserving versus undeserving' distinction and results in more payments to men than women.

Since a solidarity economy requires a commitment to universalism, these changes to the nature of welfare provision in the UK, especially when combined with a rhetoric focusing on the distinction between the deserving and undeserving poor, are inimical to its development.

Alongside this undermining of the principles of solidarity and universalism in welfare provision, we have seen arguments that rehabilitate the sense of autonomy and independence characteristic of the patchwork of mutual organisations that pre-dated the state welfare system. This explains the nostalgic recollection of the friendly societies and other working-class organisations undertaken by the Coalition government's 'poverty tsar' Frank Field (2000):

> The shift in thinking about the nature of the partnership between the voluntary and statutory sectors in the 1980s and 1990s has been profound. Government has consciously sought to promote the role of the voluntary sector as an alternative to the state, sometimes invoking the example of the late nineteenth century. (Lewis, 1999, p 16).

Coinciding with a political narrative of austerity and the inevitability of a shrinking of the state, this revival of interest in the social and voluntary provision of welfare in the UK has been greeted cynically by those who view it as at best an opportunistic Trojan Horse and at worst a thin veneer concealing an ideologically motivated assault on universal welfare provision.

It is in this context that the idea of the Big Society has emerged, first cautiously and then with greater fanfare following a speech made by the then Prime Minister David Cameron in July 2010. He portrayed this policy shift as an opportunity for liberation from the oppressive state, a chance for citizens to shake off the shackles of welfare system and soar to new heights of mutual and autonomous endeavour:

> The Big Society is about a huge culture change – where people ... don't always turn to officials, local authorities or central government for answers to the problems they face but instead feel both free and powerful enough to help themselves and their own communities.

Commentators approaching this proposal with an open mind have portrayed it as:

> ... an alternative to centralisation and state-led development ... [through which] ... the Big Society proposes a transfer of responsibility for meeting needs away from the public sector, to social enterprises, community groups, the private sector and individuals and families. (North, 2011, p 819)

Less friendly commentators have viewed it rather as a cynical rebranding of the continuation of the Thatcherite attack on the state, a deliberate political project, left incomplete when the Conservatives lost power in 1997, launched in the guise of a necessary austerity programme: '[t]he Government could not have taken up its axe with such composed ruthlessness without a story to tell about how to fill the gaps left by a retreating state' (Coote, 2011, p 82). The new brand has proved neither popular nor memorable: by September 2010 only 55% of the population had heard of it, while 57% thought it was an excuse for the government to save money by cutting public spending. In practice, rather than as rhetoric, data from the Department for Communities and Local Government (DCLG) indicate that rates of volunteering and civic participation generally are actually declining. Data collected by the Third Sector Research Centre indicates that volunteering is something of a minority sport in the UK, with 9% of people – referred to as the 'civic core' – providing 87% of the volunteer hours (Mohan and Bulloch, 2012). These are well-educated, middle-aged people, more likely to live in the south of England and be actively religious. For the majority of people, rates of participation in volunteering were lower in 2010/11 than in any year before then (33% compared with 38% and 39% for the previous two years). Formal volunteering on a monthly basis was also at its lowest since 2001 at just 25% (DCLG, 2011).

In legislative terms, the most demonstrable instantiation of the theory of the Big Society is found in the Localism Bill, introduced to parliament on 13 December 2010. The DCLG claimed that this Bill would shift power from central government back into the hands of individuals, communities and councils. The rhetoric supporting this purported shift in power is an anti-statist one around decentralising power and controlling bureaucracy. It is also an anti-government rhetoric, with an emphasis on giving power back to a range of poorly defined 'communities' such as 'neighbourhoods', as well as 'individuals' and undefined 'professionals'. In terms of services, the Bill claims to be 'putting power in the hands of individuals themselves' and that 'where services are enjoyed collectively, they should be delivered by accountable community groups' (Conservative Party, 2009, p 8). Like the example of planning cited later, this is a deceptive offer. In the age of austerity, local people are being given an opportunity within a sphere of influence that government cuts have ensured will grow narrower year on year. People are free to choose to run their own libraries, even to buy back the library they thought they already owned; they are not free to demand that the libraries they have are properly funded and remain in public control.

So how much evidence is there of the Big Society in operation in the UK? One of the first services to be cut as 'non-essential' was the library service, which had been run as a public service for more than 150 years. The Chartered Institute of Library and Information Professionals conducted a survey in 2012 and found that, in response to funding cuts, 80% of authorities had reduced the number of librarians employed in 2011/12, and 60% had done so again in 2012/13. In consequence a growing number of local governments were considering or experimenting with community-run libraries staffed by volunteers. According to data from Public Libraries News website,[1] there were 170 volunteer-run libraries in 2012, rising to 300 by the end of 2013; 12% of all public libraries have some element of volunteer staffing.

This is certainly the sort of thing that proponents had in mind when they coined the phrase Big Society: citizens meeting their needs directly without the intervention of politicians or policymakers. But can we consider it to be part of the solidarity economy? Rather than the creation of autonomous institutions based on membership and participation and in response to a need, it seems more appropriate to characterise voluntary libraries as a marginal appendage of a properly funded state service that is atrophying in response to cuts in funding levels. It is also doubtful how long the enthusiasm of the volunteer librarians will last.

If we turn from welfare services to the income-support component of the social security system in the UK, we find an even bleaker picture: cuts to benefits have had the effect of reducing many to pre-1945 levels of poverty. Evidence of the desperate levels of poverty in some of the UK's poorest communities is found in the rapidly increasing number of people now relying on foodbanks to provide them with the basic necessities of life. The Trussell Trust is the charity behind the UK's foodbanks, which have increased in number by 76% and by 170% in terms of the number of people given emergency food since April 2012. In 2008/09 the trust provided three days of emergency food rations to 26,000 people; by 2011/12 this number had risen to 128,697, and to 346,992 by 2012/13.

So do foodbanks constitute part of the SSE? The trust began working with poor people in Bulgaria and only switched its attention to the poor of the UK as demand increased. It has a religious motivation and an explicitly Christian mission. The purposes of the SSE in both North and South is to encourage independence and autonomy, whereas foodbanks are a throwback to an earlier age where the poor were forced to rely on charity to survive. In our view, foodbanks, while they may be part of the Big Society, are decidedly not part of the SSE.

Solidarity economy and welfare in Argentina

In Argentina, the SSE has always been divided into two distinct strands: one based around the idea of philanthropy and linked to Catholic Church, the other voluntaristic and communitarian, arising from working-class organisation. Immigrants, mainly from Italy and Spain, with sympathies for anarchism and socialism, set up mutual organisation alongside other workers' organisations. Mutual aid societies were mainly found in cities and were responsible for generating spaces of socialisation, workers' culture and education, through the creation of libraries as a way to tackle illiteracy, for example. Moreover, mutuals were made up of workers who might share a trade, and they provided services in terms of health insurance and social security. These organisations, which aimed primarily to enhance workers' welfare, operated as the predecessors of trade unions. Just as an example, in the late 19th century, 200,000 workers belonged to unions and had relationships with 659 mutual associations (Moirano, undated). On the other hand, cooperatives emerged as the way to help small farmers compete with larger, more powerful agricultural businesses. They appeared as an alternative to enable farmers to invest in the highly expensive machinery required by the agricultural industry and compete with larger companies (Ressel et al, 2008). Interestingly, both political and cooperative developments in Argentina can be linked to the immigrant community.

Cooperation worked in Argentina as a strategy of those who needed to solve a problem based on collective action, solidarity and a sense of social vindication that aimed to reduce economic concentration and, to some extent, work as a counterbalance in the economic struggle (Schujman, 1984). A clear example of this is the use of local cooperatives for supplying public services, such as water, electricity and gas, and telephone landlines, beginning in the 1930s. Due to the low population density of the country (Argentina's territory accounts for about 2,780,000 km², more than 11 times that of the UK, but with half the population) and the enormous cost it implied for market companies (Montes and Ressel 2003), consumers created these cooperatives themselves. Thus, cooperativism resulted in the ultimate solution for a problem that would not have been solved in another way. Therefore, the SSE was seen as a valid form of economic organisation in a country that was still in its infancy.

The biggest consumer cooperative was the Workers' Home (El Hogar Obrero). It was founded in 1905 by Juan B Justo and Dr Nicolas Repetto, and sought not only to promote projects and provide loans, but also to disseminate cooperative principles. The cooperative operated until 1991. This organisation was a key element in the social mobility process of working-class sectors that were integrated into the middle class through access to housing and household appliances provided by the cooperative. Undoubtedly, Justo made a relevant contribution to the cooperative movement in Argentina. He proposed a socialist movement based on the development of an agricultural social economy as an alternative to capitalism. For this he suggested the idea of a comprehensive agrarian reform programme based on principles of association and political organisation linking rural and urban workers. This rural-urban social block was the basis of the production and consumption cooperative movement, which aimed to improve the living conditions of different social groups (Forni et al, 2003).

By the beginning of the 20th century, the cooperative movement was established and Entrerriana Cooperative Federation was formed to bring together cooperatives from Entre Rios. In 1922, the Association of Rural Cooperatives Central Zone, the oldest federation that continues to this day, was created. At first it only involved entities of the provinces of Santa Fe and Cordoba, but later extended its scope. In the 1950s confederations, the Agricultural Cooperative Federation and the Cooperative Confederation of Argentina Ltd emerged. All of these supported the efforts of agricultural cooperatives and farmers not only in terms of production, but also the marketing and commercialisation of their products.

By the 1930s and 1940s, cooperatives were playing a key role in the development of public services in isolated rural areas that were too expensive for private companies to reach profitably. As the provision of public services, especially electricity, was in the hands of foreign private companies that did not invest in expanding services to rural areas, residents formed cooperatives that provided the service at a lower cost. At the beginning, these actions were resisted by the government and public enterprises, but quickly spread to other cities and services. In addition, during the first five-year plan of the Peron government, the number of agricultural cooperatives and consumers increased rapidly. For example, in 1937 there were 278 cooperatives composed of 42,182 workers. By 1951, this had increased to 944 cooperatives with 181,070 workers.

Given its particular understanding of state and its relations, Peronism was a turning point in Argentinian society – and this affected the SSE. Although it is disputed in the literature, it can be argued that Peronism conceived of the SSE as a 'third way' between monopolistic concentration and a local bureaucratic bourgeoisie (Elgue and Cieza, 2005), or a third way as neither capitalism nor communism but as social justice (*justicialismo*) (Vieta, 2012). Many authors consider that Peronism changed the nature of SSE. Social services in Argentina were not universal; rather they were acquired through employment. Thus, in the Peronist era, mutuals and mutual aid societies belonging to trade organisations were sucked into the national health system under the scope of trade unions, and this is still the case today (Campetella et al, 2000). To some extent, it is possible to argue that unions worked as an arm of the state, and therefore, health provision was understood as a state service. Moreover, the promotion of both rural and consumer co-operatives was included in the first five-year economic plan that was launched by Peron in 1946, reinforced in the second plan in 1952 (Levin and Verbeke, 1997). Although the plan was not entirely accomplished, being derailed by the *coup d'état* that took place in 1955, cooperatives doubled in number during the 1940s and almost doubled again in the 1950s (Arzadun, 2011).

After the anti-Peronist Liberating Revolution of 1955, two working cooperatives were created during the 1960s with the support of trade unions, and both still exist today. IMPA, a metallurgical firm, and COGTAL, a graphics company, were each created by workers who formed the cooperative with initial capital from the unions and from severance pay. Then, in the 1970s, graphics and rail workers created Ferrograf. These three examples are united by the common experience that the company they emerged from was closed for political reasons, and the workers decided to join a cooperative to keep working. While it is not the only one, Buenos Aires Graphical Federation is one of the few unions that provided support to self-management cooperatives.

As part of their commitment to the working class, the Peronists promoted cooperatives in some sectors, particularly in the consumer and agricultural sectors. This is why since the Peronist era, Argentina has been considered as a populist example of the SSE, as during this time the solidarity economy was mobilised by the state as a response to the demands of the lowest income sectors of society, and represented the consolidation of government power (Coraggio, 2002; Arzadun, 2011). Thus, although Peronism encouraged the formation of cooperatives, it merged them with the state, constraining their independence. Conversely, to some extent the decline in Peronism following the overthrow of Isabel Peron in 1976 was mirrored by a decline in the SSE. Some authors argue that the destruction of the working class and the decollectivisation this produced during the boom years of neoliberalism is the reason why the SSE took so long to resurface in Argentina (Wyczykier, 2007). Following the catastrophic financial and economic crisis that emerged in 2002, associative economic activity became a lifeline for many, and both cooperatives and other forms of alternative economic life flourished once more.

The size of the SSE fluctuated during 20th century in Argentina, and towards the end of that century it experienced a dramatic change in character, as it had become highly bureaucratic, mainly as a result of its incorporation into the state by Peronism. The legal cooperative form was distorted as a result of various tax breaks as well as the precarious nature of work relationships. Consequently in some cases the use of the cooperative form was distorted by what were known as 'false co-operatives', formed to avoid taxes and create further precarious (and cheaper) work relationships. The result was that the anarchist and socialist cooperative principles of the 19th century immigrant pioneers did not stand the test of time (Ruggeri, 2011). This misuse is reflected in available data from the National Council for Associativity and Social Economy (Instituto Nacional de Asociativismo y Economía Social), which cannot give conclusive information on the size of Argentina's SSE. Although there are 12,760 registered coops that account for 15 million members, only 5,100 have declared their economic activity. Moreover, 87.9% of them belong to public services, financial, health and agricultural sectors and the large majority of their members only make financial contributions but do not work for them. Finally, only 112,000 people work in workers' coops (INAES, 2008). This emphasises the lack of reliable information about the sector and the misuse of the legal form.

We cannot end this discussion of SSE in Argentina without a discussion of the *empresas recuperadas* (reclaimed enterprises). In the wake of the major economic, social and political crisis at the end of 2001, many examples of collective action emerged. Due to the significant increase in unemployment, workers soon understood that their best chance to tackle it was from within the workplaces rather than passively accepting redundancy (Raffaelli, 2013). Workers, faced with previous owners' neglect to take deliberate action or due to the economic failure of companies, decided to occupy the factories and bring them back into production. Reclaimed factories represented a trade-off between a defensive element that prevented them from losing their jobs and a political action that proposed the idea of autonomy (Dinerstein, 2007). Reclaimed factories became renowned in the 2000s and are still in formation, although to a lesser extent. It is not a finished process; rather it is still occurring and has been reproduced in other countries. In the latest reclaimed factories census, such organisations accounted for 311 companies (Ruggeri and Vieta, 2015).

The role that solidarity had in this process is widely recognised (North and Huber, 2004); however, with the exception of a few studies, cooperation has received less attention (Vieta, 2014). In its origins, reclaimed factories used of the cooperative legal form as a formality, but not as a consequence of the commitment with its values. Nevertheless, along with the settling down of the company and the construction of a social group that could handle it, they developed the necessary cooperation, and hence fully adopted the cooperative form (Raffaelli, 2013). In this sense, the construction of solidarity, the collective form of self-management, and cooperative relationships appeared as a consequence of practical needs rather than ideology, and are central for the understanding of Argentinian reclaimed factories. Although this type of collective action had already appeared in Argentinian history (Dinerstein, 2007; Wyczykier, 2007), the particularity of the responses to the 2001 socioeconomic crisis is given by the fact that they appeared as a worker reaction to neoliberal failure.

Finally, in an attempt to reduce unemployment, the Kirchner governments[2] included the SSE in public policies. The scope was significantly broader as it included reclaimed enterprises, existing coops, and new coops to be founded through those programmes. For instance, the Manos a la Obra (Hands to Work), Programa de Trabajo Autogestionado (Self-managed Work Programme) and the Argentina Trabaja (Argentina Works) plans sought social inclusion through productive ventures based on associative and self-managed values (Dinerstein, 2007; Neffa et al, 2012). These policies altogether created more than 7,300 worker cooperatives by 2011 (Vuotto, 2012). Although these policies demonstrate an alternative to the legitimised, mainstream economy, suggesting that some organisations can be guided neither by state nor market principles, the concern is that the sustainability of top-down initiatives contradicts the central principles of the SSE, namely the freedom of association (Dinerstein,

2007; Hopp 2011). Furthermore, despite the fact that this policy can be conceptualised in the same way as co-option in the UK, this is not the case, as Argentinian experience is fully embedded in populism (Coraggio, 2005) and the state here was more involved in the development of the SSE. Additionally, many other steps were taken, such as the introduction of a national law for SSE development, training and advice for SSE organisations, and the allocation of funding. So it was neither a stand-alone policy, nor one supported the SSE by itself. It was a form of 'assistentialist' policies that created further dependency on central government (Ruggeri and Vieta, 2015) or a tool for institutionalising social mobilisation (Dinerstein, 2007).[3]

Despite the fact that SSE became part of the policy agenda, its scope remains limited. Some authors, such as North and Huber (2004) (writing about the situation in 2002/03) were concerned that the anti-neoliberal experiences in Argentina, such as neighbourhood assemblies and Trueque (barter networks), might turn out to be transitory and not resilient. However, the case of reclaimed enterprises, worker cooperatives and the picket movement is different. Coraggio (2011) acknowledges that the limited number of organisations involved and the lack of a strong national movement act against the construction of a 'different economy'. Nonetheless, he still recognises the potentiality of SSE. Moreover, as Coraggio (2011; Chapter Two in this volume) points out wisely, the SSE should be recognised as a fundamental part of the economy in developing countries due to the significance of the informal sector in the satisfaction of needs, which means that we should recognise the existence of a three-sector, mixed economy.

Sustainability and social justice

Alternative trajectories for SSE in the UK and Argentina may seem like two separate and distinct narratives, linked only by their aspiration to claim a separate space within a capitalist economy, but we would argue that there are common themes that we can describe in terms of autonomy, solidarity and participation. To these we seek to add another perspective where we believe the SSE has something to offer: sustainability. SSE organisations in Latin America seek to achieve social, economic and to some extent, political sustainability. However, they are not able to achieve ecological goals. According to some theoretical perspectives, the potential of the SSE to contribute to sustainable forms of development in Latin America is limited as a consequence of poverty, unsustainable management of natural resources, a negative institutional environment, high population growth, and lack of social consensus on the meaning of sustainable growth. These five aspects are mutually interlinked, given as a result a complex issue (Gabaldón, 2000). Thus, in a region with more urgent problems to be solved, ecological issues are not considered important.

In the context of the most urgent sustainability problem the world faces – climate change – the conflict between those who enjoy post-industrial comfort and those without access to electricity and running water have so far stood in the way of consensus in discussions on the United Nations' Framework Convention on Climate Change. In the case of relationships between Europe and Latin America, the parliamentary assembly known as EuroLat, supported by the Heinrich Böll Foundation, affiliated to the German Green Party, attempted to bridge this gap by producing a motion that parliamentarians from both sides of the Atlantic were able to sign up to in June 2015.

The motion tackled head on some of the key areas of disagreement, placing particular responsibility on the industrialised and wealthy Western countries to facilitate the transfer of the technologies that the fossil-fuel era had enabled them to develop, while simultaneously noting the important responsibility of Latin American societies to preserve their natural forests. It also attempted to valorise attempts in several Latin American societies to develop 'a new paradigm of human well-being that reconciles the twin challenges of fighting climate change and enhancing equality and social cohesion; encourages governments to strengthen bi-regional exchange using concepts such as "Buen Vivir" [living well]' (EuroLat, 2015, p 2).

It should also be noted that the process of negotiation at the Paris talks could also be argued to have responded to an agenda of solidarity and particularly to the bottom-up process favoured by those who support the idea of a solidarity economy. Rather than leaders negotiating in a zero-sum game, it was left to individual countries, no matter how small, to make their best offer for reducing carbon dioxide emissions and implementing measures to make the transition towards a clean energy future. It was the bottom-up nature of the negotiations that enabled a deal.

It is difficult to know what effect the intervention by Pope Francis into the discussion on sustainability will have, although one can assume that in a continent with some half a billion Catholics, and with which the Pope is well acquainted, his impassioned plea for a holistic approach to global environmental policymaking must have had some impact. Pope Francis, with his background as a Jesuit and his choice of Saint Francis as his theological inspiration, has demonstrated the impact that liberation theology has had on his teaching. In the extraordinary papal encyclical, 'Laudato Si: On Care for Our Common Home', it effectively extends the mission to the poor to a mission to the poor of the whole planet, with all its multiple and varied species. Hence, in connection with climate change, Pope Francis notes:

> Many of the poor live in areas particularly affected by phenomena related to warming, and their means of subsistence are largely dependent on natural reserves and ecosystemic services such as agriculture, fishing and forestry. They have no other financial activities or resources which can enable them to adapt to climate change or to face natural disasters, and their access to social services and protection is very limited. For example, changes in climate, to which animals and plants cannot adapt, lead them to migrate; this in turn affects the livelihood of the poor, who are then forced to leave their homes, with great uncertainty for their future and that of their children. (Pope Francis, 2015, p 25)

His message is that the planet and the climate must be conceived as common goods, gifts of God to be shared. This message is remarkably similar to that of the contraction and convergence model of climate justice. A mutual, global solution requires the recognition of the global atmosphere as a 'common heritage' that should be equally shared among all citizens of the world. This is what is proposed as the contraction and convergence model, moving towards an emissions total in 2050 that is compatible with continued human life on the planet and shares the CO_2 emissions in per capita terms.

Conclusion: diverse history but shared future?

We need not be surprised to find common motivations for the growth of social and solidarity economies in the UK and Argentina, since it is intrinsic to mutual economic organisation that those who face difficulties join together to solve their problems in solidarity and justice. But beyond this common impulse to find shared solutions to economic problems, what common threads can we find between the experiences of these two very different societies?

The most obvious difference between the UK and Argentina is that in the former the consumer and welfare cooperative or mutual society predominated historically, whereas in Argentina, under the influence of the influx of European migrants who brought their associative and syndicalist traditions with them, it was the worker cooperative that was most influential. However, in both cases we witness the institutionalisation of working-class solidarity and the establishment of autonomous economic organisations to provide livelihoods and welfare to their members based on the Rochdale principles[4] of open access and equality.

In terms of our theme about the role that the SSE can play in substituting for a state-funded welfare state, we see a commonality in terms of how the dominant political ideology has attempted to co-opt what is essentially an autonomous social form to serve its own political ends. In the UK, this is how we would characterise the emergence of the idea of the Big Society, which, while it may sound like material from which a solidarity economy might be fashioned, is in reality the reverse. Rather than a society of shared values and social security guaranteed through a social contract, the Big Society represents a return to the 19th-century values of self-help and philanthropy, especially when implemented against the backdrop of a politics of austerity that guarantees the shrinking of the state and a continual reduction in public funding. So while the UK coalition government has co-opted the idea of social enterprise and the social economy, its policies are in fact inimical to the development of a genuinely autonomous and solidarity economy. In Argentina, we can see a similar co-option of mutualism through the significant involvement of the Peronist Party. In Argentina, the origins of the SSE can be more directly linked to the need to provide for one's livelihood in a society where survival required and for most still requires the production of economic value and that does not have a social security safety-net. Thus there is evidence that in Argentina, rather than the welfare state meaning direct cash payments, it means providing subsidy and tax advantages to solidarity workplaces.

As in the UK, the cooperative form grew up in response to the socioeconomic times and the institutional problems that Argentina was experiencing during its period of rapid industrialisation. It was born out of the working class who suffered harsh living conditions and poor pay. From its earliest origins, the SSE in Argentina demonstrated its commitment to solidarity and cooperation as a way to improve the living conditions of workers through the establishment of mutual societies and cooperatives.

The history of the SSE in Argentina cannot be told without an understanding of the peculiar nature of Argentinian politics and the dominant role of the Peronist Party since the 1940s. Before that, government did not have institutions that provided welfare to the citizens. This is because Peronism argued that workers should belong to mutual aid associations to be protected. Peronism quickly understood this situation and the state provided welfare services to all citizens. Thus, this significant increase in the population's welfare was decisive for the consolidation of the party. In turn, the increase in local production due to the need to replace imported goods from Europe, led to a rise in employment and a 'democratisation of welfare' (James, 1990; Torre and Pastoriza, 2002). The response of Peronism to the claims that labour unions had made for over 20 years was essential to the bond that emerged between the unions and Peronism (James, 1990).

It is always difficult to judge the extent to which neoliberal politics are driven by cynicism, but it is important not to underestimate the potential for this. In this context, we would argue that we should consider the possibility that the much-vaunted Big Society programme in the UK was merely a softening-up exercise for the policies of austerity that were to follow. The idea of solidarity has never found such fertile ground in the UK as in our Southern neighbours, but the concept of Big Society helped to move us from a society where we had learned to take responsibility for one another to one where we are encouraged to fend for ourselves and where a state of destitution is our own responsibility. In such a cultural context, it is much easier for politicians to cut welfare benefits, particularly when they are simultaneously blaming what they have now portrayed as the 'undeserving poor'.

All in all, although it is possible to establish some similarities between SSE in Argentina and the UK, many divergences can be identified. The history of SSE in Argentina includes as many bottom-up as top-down organisations. Moreover, the SSE in Argentina was never understood as a civic responsibility in abstract terms in which the well-off had to help the worst-off, as was the case in the UK; SSE in Argentina implied taking the bull by its horns and creating a solution. Indeed, associativity and self-management were part of workers' cultural capital and it was developed in many different forms according to the need (Raffaelli, 2015). This establishes a distinction between how SSE was structured in the UK and Argentina; whereas in the UK it was to a large extent encouraged by the state, in Argentina it was the consequence of rebellion. Moreover, these differences might manifest as a consequence of the success of the market economy and welfare state in the UK, and their limitations in the Argentinian setting.

Notes

[1] http://www.publiclibrariesnews.com.

[2] Nestor Kircher was in office from 2003 until 2007. He was followed by his wife, Cristina Fernandez de Kirchner, for two consecutive periods: 2007–11 and 2011–15.

[3] The impact of the election of the right-wing Macri government is unknown at the time of writing.

[4] The principles formulated by Rochdale weavers, in 1844, considered the pioneers of the modern cooperative movement.

References

Arzadun, P. (2011) 'Globalización económica y cooperativismo. Estudio empírico sobre el sector cooperativo argentino', *Revista de Economía Pública, Social y Cooperativa*, 72: 215-235.

Beveridge, W.H.B. (1942) *Social Insurance and Allied Services*, Report by Sir William Beveridge, London: HMSO.

Campetella, A., González Bombal, I. and Roitter, M. (2000) 'Definiendo el sector sin fines de lucro en Argentina', Buenos Aires: CEDES/John Hopkins University.

Chartered Institute of Library and Information Professionals (2012) 'A changing landscape: A survey of public library authorities in England, Wales and Northern Ireland 2012-13', available at www.cilip.org. uk/sites/default/files/documents/CILIP_Public_Library_Survey_ Full_Report_A_Changing_Landscape_2012-13_1.pdf (accessed 28 December 2013).

Conservative Party (2009) 'Control shift returning power to local communities', Responsible Agenda, Policy Green Paper No. 9, available at www.isitfair.co.uk/Downloads/Returning_Power_Local_ Communities.pdf.

Coote, A. (2010) *Cutting it: The 'Big Society' and the new austerity*. London: nef.

Coote, A. (2011) 'Big Society and the New Austerity', in M. Stott (ed) *Big Society in Context*. Thetford: Keystone Development Trust Publications.

Coraggio, J.L. (2005) 'Economía social como vía para otro desarrollo social',n *Boletín Tecnología para la Organización Pública*, Vol 12.

Coraggio, J.L. (2011) *La presencia de la economía social y solidaria (ESS) y su institucionalización en America Latina*. Paris: Estados Generales de la Economía Social y Solidaria.

DCLG (Department for Communities and Local Government) (2011) 'Citizenship Survey: Headline Findings, April-December 2010, England', available at http://webarchive.nationalarchives. gov.uk/20120919132719/http://www.communities.gov.uk/ publications/communities/citizenshipsurveyq3201011 (accessed 28 December 2013).

Dinerstein, A.C. (2007) 'Workers' factory takeovers and new state policies in Argentina: Towards an "institutionalisation" of non-governmental public action', *Policy & Politics*, 35(3): 529-550.

Elgue, M.C. and Cieza, D. (2005) 'La economía social y el peronismo histórico'. Paper presented at Foro Federal de Investigadores y docentes. La Universidad y la Economía Social en el Desarrollo Local, 2° Encuentro, Buenos Aires: Ministerio de Desarrollo Social, pp 145-161.

EuroLat (2015) 'Resolution by the Euro-Latin American Parliamentary Assembly on "The Europe-Latin America position on issues related to climate and climate change in the context of the Summit of 2015 in Paris (COP 21)", Article 8(3)', available at www.europarl.europa.eu/intcoop/eurolat/assembly/plenary_sessions/brussels_2015/urgent_resol_def_en.pdf.

Field, F. (2000) *The state of dependency: welfare under Labour*. London: Social Market Foundation.

Forni, F., Angélico, H. and Roldan, L. (2003) 'La economía social y solidaria. Continuidades y rupturas desde una interpretación de la literatura', Paper presented at 6° Congreso Nacional de Estudios del Trabajo, Buenos Aires.

Gabaldón, A.J. (2000) 'Sustainable development in Latin America and the Caribbean: Perspectives and future', available at http://www.eolss.net/Sample-Chapters/C16/E1-58-50.pdf.

Hopp, M.V. (2011) 'Relación Estado-sociedad civil en las políticas de desarrollo socio-productivo en Argentina contemporánea', *Revista Katálysis*, 14(1): 13-22.

INAES (Instituto Nacional de Asociativismo y Economia Social) (2008) 'Las cooperativas y Mutuales en la República Argentina. Reempadronamiento Nacional y Censo Económico Sectorial de Cooperativas y Mutuales', available at www.inaes.gov.ar.

James, D. (1990) *Resistencia e Integración. El peronismo y la clase trabajadora argentina 1946-1976*. Buenos Aires: Sudamericana.

Levín, A. and Verbeke, G. (1997) 'El cooperativismo argentino en cifras: tendencias en su evolución: 1927–1997', *Realidad Económica*, 152: 18-33.

Lewis, J. (1999) 'The Voluntary Sector in the Mixed Economy of Welfare', in Gladston, D. (ed) *Before Beveridge: Welfare before the Welfare State*. London: Civitas, pp 10-17.

Mohan, J. and Bulloch, S. (2012) *The idea of a 'civic core': what are the overlaps between charitable giving, volunteering, and civic participation in England and Wales?*, TSRC Working Paper 73, Birmingham: TSRC.

Moirano, A.A. (undated) 'Apuntes para una historia del mutualismo', available at www.fundacioncieso.org.ar/testing-wp/wp-content/uploads/Apuntes_para_una_historia_del_mutualismo.pdf.

Montes, V.L. and Ressel, A.B. (2003) 'Presencia del cooperativismo en Argentina', *Revista UniRcoop*, 1, pp 9-26.

Neffa, Julio César, Brenda Brown y Emiliano López (2012) 'Políticas activas de empleo durante la posconvertibilidad', *Empleo, Desempleo & Políticas de Empleo*, No 10, Buenos Aires, CEIL - PIETTE CONICET.

North, P. and Huber, U. (2004) 'Alternative spaces of the "Argentinazo"', *Antipode*, 36(5): 963-984.

North, P. (2011) 'Geographies and utopias of Cameron's Big Society', *Social and Cultural Geography*, 12(8): 817-827.

Pope Francis (2015) 'Laudato Si: On Care for Our Common Home', Encyclical Letter, available at http://w2.vatican.va/content/francesco/en/encyclicals/documents/papa-francesco_20150524_enciclica-laudato-si.html.

Raffaelli, P. (2013) 'Modalidades de gestión organizacional en cooperativas de trabajo pertenecientes a la Federación Red Gráfica Cooperativa', Master's dissertation. Tesis de Maestría en Ciencias Sociales del Trabajo UBA-CEIL PIETTE, available at www.ceil-conicet.gov.ar/formacion/maestria-en-ciencias-sociales-del-trabajo-uba

Raffaelli, P. (2015) 'Joining workers' co-operatives. The case of the Argentine Co-operative Graphic Network Federation', *International Review of Co-operation*, Youth Scholars special edition, available at http://ccr.ica.coop/sites/ccr.ica.coop/files/attachments/InternationalCoopReview2014%20(00000002)_for%20web.pdf.

Ressel, A.B., Silva, N.C. and Martí, J.P. (2008) 'Estudio de las cooperativas agrarias en Argentina'. Working Paper No 3, available at http://sedici.unlp.edu.ar/bitstream/handle/10915/42971/Documento_completo.pdf?sequence=1

Ruggeri, A. (2011) 'Reflexiones sobre la autogestión en las empresas recuperadas argentinas. Estudios', *Revista de Pensamiento Libertario*, 1: 60-79.

Ruggeri, A. and Vieta, M. (2015) 'Argentina's Worker-Recuperated Enterprises, 2010–2013: A Synthesis of Recent Empirical Findings', *Journal of Entrepreneurial and Organizational Diversity*, 4(1): 75-103.

Schujman, L. (1984) 'El cooperativismo en la Argentina', *Estudios cooperativos*, 52: 125-136.

Torre, J.C. and Pastoriza, E. (2002) 'La democratización del bienestar', in J.C. Torre (ed) *Los años peronistas (1943–1955)*. Buenos Aires: Sudamericana, pp 257-312.

Vieta, M. (2012) 'From Managed Employees to Self-Managed Workers: e Transformations of Labour at Argentina's Worker-Recuperated Enterprises', in M. Atzeni (ed) *Alternative Work Organizations*. Basingstoke: Palgrave Macmillan, pp 129-156.

Vieta, M. (2014) 'Learning in struggle: Argentina's new worker cooperatives as transformative learning organizations', *Industrial Relations*, 69(1): 186-218.

Vuotto, M. (2012) 'Acerca de las orientaciones del cooperativismo de trabajo: el caso argentino', *Sociedade em Debate*, 13(1): 101-120.

Wyczykier, G. (2007) 'De la dependencia a la autogestión laboral: sobre la reconstrucción de experiencias colectivas de trabajo en la Argentina contemporánea', available at http://flacsoandes.org/dspace/handle/10469/1058#.UjtU4rUz0Yo.

Yeo, S. (1976) *Religion and Voluntary Organisations in Crisis*. London: Croom Helm.

SIXTEEN

Conclusion: lessons learned and tensions exposed

Peter North, Molly Scott Cato, and the participants in our discussions (Liverpool and Buenos Aires)

In this conclusion, we do not try to put an artificial coherence on what is still a conversation, while walking, talking and working together. We just raise some themes and questions, perhaps better questions than we had when we wrote the grant bid that led to this book. Different histories, politics and culture mean that Latin Americans and Europeans are starting from different places. Whether we think in terms of the contrast between the big-dealing suited men in the City of London and the social enterprise sector in Liverpool that is people-centred and where women play such an important role, or whether we think about the contrast between the massive high-rise developments of São Paulo and the small enterprises supported in a Brazilian *favela* by a solidarity economy incubator, the distances in terms of scale, scope and speed are huge. Are we realistically proposing that the edifice of global capital should be dismantled and replaced by a much larger number of homespun businesses run as cooperatives or social enterprises? A diverse economies and non-paranoid stance that refuses to concede overwhelming power to capitalism, and the emphasis on developing our power 'to create the world we want to see' offers a way out of this trap, in both the global South and North. It is the legacy the Zapatistas, *piqueteros* and land occupiers have given us.

As the chapters in this book show, Europeans are inspired by the creativity, energy and political focus of Latin Americans, especially in the current hard economic times that Latin Americans have experienced for much longer. The chapters demonstrate that scholars and activists in Latin America have pushed ahead much further and with wider public appeal in their efforts to develop deeper concepts of alternatives than their counterparts in Europe. That being the case, since we started these discussions, austerity and the Eurozone crisis have ground on, and we have seen significant levels of mobilisation in Greece and Spain (in particular) that suggest that these two countries might be societies in movement, while there have been setbacks in Argentina and Brazil. Of course, at the time of writing we cannot know what economic turbulence the UK is in for given Brexit. The climate crisis continues to be the elephant in the room where growth continues to be the object of economic development.

Thus it is easier to address this question if we begin by thinking what it is that attracts us to the social and solidarity economy in terms of its values and motivations. It is these we seek to spread throughout the varied economies of the world. Of these, the most important is the motivation to have a livelihood that engenders dignity and respect; very few people can claim this about their daily life, North *and* South. Second, we feel that the cooperation between people in their work, a shared project of collaboration and mutual trust to achieve a shared goal, is what is most lacking from the lives of those of us who live in the North, and helps to explain the continuing sense of social dis-ease and its evidence in the form of unprecedented levels of mental illness. Third, we would cite the satisfaction that comes from knowing your work serves not just yourself but the community you feel yourself to be a member of; it is this ability to work for the common good, alongside collectively owning the means of production, that most strongly characterises the structure of the solidarity economy.

The transition that we need to effect – away from a fossil-dependent, individualist and consumerist paradigm of economic success and towards one based on *buen vivir*, dignity and sustainability – must have inspirational guiding principles, and it is these that we find in the examples of solidarity and social enterprises described in this collection. It was the sense that people were able to respond to their own needs and find collaborative solutions that did not involve social or environmental exploitation that drove our research in this field. What we learned was that economic activity motivated in this way is also far more capable of generating contented human communities than the turbo-charged model of global capitalism, for all its material splendour.

Critics of post-colonial societies who have struggled to develop their own unique paths towards human development in the face of hegemonic power from 19th-century imperialism to contemporary neoliberal globalism have used the phrase 'decolonising the mind' to describe the necessity of not being overwhelmed by a dominant belief system that, while violently exploitative and socially destructive, is nonetheless supremely self-confident and intellectually hegemonic. We see the need to challenge the ideological hegemony of neoliberal global capitalism as a parallel undertaking: communities North and South need to find ways to counteract this colonisation of the mind. We do not underestimate the magnitude of this task: the dominant economic model has the concerted power of capital and its ideological servant, the advertising industry, at its disposal. But neither must we assume in advance that we will lose. To counter the dominant model, we have the innate human need for community and to work cooperatively and the unquenchable determination of the human spirit. We have millions of examples of people doing things, challenging neoliberal nostrums, not caring about the odds. Our future as a species, and the health of our planet, depend on the outcome of the battle between these irreconcilable forces.

Trying to understand why this is the case, and why social economy activities have been successful or otherwise, has been very important. In particular, the transformational aspirations of the solidarity economy compared with a market-focused role in the UK raised the question of how social economy organisations could become more transformational. UK-based social economy practitioners in particular find this challenging.

Private or public? Market or state?

In both Europe and Latin America, we are having to understand the role of the state, and think more deeply about when the state facilitates or crushes grassroots activity. Latin American experience shows that solidarity economy activities cannot replace the state, despite the blandishments of the Big Society and the attraction of right-wing libertarianism to many (often young) globally privileged actors, especially in the US. Perhaps some otherwise globally privileged actors that do have many resources in the global North (such as Transition Towns, and the large numbers of food and energy coops) can act independently of the state to some extent, as can middle-class actors in Latin America (as the experience of Argentina's barter networks shows). But it is much harder for the very poorest. Chapter Ten suggests that the state can foster a community sector, while Chapter Twelve shows that, even with the best intentions, the Venezuelan state could smother grassroots actions.

The dominant neoliberal ideology and the politics of austerity has challenged the state on both sides of the Atlantic. Thinking about a reduced role for the state and about entrepreneurialism in different ways can be seen as an unwelcome introduction of neoliberal constructs into the debate. Latin America had its lost decade in the 1980s, and Argentina went through a profound economic crisis at the turn of the century; given this, many with a profound critique of neoliberal globalisation want to reject in in its entirety, and discuss alternatives. 'Entrepreneurialism' = 'big business' = 'part of the problem', even though, we would argue, many grassroots actors are incredibly entrepreneurial, and we should recognise this. Think back to Marina Sitrin's description of 'Nac & Pop sín patrón' in Chapter Fourteen.

A significant difference between the UK and many Latin American societies is that in the global North demands for higher standards of welfare and employment have been won through a well-developed public sector in the post-Second World War Keynesian settlement – although the high standards of welfare achieved in Argentina before Menemismo and the crisis of 2001 are comparable with European welfare levels, and thus stand as a point of difference between Argentina and other parts of Latin America. Much of the focus of recent struggles in the global North, especially since 2008 introduced a new era of austerity, has been on defending state payments for children and unemployed, sick and retired people, and defending the National Health Service. Universal welfare is both under attack and little defended by many who are not convinced of the benefits of social inclusion and a well-funded public sector achieved by the 'buy-in' of universal benefits paid to seemingly well-off people. Benefits for poor people are inevitably poor benefits. Northerners are thus defending levels of welfare that Latin Americans have never had to the same degree.

Thus in a neoliberalising environment where the public sector is retreating we must not be naïve. The social and solidarity economy *can* be seen as second rate, with poor people struggling on their own. If the solidarity of social economy is not supported and taken seriously by states, the outcomes can be inadequate – at best useful empowering visions of what could be, critique, and spaces for grassroots innovation that their participants get a lot out of. But if the challenge is to provide livelihoods with dignity for millions that don't have it, perhaps the practices are not up to scratch yet, in both the global North and South. In the North involving social economy organisations in initiatives where they are unable to deliver quality services is often simply a case of setting them up to fail. Contracts are then taken over by the private sector, so the social economy is merely a cynical way to smooth the path to privatisation. State withdrawal of services is also accompanied by increasingly long hours of work for lower pay, meaning people increasingly lack the time, energy of commitment to third sector activities, while the infrastructure that supports the third sector – meeting rooms, public libraries, a grant and support infrastructure and so on – are increasingly undermined.

Similarly, the strengthening of the solidarity economy movement in Brazil is linked to the decline of formal employment and a growth of autonomous and informal work that started in the 1980s and was further accentuated by the productive restructuring of companies in response to globalisation processes in the 1990s. The experience of the solidarity economy in Venezuela is a reminder of how a great number of people in Latin America are still experiencing a lack of infrastructure. In this context, while the critique of neoliberalism and mobilisations for a better world are inspirational, questions can be raised about the extent to which the dispossessed in the global North should look to Latin America for real-world, liveable alternatives to neoliberal policies – just yet.

Conversely, if state support is serious about providing dignified lives for the many and the solidarity economy sector is well supported, it can be a powerful bridge to developing a convivial and inclusive low carbon economy and society. Inspiration can be drawn not only from work in Venezuela's *barrios* where critical infrastructure, education and health needs are being met by a facilitating state, but also from state and university support for the social and solidarity economy in Brazil. The same can be said for new constitutional developments such as the prominence of the right to an economic life in the Bolivian, Ecuadorian and Venezuelan constitutions. This is of interest in the context of recent debates in the global North about the right to a city that provides a good life. It is a tragedy that social democrats in the global North have not yet reacted to the awful implications of the infatuation of the 'third way' with globalisation and markets that has resulted in the destruction of many powerful social democrat parties through what we now call 'pasokification'. Perhaps a social democracy that engaged with the grassroots, which some call 45° politics and which combines the democracy of horizontalism with the effectiveness, resources and universalism of the state, can provide a recipe for a revived social democracy.

Building a good life in harmony with the planet

Distinct conceptualisations of the environmental crisis and especially climate change led to the fiercest disagreements during our debates with participants. Climate change was seen by many of our Latin American discussants as the latest of a long line of Northern concepts designed to limit development opportunities in the global South. Extreme weather events were a more accepted part of life for Latin Americans – a flash flood that occurred while we were in Buenos Aires resulted in 80 deaths. The main issue, for Latin Americans, was for global Northerners to take action to reduce their over-consumption of planetary resources – something that, as the Uruguyan writer Eduardo Galeano famously pointed out, they have been doing for 500 years. The everyday realities of meeting the needs of those struggling to get by in Latin American cities are obviously more pressing and could act to minimise the questions chosen to orient our joint seminars, such as 'How might finding a future where our need for material satisfaction be better balanced with our need to respect the natural world on which all our wellbeing depends?' Our discussions revealed that there are debates about the extent to which the transition to a low carbon economy is an issue in parts of Latin America. Some indigenous groups, especially in the Andean highlands and Amazonia, are very clear about the immediacy and potentially catastrophic nature of climate change within a range that would be tolerable at higher latitudes, and are developing an exciting new politics based on indigenous conceptions of earth stewardship. However, to urban unemployed people, climate change can seem to be a Northern issue, or worse, as the latest version of a long line of Northern neo-imperialist strategies to maintain Latin America in a disadvantageous relationship with the Global North. There are few conceptions of a practical politics of the right to development in a climate- and resource-constrained world.

One of the perspectives we benefit from but were unable to include in this collection is the indigenous idea of *buen vivir*, an indigenous conception of 'the good life' that is central to the new Bolivian Constitution, which includes a commitment to human rights and participatory democracy, a radical reduction in social inequality and a shift from an anthropocentric to a holistic worldview. This rethinking of how to evolve towards a good life that does not threaten the limits of the planet is providing fruitful political insights in the Andean polities, especially in Bolivia and Ecuador, and is also influencing European policymaking in the context of climate change. A motion written jointly by the European Parliament and the Andean Parliament (Parlandino) in advance of the Paris climate negotiations in December 2015 underlines:

> … the importance of the search for a new paradigm of human well-being that reconciles the twin challenges of fighting climate change and enhancing equality and social cohesion; encourages governments to strengthen bi-regional exchange using concepts such as 'Buen Vivir' and themes concerned with managing the transition

towards resilient low-carbon societies; considers that the global transition to low emissions can provide significant opportunities to revitalise economies in Europe, Latin America and globally. Action to tackle climate change also brings significant benefits in terms of public well-being.[1]

During our discussions, our focus was on how we manage the contradictions of centre-periphery inequality and different cultures in the context of climate change. This was in part due to the location of the seminar; Buenos Aires, and Argentina, are, of course, not representative of Latin America as a whole – although we do believe we had participants with experiences of a wide range of Latin American environments. A seminar in Ecuador or Bolivia might have engaged more with indigenous knowledges of climate change. A seminar in Brazil might have focused more on developing the organisational capacity of the solidarity economy rather than on the solidarity economy as a counter-power. That said, more agreement was found on the need for action to mitigate against dangerous climate change and adapt to what was inevitable through the construction of networks of activists from the social and solidarity economies North and South. Networks were developed and literature was exchanged that will enable research on this issue to be continued in the future.

Meanwhile, some of the partners in our seminar felt that Latin Americans *do* need to think more about climate change and the place of nature in development. Latin Americans wanted to think more deeply about what development means, and how ecological issues could be integrated into development models, rather than a more explicit politics of mitigation of and adaptation to climate change. Inevitable climate change of 3°C in the Andes would have catastrophic effects on the development opportunities of much of Latin America that depends on the Andean snow pack for its water supply. Consequently, seminar participants from Latin America were as inspired by many of the practical grassroots initiatives in the global North focusing on climate change, environmental sustainability and renewable energy as the visitors were by Latin American experiences of self-management and of *autogestión*.

For some UK social economy organisations, responses to the climate and energy crisis have been primarily pragmatic, driven by the need to cut costs. Given the lack of state investment in solidarity economy models here, an attention to energy efficiency as a way to improve the efficiency and hence the longevity of solidarity economy projects might be useful. At the time of the seminar, our Latin American partners felt that energy efficiency was not on the agenda at all: in Argentina, the state subsidised gas, which was very cheap, and when the Macri government liberalised energy prices in 2016 many solidarity economy enterprises struggled to cope with price hikes of between 200% and 400% for electricity, and 1,300% for gas (Ruggeri, 2016: 18). The Kirchner government focused on developing shale gas resources rather than reducing demand or cutting carbon emissions. The solar technology in Argentina was felt to be expensive, rudimentary and unreliable. Given concerns about the unequal global division of labour, and pride in Argentina's nuclear technology as a symbol of national dignity and independence, our Argentine partners were critical of the power relations inherent in Africa's experiences with Chinese solar power. However, given the abundant free resource of solar power and the rapidly declining cost and improved efficiency of solar power, this seems to be missing a trick. Northern grassroots innovations in this field were of considerable interest, as was the experience of grassroots organisations organising to develop prefigurative low carbon societies such as Transition Towns.

In both societies, there is an understanding that balancing material wellbeing with environmental respect may require us to re-evaluate systems of ownership and challenge the private, capital-driven model of economy that dominates the contemporary global economy. In this context, the description in Chapter Nine of systems of communal land ownership in the *fundos de pasto* over Brazil's north-eastern Bahia state, provides some useful pointers. In this extremely poor and arid area, the local people who manage the land communally not only accept national legislation that requires 40% of land to be set aside as wilderness but have voluntarily left a larger area outside their cultivation. In Chapter Eleven, Paul Singer and Heloisa Primavera also note that the landless workers' movement in Brazil (MST) follows the principle of organic agriculture.

Shared challenges, shared solutions?

There is a perceived crisis of thinking on the left in both global North and South. While austerity and the Eurozone crisis have meant that many social movement actors in the global North now challenge the forces of capital in ways that Argentine pickets or Brazilian land occupiers have done for many years, both continents are starting to think more about alternatives to capitalism, less about domination, more about grassroots power. A Northern movement thinking more about solidarity economy-based conceptions of a transition to a convivial economy could mirror developments in the global South in powerful ways.

While many of the challenges that drove our debates were shared – precarious employment, weakened public and social services, pressure on resources, climate change – old tensions resurfaced and the Western participants learned that it is difficult to transcend the post-colonial framing that colours so much thinking in Latin America. In other ways, things are coming together. Both continents are dealing with globalising forces and increasingly with financial crisis. Continued austerity North and South and the ongoing crisis of free market economics mean that there is an emergence of changed thinking in both. North and South, walking together, we both ask the following.

The state cannot or will not provide. When it did provide, it could crowd out grassroots activism and introduce dependency and domination. There are no jobs, but there are still things can be done. What can we do, together? How *could* the state help us, not get in the way?

The experience of the social and solidarity economy that emerged from our discussions should not been seen as either a perfect utopia or problematic neoliberalisation, but as bricolage. A mix of left and right, solidarity and entrepreneurialism, state support but not domination, a journey not an end-point. A social economy perspective of using business skills and techniques to meet needs and to generate a surplus for social good, and a solidarity economy perspective that focuses more on how we want to live and work are different ways of coming at the same question. How can we create low carbon jobs, businesses, cooperatives and livelihoods? Both an alternative to, or as a bridge to conventional ways of providing livelihoods, North and South.

Neoliberal hegemony has been broken, but we are still in the very early days of a better world.

Note

[1] Urgent Resolution on the Europe-Latin America position on issues related to climate and climate change in the context of the 2015 summit in Paris (COP 21), by the Parlandino and European Parliament.

References

Ruggeri, A (2016) *Worker-recovered enterprises at the beginning of the government of Mauricio Macri*, Buenos Aires: Callao Cooperativa Cultural.

Index

Page numbers in *italics* refer to figures or tables.